GLOBALIZATION

SERIES EDITORS
MANFRED B. STEGER
ROYAL MELBOURNE INSTITUTE OF TECHNOLOGY AND UNIVERSITY OF HAWAI'I–MĀNOA
AND
TERRELL CARVER
UNIVERSITY OF BRISTOL

"Globalization" has become *the* buzzword of our time. But what does it mean? Rather than forcing a complicated social phenomenon into a single analytical framework, this series seeks to present globalization as a multidimensional process constituted by complex, often contradictory interactions of global, regional, and local aspects of social life. Since conventional disciplinary borders and lines of demarcation are losing their old rationales in a globalizing world, authors in this series apply an interdisciplinary framework to the study of globalization. In short, the main purpose and objective of this series is to support subject-specific inquiries into the dynamics and effects of contemporary globalization and its varying impacts across, between, and within societies.

Globalization and Sovereignty
John Agnew

Globalization and War
Tarak Barkawi

Globalization and Human Security
Paul Battersby and Joseph M. Siracusa

*Globalization and American Popular Culture,
3rd ed.*
Lane Crothers

Globalization and Militarism
Cynthia Enloe

Globalization and Law
Adam Gearey

Globalization and Feminist Activism
Mary E. Hawkesworth

Globalization and Postcolonialism
Sankaran Krishna

Globalization and Media
Jack Lule

Globalization and Social Movements, 2nd ed.
Valentine M. Moghadam

Globalization and Terrorism, 2nd ed.
Jamal R. Nassar

Globalization and Culture, 2nd ed.
Jan Nederveen Pieterse

*Globalization and International
Political Economy*
Mark Rupert and M. Scott Solomon

Globalization and Citizenship
Hans Schattle

Globalization and Islamism
Nevzat Soguk

Globalisms, 3rd ed.
Manfred B. Steger

Rethinking Globalism
Edited by Manfred B. Steger

Globalization and Labor
Dimitris Stevis and Terry Boswell

Globaloney 2.0
Michael Veseth

Supported by the Globalization Research Center at the University of Hawai'i–Mānoa

GLOBALIZATION AND SOCIAL MOVEMENTS

ISLAMISM, FEMINISM, AND THE GLOBAL JUSTICE MOVEMENT

SECOND EDITION

VALENTINE M. MOGHADAM

ROWMAN & LITTLEFIELD PUBLISHERS, INC.
Lanham • Boulder • New York • Toronto • Plymouth, UK

Published by Rowman & Littlefield Publishers, Inc.
A wholly owned subsidiary of The Rowman & Littlefield Publishing Group, Inc.
4501 Forbes Boulevard, Suite 200, Lanham, Maryland 20706
www.rowman.com

10 Thornbury Road, Plymouth PL6 7PP, United Kingdom

British Library Cataloguing in Publication Information Available

Library of Congress Cataloging-in-Publication Data

Moghadam, Valentine M.
  Globalization and social movements : Islamism, feminism, and the global justice
movement / Valentine M. Moghadam. — 2nd ed.
    p. cm. — (Globalization)
  Includes bibliographical references and index.
  ISBN 978-1-4422-1418-7 (cloth : alk. paper) — ISBN 978-1-4422-1419-4 (pbk. :
alk. paper) — ISBN 978-1-4422-1420-0 (electronic)
    1. Social movements. 2. Transnationalism. 3. Globalization. 4. Anti-globalization
movement. I. Title.
  HM881.M64 2012
  303.48'4—dc23

                                                                2012020636

Printed in the United States of America

CONTENTS

List of Figures and Tables — vii

Preface to the Second Edition — ix

List of Acronyms — xiii

1 Introduction and Overview: Social Movements and Contemporary Politics — 1

2 Globalization and Collective Action — 31

3 Social Movements and Democratization — 61

4 Islamist Movements — 99

5 Feminism on a World Scale — 133

6 The Global Justice Movement — 171

7 Conclusions and Prognostication — 203

Notes — 217

References — 233

Index — 253

About the Author — 267

Figures and Tables

FIGURE

2.1 The Making of a Global Social Movement   55

TABLES

1.1 The World-System, Globalization, and Social Movements: A "Long Twentieth Century" Timeline   15

1.2 Social Movement Features of Feminist, Islamist, and Global Justice Movements   23

2.1 Balance Sheet of Globalization   37

2.2 Globalization: Features, Agents, and Challengers   41

3.1 Four Waves of Democratization: Successes, Failures, and External Impositions   72

3.2 "Third Wave and Fourth Wave" Pro-Democracy Sociopolitical Movements: World-System Location, Frames, and Outcomes   73

3.3 Internet Usage in Egypt, Morocco, and Tunisia, circa 2011   90

4.1 Types of Islamist or Muslim Movements and Organizations, 1980s–Present   103

5.1 Types of Transnational Feminist Networks   140

5.2 Strategies Deployed by Transnational Feminist Networks   145

6.1 The Global Justice Movement: Issues and Types of
Movements and Networks   172

6.2 Number of Protests against Structural Adjustment by Country
and Date   176

6.3 UN Conferences of the 1990s: Transnational Opportunities
for Mobilizations and Framings   181

6.4 Global Justice Movement Protests since the Battle of Seattle   185

PREFACE TO THE SECOND EDITION

This book originates in an invitation extended by Manfred Steger when we were both at Illinois State University and he had just taken on the co-editorship of this book series. It took me several years to finally begin the project, and I am grateful to Manfred, and to the other series editor, Terrell Carver, and acquisitions editor Susan McEachern, for their patience, encouragement, and support. To the anonymous reader: thank you for very helpful comments on the first edition. For this edition, I am grateful to Chris Chase-Dunn and Jackie Smith, the students in my political sociology graduate seminar in fall 2011, and Darien Hutson, undergraduate research assistant through the Wilke program at Purdue.

The topic of this book is globalization and transnational social movements. A social movement is constituted by large numbers of individuals, networks, and groups that express grievances and make claims on power holders in a sustained form of contentious and unconventional politics. A transnational social movement brings together people and networks from several countries around shared goals. While today's transnational social movements are not historically unprecedented, aspects of globalization have provided them with more advantages as well as challenges. I define globalization as a complex economic, political, cultural, and geographic process in which the mobility of capital, peoples, organizations, movements, ideas, and discourses takes on an increasingly transnational or global form. The Internet—a "gift" of globalization—has made possible rapid communication, transfers, and mobilizations. And yet, the type of economic globalization that has emerged is neoliberal capitalism, with its features of denationalization, privatization, "flexible" labor markets, and deregulated capital markets. Its deficits lie in the areas of labor rights, human rights, women's rights, and environmental protection. It thus devolves upon activists, mobilized in local or transnational networks, to form movements for change. Thus, just as globalization has engendered the spread of neoliberal capitalism across the world, it has also stoked opposition, collective action, and contentious and noninstitutional politics. And while the Internet has allowed capitalists to speculate, buy, and sell across space and time, it also allows activists to organize and mobilize rapidly and effectively.

This became evident with the democracy movements in the Middle East and North Africa, including the Green Protests in Iran in June 2009 and the mass social protests in Tunisia and Egypt in early 2011 that led to the collapse of the governments in those two countries. In all three countries, activists made extensive use of social-networking media to connect with each other, mobilize citizens, and transmit their messages across the globe. What is more, the protest movements in Iran, Tunisia, and Egypt were initiated by technologically savvy young people motivated by social grievances to demand political change.

In this second edition, I update each of the chapters while also adding an analysis of the democratic demands of contemporary social movements, highlighting the way in which social movements contribute to the democratization of their societies. I interrogate conventional definitions and practices of democracy, pointing out that demands for a robust democracy must include economic rights as well as civil and political rights. Such demands were evident in the social protests and opposition movements of Tunisia and Egypt, and they figure prominently in the critiques and stated solutions offered by the transnational feminist networks and the global justice movement discussed in this book. The new chapter shows that transnational movements for democracy are both an outgrowth of globalization and a challenge to "business as usual."

2011—what a year for social movements! We saw the Arab Spring, the European Summer, and the American Autumn. The global justice movement, which usually meets at the World Social Forum in Brazil or other parts of the world, expanded when Europeans protested austerity measures in the wake of the global economic crisis, students in the United Kingdom and Chile protested the rising costs of education, and the *indignados* mounted massive demonstrations in Madrid against unemployment and welfare cuts. In the fall of 2011, the call for democracy and social justice seemed to engulf the world, as the Occupy Wall Street campaign, which began with activists in New York City protesting the injustices of Wall Street practices, went global. The protests were a direct result of the global economic crisis, which originated in the financial sector of the advanced countries, beginning with the 2007–2008 subprime mortgage problem and the meltdown of mortgage-based securities in the United States. The financial crisis had immediate reverberations in those developing countries that were closely linked to the global financial markets. Soaring food prices and rising unemployment, coupled with knowledge of the stratospheric incomes of economic elites, brought into sharp relief the complicity of states with a capitalist model—neoliberalism—that had wreaked havoc on economies and households.

We are living in times of insecurity, instability, and risk, but equally in times of opportunity and possibility. Climate change, war, and economic crisis loom large, while increased militarization by states and violent contention by nonstate actors contribute to a seemingly dangerous world. But these developments have been met by sustained opposition and mobilization for change: the transformation of the status quo and the building of "another world" that is peaceful, environmentally sound, and egalitarian. Networks and communities of activists across borders—notably feminists, environmentalists, human rights advocates, and economic justice activists who constitute transnational social movements—have initiated sustained critiques of the contemporary world-system and have offered rational and feasible alternatives.

This book is dedicated to all such activists.

Acronyms

AKP   Justice and Development Party (Turkey)
ASEAN   Association of Southeast Asian Nations
ATTAC   Association for the Taxation of Financial Transactions and
         for Citizens' Action
AWID   Association for Women's Rights in Development
BRIC   Brazil, Russia, India, China
CEDAW   Convention on the Elimination of All Forms of Discrimi-
         nation against Women; also Committee on the Elimina-
         tion of Discrimination against Women (UN)
CFTC   Commodity Futures Trading Commission (U.S.)
COSATU   Congress of South African Trade Unions
DAWN   Development Alternatives with Women for a New Era
ECOSOC   Economic and Social Committee (UN)
ENDA   Environnement et Développement du Tiers Monde
EU   European Union
FIS   Front Islamique du Salut (Islamic Salvation Front, Algeria)
FTAA   Free Trade Area of the Americas
GCC   Gulf Cooperation Council
GIA   Groupe Islamique Armée
GJM   global justice movement
IAW   International Alliance of Women
ICFTU   International Confederation of Free Trade Unions
ICPD   UN International Conference on Population and Develop-
         ment (Cairo, 1994)
IGO   intergovernmental organization

IGTN	International Gender and Trade Network
ILO	International Labour Organization (UN)
IMF	International Monetary Fund
INGO	international nongovernmental organization
IROWS	Institute for Research on World-Systems
ISIS	International Women's Information and Communication Service
MAI	Multilateral Agreement on Investment
MDGs	Millennium Development Goals
MDS	Movement of Socialist Democrats (Tunisia)
MENA	Middle East and North Africa
NAFTA	North American Free Trade Association
NATO	North Atlantic Treaty Organization
NGO	nongovernmental organization
NIEO	New International Economic Order
NWICO	New World Information and Communication Order
OECD	Organization for Economic Cooperation and Development
OWS	Occupy Wall Street
PAS	Pan-Malaysian Islamic Party/Parti Islam Se-Malaysia
PJD	Parti du Justice et Dévéloppement (Morocco)
PT	Partido dos Trabalhadores (Workers' Party, Brazil)
SAP	structural adjustment policy
SEN	Solidarity Economy Network (U.S.)
SIGI	Sisterhood Is Global Institute
SMO	social movement organization
TARP	Troubled Asset Relief Program
TCC	transnational capitalist class
TFN	transnational feminist network
UNCED	United Nations Conference on Environment and Development
UNCTAD	United Nations Conference on Trade and Development
UNDP	United Nations Development Programme
UNU	United Nations University
WEDO	Women's Environment and Development Organization
WICEJ	Women's International Coalition for Economic Justice
WIDE	Network Women in Development in Europe
WIDF	Women's International Democratic Federation
WILPF	Women's International League for Peace and Freedom
WLP	Women's Learning Partnership
WLUML	Women Living under Muslim Laws
WSF	World Social Forum
WTO	World Trade Organization

CHAPTER 1

INTRODUCTION AND OVERVIEW

SOCIAL MOVEMENTS AND CONTEMPORARY POLITICS

Men and women make history, but not under conditions of their own choosing.

—adapted from Karl Marx, *The Eighteenth Brumaire of Louis Bonaparte*

What is the connection between globalization and social movements? How have people collectively responded to globalization? Have social movements changed to better confront globalization's economic, political, and cultural manifestations and challenges? And how are contemporary social movements and networks affecting the progression of globalization? These are the principal questions posed and addressed in this book through a focus on three transnational or global social movements: the global women's movement and transnational feminist networks; transnational Islamist movements and networks; and the global justice movement (GJM) against neoliberalism. In addition to exploring the interrelationship of globalization and social movements, this book examines the ways that the social sciences have sought to address changing sociopolitical realities.

The social sciences have long focused on processes and institutions within single states, societies, and economies. Until the 1990s, the terms "global" and "transnational" represented concepts that were either alien or marginal to mainstream social science theories. "International" and "world" were of course understood, but supranational developments could hardly be fathomed. The post–World War II, Cold War world order consisted of what came to be called the First World, Second World, and Third World—also known as the rich capitalist countries of the West, the countries of the communist bloc, and the developing countries of Africa, Asia, and Latin America. When scholars studied these political and economic regions, analytical frameworks—such as modernization theory, theories of international relations, studies of international development, or even the relatively new field known as women-in-development (WID)—tended to focus on single societies and economies.

Dependency theory and its more sophisticated variant, world-system theory, challenged mainstream social science theorizing as well as Marxism's emphasis on class conflicts within single societies, drawing attention to the transnational nature of capital and labor flows and the implications thereof for economic and political processes at the societal level, as well as for the reproduction of global inequalities. (However, in *The Communist Manifesto*, Karl Marx and Friedrich Engels were absolutely correct in predicting the ever-growing concentration of capital and its expansion across the globe. And toward the end of volume 1 of *Capital*, Marx's sardonic comments about the "bankocracy" presage the 2008 global financial meltdown.[1]) World-system theory in particular was unique in its conceptual and methodological approach. Though it posited the existence of hierarchical "economic zones" of core, periphery, and semiperiphery, it insisted that the analytical point of departure should be the structures of the world-system in its entirety. Back in the mainstream, theories of social movements and "new social movements" focused on national-level dynamics—and mainly in the West or in "postindustrial society."[2] But no sooner had these theories gained prominence in the 1980s than new developments began to challenge some of their basic assumptions.

The new developments included forms of governance and activism on a world scale, as well as global shifts in political economy. New governance structures included the ever-growing power and influence of multinational corporations, the World Bank, the International Monetary Fund (IMF), and (later) the World Trade Organization (WTO), along with the emergence of regional blocs such as the European Union (EU) and the North American Free Trade Agreement (NAFTA), as well as less powerful trade groupings such as the Association of Southeast Asian Nations (ASEAN) and the Gulf Cooperation Council (GCC). These institutions of global and regional governance were also behind shifts in the international political economy, which entailed the move from Keynesian or state-directed economic models to neoliberal or free market economic strategies. Thus the "structural adjustment and stabilization" policies that were advocated for and implemented in debt-ridden Third World countries in the 1980s and 1990s, the transition from socialism to capitalism in the Second World, and the free market imprint of Reaganism and Thatcherism in the First World all seemed to be part of a global process of economic restructuring. Along with these changes arose a powerful ideology of free market capitalism and consumerism.[3]

As globalization was being observed in its economic, political, and cultural dimensions, certain scholars came to analyze what they viewed as a global tendency toward common values. Echoing some arguments made earlier by modernization theorists, proponents of "world society" maintained that structures, institutions, and processes are explicit or implicit carriers of modern values such as rationality and individuality. These carriers include rationalized state tax and management systems, formal organizations, bureaucratized legal systems, and formal schooling. In the 1990s, emphasis began to be placed on the role of international organizations in the construction of world values. World polity theory places primacy on cultural and political institutions and norms, emphasizing norm diffusion and convergences in political and cultural developments, which is interpreted as a kind of global westernization. It posits a tendency toward "isomorphism" in institutions, values, practices, and norms across the globe, indicated by states' membership in intergovernmental organizations and their adoption of all manner of international instruments, along with the exponential growth and increased prominence of national and international nongovernmental organizations (NGOs and INGOs). Theorists argued that these were measures of a "world culture" and a kind of "world polity." In this perspective, world culture encourages countries to adopt similar strategies for addressing common problems. World organizations are viewed as "primary instruments of shared modernity," disseminating standards and practices, and international conventions and treaties often provide declarations of common causes and blueprints for change. Social movements and civil society organizations—including human rights and women's rights associations, environmental protection groups, and various other advocacy groups—are regarded as active agents in the deepening of the cultural and normative features of world society. What is more, the global diffusion of increasingly sophisticated mobile phones and the use of social-networking media such as Facebook, YouTube, and Twitter, especially by youth, are further indicators of world culture.[4]

Parallel with the economic shifts that were unfolding in the 1980s, a new phenomenon occurred that the theorists of new social movements had some difficulty addressing, focused as they were on presumed emancipatory, postclass, postmaterial, and postideological new social movements in the democratic West. The new phenomenon was the seeming revival of religious movements across the globe that appeared also to take on a political character. In the United States, this movement came to be analyzed as the New Religious Right, and it gave rise to questions about the validity of the "secularization" thesis associated with Max Weber and some tenets of modernization theory. Robert Wuthnow discussed the increasing tendency of American evangelicals to enter the political arena after 1976, and Rebecca Klatch examined the American New Right, including the role of women within it, as a kind of countermovement to the progressive social changes of the 1960s and beyond. Kathleen Blee and Kimberly Creasap situate the American New Right in "the alliance of free market advocates and social conservatives . . . [and] the entry of large numbers of conservative Protestant evangelicals into secular political life." In explaining the emergence of Islamic fundamentalism and political Islam, Said Amir Arjomand examined five broad processes of social change generally associated with secularization—integration into the international system; development of transport, communication, and the mass media; urbanization; the spread of literacy and education; and the incorporation of citizens into political society—and showed how these in fact had "fostered a variety of movements of revitalization in the Islamic world."[5]

In the Middle East, North Africa, and South Asia, Islamic movements sought to reinforce religious values, recuperate traditional social and gender norms, and curb Western political and cultural influences. The theorization of these movements fell largely to scholars within Middle East studies and Middle East women's studies, although Benjamin Barber later included them under the rubric of "jihad" movements against "McWorld." Those who studied Muslim-majority countries, as well as scholars of Islam, sought to understand the new movements in terms such as "political Islam," "fundamentalism," "Islamist movements," or "resurgent Islam." The focus tended to be on the dynamics within particular countries that had led to the growth of such opposition movements—for example, in the Middle East—but some studies also noted region-wide factors, such as a shared religio-cultural civilization, the presence of authoritarian governments, reaction to changing gender relations, and a shared antipathy toward Israel and its handling of the Palestinian question. Following the al-Qaeda attacks on the United States on September 11, 2001, "terrorism studies" became widespread, but social scientists such as Quintan Wiktorowicz and Mohammed Hafez studied Islamist movements in terms of social movement dynamics or as conservative political movements. Rarely, though, were Islamist movements studied in terms of their relationship to the changing global political economy, although an early work of mine did situate the growth of Islamist movements in global restructuring.[6] Inasmuch as the scholarship on new social movements focused on collective identity as a mobilizing force and on cultural issues as the main concern, the framework could be usefully extended to explain Islamic/Islamist movements. On the other hand, Islamic/Islamist movements generally did not fit the presumption of emancipatory movements found in much of the literature on new social movements, and they had a relationship to the global political economy that was missing in new social movement theorizing.

Another apparent outcome of globalization and a challenge to conventional theories of social movements was the rise in the late 1990s of what have been variously called transnational advocacy networks, transnational social movements, and global social movements. Social movement theorists previously had focused on domestic processes and movement characteristics, but it became increasingly clear that the analytical point of departure would have to take account of the transnational and that local-global linkages would have to be theorized. Early theorists of transnational advocacy networks focused on ideational and ethical motivations for the emergence of the human rights, environmental, and solidarity movements. Margaret Keck and Kathryn Sikkink, for example, defined a transnational advocacy network (TAN) as a set of "relevant actors working internationally on an issue who are bound together by shared values, a common discourse and dense exchanges of information and services. . . . Activists in networks try not only to influence policy outcomes but to transform the terms and nature of the debate." They also emphasized the research, lobbying, and advocacy activities of the TANs that they studied.[7] However, the 1997–1998 mobilization against the Multilateral Agreement on Investment (MAI) in the United States and the Battle of Seattle in late 1999 confirmed that movement interest in economic, inequality, and class issues had returned. A new body of literature emerged, therefore, taking these novel departures into consideration. There is now some consensus among scholars that the response to global economic, political, and cultural developments—notably, neoliberalism, war, the decline of the welfare state, and growing inequalities—has taken the form of transnational collective action, including the emergence of transnational social movements and advocacy networks that focus on human rights, the environment, and economic justice. As discussed later in this chapter, such movements and networks are not historically unprecedented, but they became prominent in the early part of the new century. In the wake of the financial crisis of 2008 and the ensuing economic recession that engulfed the world-economy, and with confidence and trust in government declining in the West as well as in developing countries, lobbying no longer made sense, and global social movements developed new tactics, strategies, and frames. In particular, social/economic justice frames have seen global transmission and diffusion.

TRANSNATIONAL SOCIAL MOVEMENTS

Economists and some world-system sociologists tend to view globalization in largely economic terms (e.g., in terms of trade, investment, and capital-accumulation patterns), but for many observers it is a multifaceted phenomenon. It refers, inter alia, to time-space compression, world culture, the increase in the available modes of organization, the emergence of multiple and overlapping identities, and the arising of hybrid sites such as world cities, free trade zones, offshore banking facilities, border zones, and ethnic mélange neighborhoods. Jan Aart Scholte discusses globalization as deterritorialization, producing and diffusing "supraterritorial," "transworld," and "transborder" relations between people. He and Jan Nederveen Pieterse regard "hybridization" to be an important facet of globalization, although both also highlight the unevenness, asymmetry, and inequality that are embedded in the new global mélange.[8] These observations have implications for social movements and transnational networks. Among other things, these aspects of globalization permit interactions, connections, and mobilizations conducive to transnational collective action.

A transnational social movement has come to be understood as a mass mobilization uniting people in three or more countries, engaged in sustained contentious interactions with political elites, international organizations, or multinational corporations.[9] A transnational social movement is analytically distinct from, though related to, an international solidarity network or a transnational advocacy network; the latter may identify themselves with social movements, such as the feminist, environmentalist, human rights, or peace and justice movements, and thus may be oriented toward social change. In the perspective taken in this book, transnational social movements and transnational advocacy networks alike are structurally linked to globalization, though in somewhat different ways, and they constitute important sectors in what scholars call "global civil society." These points are elaborated further in chapter 2.

Along with such features of collective action, new transnational political spaces have opened, in the form of the World Social Forum (WSF) and the regional forums. I regard these as key institutions of at least two transnational social movements: the global justice movement against neoliberalism and the global feminist movement for women's participation and rights. Whereas theorists of new social movements had projected feminist movements as localized and identity focused, the 1990s saw women organizing and mobilizing across borders in transnational feminist networks, particularly around the effects of economic restructuring, patriarchal fundamentalisms, and violence against women. In the Middle East and North Africa, movements for women's rights spread, and one transnational feminist network, the Collectif Maghreb Egalité 95, based in North Africa and linking feminist groups in Algeria, Morocco, and Tunisia, mobilized for the reform of patriarchal family laws, criminalization of domestic violence and sexual harassment, equal nationality rights, and greater political and economic participation.[10]

In the new millennium, therefore, a growing body of literature was examining both globalization processes and transnational social movements. As noted, the attacks of September 11, 2001, broadened the scope of the study of Islamist movements beyond the purview of area specialists. Conventional social scientists became interested in analyzing militant Islam and the "war on terror," while the 2003 invasion of Iraq by the United States and Great Britain spurred numerous studies on war, "empire," and the new imperialism. And although the Middle East and North Africa (MENA) region had been widely and long identified with political authoritarianism, Islamic fundamentalism, conflict, and patriarchal gender relations, the emergence of democracy movements in Iran, Tunisia, Egypt, Morocco, and elsewhere seemed to shatter popular and social science stereotypes of the region. At the same time, the NATO intervention in Libya in 2011—in which air power was used to support armed rebels and force the collapse of the regime of Muammar Ghaddafi—spawned debates about the legitimacy of such action, appropriate responses from the Left, and the role of violence in this particular "pro-democracy" movement.[11]

ACTIVISM AND THE INTERNET

The new century also saw increasing usage of the Internet, mobile phones, blogs, and new social-networking media for purposes of political mobilization and engagement in the public sphere. Scholars have long examined the extent to which social networks—whether formal or informal—affect movement recruitment and organizational growth. The Internet and especially social-networking media came to be seen as significant new mobilizing technologies that helped to create "virtual communities" or connect various movements, networks, and individuals for collective action framed by a collective identity. For example, in the United States, MoveOn.org—a nonprofit organization and political action committee founded in 1998 to focus on education about and advocacy for national issues—has utilized the Internet extensively and effectively to mobilize public action on specific bills, policies, or candidates in favor of progressive politics. In addition to the virtual communities that it creates, MoveOn.org encourages the formation of local discussion and activist groups. Avaaz.org, launched in 2007, is a global campaigning organization with a strong antiwar stance. According to its website, "Avaaz is a global web movement to bring people-powered politics to decision-making everywhere." It uses the model of Internet organizing "to mobilize thousands of individuals to take action on pressing global and national issues and to create a powerful collective force." Avaaz campaigns in fifteen languages with thousands of volunteers. The principal value that underlies their campaigns is "the conviction that we are all human beings first, and privileged with responsibilities to each other, to future generations, and to the planet."[12]

The new information and communication technologies have affected research on protest participation as well as on social movements themselves. One study of the social and political implications of mobile phones shows how they were used for various political mobilization processes, such as the deposing of Philippine president Joseph Estrada in 2002, the election campaign in South Korea in 2002, the 2004 elections in Spain following the terrorist bombing attack in Madrid, and the protest events at the 2004 Republican National Convention in the United States. Young people in particular have come to rely on mobile phones, instant messaging, and other new technologies not only for information and entertainment but also for mobilization purposes. Social-networking media such as Facebook and Twitter, very popular among young people, are especially useful for purposes of rapid communication during protest periods. In Iran's Green Protests of June 2009, mobile phones and tweets were used to mobilize people for the street protests, record and document the massive nature of the demonstrations, warn activists about the presence of police, photograph police brutality, and disseminate visual and aural images globally.[13] Throughout the Arab Spring of early 2011, young people received information and were mobilized via YouTube, Facebook, and Twitter; they captured police brutality on their smart phones, posted images on the various social-networking media, and celebrated their victory on the Web as well as on the streets of Tunis, Cairo, and elsewhere. On October 15,

2011, one month after Occupy Wall Street emerged in New York City, a global day of solidarity took place, with nine hundred protests across eighty-two countries—all coordinated via the Internet. Among other things, these examples illustrate how the new information and communication technologies (ICTs) play a role in facilitating rapid horizontal communication and coordination.

Lauren Langman and Douglas Morris have argued that ICTs permit "internetworking," or connections to diverse networks and movements for social change. Similarly, research by Stefaan Walgrave and colleagues has examined the ways in which ICTs may "lower networking costs, extend the reach and diversity of networks, and increase levels and scale of participation," as well as the extent to which digital media "allow activists to combine multiple engagements with diverse causes." They contend that

> ICTs, due to their flexible utilization and asynchronous character, permit people in general and activists in particular to maintain multiple contacts and to hold various engagements for different causes at the same time. . . . ICTs help activists with multiple engagements cope with their complex, multi-issue, multi-protest, and multi-movement commitments.[14]

Such observations hold true for the transnational feminist movement and the global justice movement examined in this book, though arguably less so for activists in Iran, Egypt, and Tunisia. Although ICTs played a significant mobilizing role in the protest movements of the three countries, and activists did have external links, those protest movements were more focused on a single, domestic issue (challenging authoritarian government and calling for democracy) than has been the case with transnational feminist networks or Occupy Wall Street.

In another expression of cyberactivism, WikiLeaks—part of a longer tradition and principle of free publication, "open source" information, and news distribution—challenged authorities and governments the world over by releasing classified U.S. documents revealing malfeasance in wars, foreign policy, and global business. According to one report, WikiLeaks had changed whistle-blowing, dissident journalism, and the new phenomenon of "citizen journalism" through its regular exposés of state or corporate crimes. Its founder, Julian Assange, an Australian national, unveiled WikiLeaks.org in January

2007, and in publications that were picked by the *New York Times*, the *Guardian*, *El País*, *Der Spiegel*, and *Le Monde*, it exposed evidence of corruption in the family of former Kenyan president Daniel arap Moi, published the standard operating principles for the Guantánamo Bay detention center, and, most significantly, released in April 2010 a video of a U.S. helicopter attack in Baghdad in July 2007, which killed a number of Iraqi civilians and two Iraqi-born Reuters personnel. An eighteen-minute film called "Collateral Murder" gave a chilling insight into what could be perceived as U.S. war crimes. Assange maintained that an explicit part of WikiLeaks' purpose in exposing U.S. State Department cables and other government documents was to highlight human rights abuses. Subsequently, both the website and its founder became the subject of investigation, personal attacks, and a financial blockade that impeded supporter donations. In response, the chimerical Anonymous collective retaliated by hacking into government, police, and corporate files.[15]

As one of the "gifts" of globalization, the Internet has been an indispensable tool for activists. It has allowed for rapid communication and coordination; Internet-savvy transnational networks have set up extensive, interactive, and increasingly sophisticated multimedia websites, where one can find statements, research reports, and manifestoes, as well as discussion forums, chat rooms, blogs, tutorials, and digital libraries. Such websites, many of which are linked to each other, create or support communities of activists while also providing them with resources. Cyberactivism can cross generational lines, but it is the vehicle par excellence of the younger generation, with their affinity for, and expertise in, social-networking media. As such, the "biographical availability" of youth for protest activity is enhanced by their immersion in the world of ICTs, creating a demographic pool with a potential for rapid mobilization and protest activity.[16] It is important to note, however, that the Internet also has been used by right-wing and violent networks, and it is under constant surveillance by state agencies. (See further discussion on this aspect in chapter 2.)

All these developments—the rise of transnational social movements and networks for democracy, justice, and human rights; the growth of militant networks that draw on Islamic symbols; the spread of women's rights movements; the invasion and occupation of Afghanistan and Iraq; the political revolutions and democracy movements in Egypt and Tunisia; the NATO intervention to support the armed uprising in Libya; the extensive use of the new information and communication technologies—are pertinent to the study of globalization and social movements. They present questions about opportunities and resources for movement building, the use of violence in social/political movements and transnational networks, the relationship of war to the global capitalist order, the changing dynamics of the world-system and the role of the hegemon, the salience of masculinities in global processes, and prospects for women-friendly democratic transitions that institutionalize the economic as well as civil and political rights of citizens. These questions are addressed in the book's subsequent chapters.

This book integrates a discussion of theories and empirical documentation of social movements in an era of globalization while also offering an explanatory framework. It examines the relationship between globalization (in its economic, political, and cultural manifestations) and social movements, including the new forms of transnational collective action. The book also examines the relations among globalization, social movements, and democratization, inspired by the MENA democracy movements but also by the democratic practices of transnational social movements such as global feminism and the global justice movement, including Occupy Wall Street. As will become evident, the MENA social movements are linked to globalization in at least three ways. First, they are rooted in grievances concerning the unemployment, high costs of living, and deteriorating public services that have accompanied the neoliberal policy model implemented across the globe. Second, they have "caught up" with the so-called third wave of democratization (a theory associated with political scientist Samuel Huntington); as such, democracy movements in MENA are part of a global trend. Third, they are transnational in their use of social-networking media, their connections with the MENA diaspora, and the support they have received from transnational advocacy and activist networks. Chapter 3 takes up such sociological issues as the agents of the democracy movements; democracy "frames"; mobilization processes and organizational features; and prospects for a global democracy.

The empirical chapters—chapters 4, 5, and 6—focus on three transnational social movements that emerged under the conditions of late capitalism/neoliberal globalization: political Islam, the women's movement, and the global justice movement. Undoubtedly, these are among the most vocal and visible of transnational movements and networks. Each constitutes a transnational social movement inasmuch as it connects people across borders around a common agenda and collective identity; mobilizes large numbers of supporters and activists, whether as individuals or as members of networks, groups, and organizations; and engages in sustained oppositional politics with states or other power holders. Despite this overarching similarity, however, it will become apparent in the course of this book that although Islamist movements are internally differentiated, their grievances, methods, and goals differ in profound ways from those of the radical democratic or socialistic visions of global feminism and the global justice movement. One key difference is that many Islamist movements seek state power and, like revolutionary movements before them, are willing to use violence to achieve this aim. In contrast, both the feminist and global justice movements are disinterested in state power, although they do seek wide-ranging institutional and normative changes, and they eschew violence.

ISLAMISM, FEMINISM, GLOBAL JUSTICE: ORIGINS AND ANTECEDENTS

Transnational social movements date back to the late eighteenth century, although in recent decades the scope of transnationalization and the scale of international ties among activists have risen dramatically. Sidney Tarrow has noted that social movements emerged in the eighteenth century from "structural changes that were associated with capitalism," such as "new forms of association, regular communication linking center and periphery, and the spread of print and literacy." Social movements—like revolutions—are thus associated with modernity and capitalism; they are rooted in and triggered by the contradictions of the capitalist world-system. In a Marxian dialectical sense, these contradictions entail both oppressive conditions and opportunities for action, resistance, and change. In her study of historical resistance to economic globalization, Zahara Heckscher identifies five episodes between the 1780s and the early 1900s: the Tupac Amaru II uprising in what is now Peru against the Spanish colonialists; the international movement against the Atlantic slave trade; European workers and the First International Workingman's Association; the campaign against the colonization of the Congo; and United States–Philippines solidarity in the anti-imperialist movement of the late nineteenth century.[17] These cases of what world-system analysts call "antisystemic resistance" confirm Marx's many apposite observations about human action and societal constraints, including the famous line from the *Eighteenth Brumaire of Louis Bonaparte*: "Men make their own history," he noted, "but not in circumstances of their own choosing."

World-system theorists point out that history proceeds in a series of waves. Capitalist expansions ebb and flow in waves of globalization and deglobalization, and egalitarian and humanistic countermovements emerge in a cyclical dialectical struggle. Karl Polanyi called this the "double-movement." As noted above, world-system analysts refer to antisystemic movements, and Terry Boswell and Christopher Chase-Dunn termed this "the spiral of capitalism and socialism."[18] Table 1.1, which I prepared for classroom use in 2007 and have updated since, summarizes some of the key events associated with the global spread of capitalism and its challengers during the "long twentieth century," that is, from the late 1800s to the current century. It draws attention to the salience of, and relations among, political economy, states, and resistance. It also includes some of the key institutions of global governance and international organizations that belong to what sociologist Jackie Smith has identified as two contending global networks: the global neoliberal network and the global pro-democracy network.[19]

The choice of the global justice, Islamist, and feminist movements analyzed in this book is neither accidental nor arbitrary. Apart from the fact that they are among the most prominent and visible of contemporary social movements, they also have historical antecedents in the eighteenth, nineteenth, and early twentieth centuries. The global justice movement of today can be linked back to transnational movements of workers, socialists, communists, progressives, and anarchists during an economic period that Polanyi called the "great transformation." Many of the older activists in the contemporary global justice movement were once affiliated with left-wing organizations or solidarity movements, many of the younger activists are involved in labor and economic justice causes, and the writings of Karl Marx are well known to many activists. Human rights groups also abound in the global justice movement, and some scholars have found similarities between their moral discourse, tactics, and strategies and those of

Table 1.1. The World-System, Globalization, and Social Movements: A "Long Twentieth Century" Timeline

1870–1914	Economic liberalism, free trade, British Empire, colonialism, competition (France, Germany, British, Austro-Hungarian and Ottoman empires)
1914–1918	World War I; suffrage movement, socialism/communism
1920s–1930s	Aftermath of war: breakup of empires; modernity and its discontents; Great Depression; socialism/communism, labor, League of Nations; fascism
1939–1945	World War II (United States, United Kingdom, Soviet Union versus Germany, Italy, Japan)
1945	Beginning of decolonization; decline of British Empire, rise of United States as hegemon (especially after 1953 coup in Iran)
1950s	Cold War (including coups and CIA dirty tricks); emergence of the "three worlds," including the nonaligned movement (Bandung Conference)
1950s–1970s	Theories and policies of development (balanced growth, basic needs, dependency, ISI, etc.); era of state-led development (industrialization, etc.); Fordist/Keynesian economics; deficit financing; influence of CEPAL/ECLAC, NAM, NIEO, UNIDO, UNCTAD, ILO, and UNESCO[a]
1960s–1980s	Third World revolutions and Western social movements: anti–Vietnam War, student movements across globe; feminist, environmental, antinuclear, animal rights movements
1980s	End of Keynesianism; rise of monetarism and neoliberalism; structural adjustment in Third World; debt increases due to interest rate increases; Contra Wars in Central America; Afghan war; Islamic fundamentalism; slow decline of Soviet Union; emergence of transnational feminist networks
1989–1990	End of communism in Eastern Europe and Soviet Union; end of Three Worlds; publication of first UNDP Human Development Report
1990s	Iraq sanctions, Yugoslav wars, Rwanda genocide; consolidation of European Union, end of apartheid in South Africa; Fourth World Conference on Women; globalization through new information and communication technologies and spread of neoliberalism, flexible labor markets, North American Free Trade Agreement (NAFTA), shift from the General Agreement on Tariffs and Trade (GATT) to the World Trade Organization (WTO). Transnational capitalism: class and global governance; rise of NGOs, INGOs, transnational advocacy networks; the UN's Fourth World Conference on Women. Mobilizations against neoliberal globalization: anti-MAI, "Battle of Seattle."
2000	Beginning of cycle of antiglobalization protests; enactment by global elites of Millennium Declaration and MDGs; Security Council Resolution 1325
2001	September 11, al-Qaeda, invasion of Afghanistan; spread of global Arab media
2003	War on terror and invasion of Iraq
2007–	Defeat of the Doha round, rise of Brazil, Russia, India, China (BRIC); mortgage crisis in United States; start of global financial crisis and economic recession; declining U.S. hegemony? world-system transition?
2011–2012	Arab Spring; European protests against austerity; Occupy Wall Street

[a]CEPAL/ECLAC refers to the UN's Economic Commission for Latin America; NAM is the Nonaligned Movement; NIEO is the New International Economic Order; UNIDO is the UN Industrial Development Organization; ILO is the International Labour Organization; UNESCO is the UN Educational, Scientific and Cultural Organization.

the much earlier antislavery movement in the United States and the United Kingdom. Margaret Keck and Kathryn Sikkink have noted that the backbone of the antislavery movement was made up of Quakers and the "dissenting denominations"—Methodists, Presbyterians, and Unitarians—who used reportage, conferences, and novels to push for abolition.[20] These tactics are still used in the human rights movement and in the global justice movement in general, even though the Internet revolution has broadened the scope of their mobilizing mechanisms and tactics and added to their collective action repertoire. An important difference between the contemporary global justice movement and the movements of the nineteenth and twentieth centuries, however, pertains to the far more decentralized, diffuse, fluid, and internetworked nature of global justice.

The Islamist movements that burst onto the international scene in the late 1970s and spread in the 1980s were rooted in eighteenth-, nineteenth-, and early-twentieth-century revival movements, which in turn claimed to be following the path taken by the Prophet Muhammad in the seventh century AD. Sociologist Mansoor Moaddel has traced the evolution of Islamic modernism, liberal nationalism, and Islamic fundamentalism, arguing that the movements arose in the context of different global developments, resources, cultural capital, and institutional ties. He adds,

> Yet Muslims reached no lasting agreement on the form government should take, the appropriate economic model, the relationship of Muslim nations with the outside world, the status of women, their national identities, and the relation of Islam to rational analysis and rule making. Instead, Islamic societies experienced a sequence of diverse cultural episodes characterized by serious ideological disputes and acrimonious debates followed by sociopolitical crises, ending in revolutions or military coups.

Hugh Roberts has shown how Algeria's Front Islamique du Salut (FIS) was part of the legacy of orthodox, urban-based Islamic reformists associated with the Salafists of the early decades of the twentieth century against rural-based maraboutic Islam. John Voll identified contemporary Islamic fundamentalism in Egypt and the Sudan with eighteenth- and nineteenth-century Wahhabist and Mahdist movements. Today's militant Islamists are inspired by the rigid and puritanical legacies of Ibn Taymiyyah, a medieval Hanbali jurist, and Ibn Abd-al-Wahhab, an eighteenth-century theologian who formed an alliance with Muhammad Ibn Saud and built a religio-political movement that was defeated by the Ottomans but in the twentieth century formed the foundation of the new state of Saudi Arabia. Other sources of inspiration and guidance are the writings of Abul Ala Mawdudi (who founded the Jamiat-e Islami in India in 1941), the Egyptians Rashid Rida and Hassan al-Banna (who founded the Muslim Brotherhood in 1929), and Sayyid Qutb of Egypt, all of whom took issue with modernity as it was proceeding in their countries and called for a return to strict implementation of sharia law. Sayyid Qutb's 1948–1950 stay in the United States convinced him that the *jahiliyya*—the so-called age of darkness that characterized pre-Islamic Arabia—had returned and needed to be combated. Today's militant Islamists use the term *jahiliyya* to describe the state of the world and justify their aggressive tactics. From Ibn Taymiyyah they adopted the duty to wage jihad against apostates and unbelievers.[21]

Islamist movements became prominent in the 1980s, but clearly Islam had been a mobilizing frame in the decades before. Both Islamic and nationalist frames were used in anticolonial struggles, but on occasion Islamist groups opposed progressive nationalist leaders. Thus, in the 1950s, Iranian premier Mohammad Mossadegh and Egypt's Gamal Abdel Nasser incurred the opposition, respectively, of Sheikh Fazlollah Nouri and the Muslim Brotherhood. Self-described Islamic governments have come to power in Iran, Sudan, and Turkey, though only in Turkey has the ruling party—the Justice and Development Party, or AKP as per the Turkish acronym—been discussed in terms of an example of the compatibility of Islam and democracy. The Arab Spring in Tunisia and Egypt has been accompanied by the political prominence of Islamic groups such as Egypt's Muslim Brotherhood and Tunisia's an-Nahda. Questions that may be posed are, Can Islamic movements be democratic? Can they contribute to democratization in MENA? Are they agents of democratization or a new form of authoritarianism? As we will see, Turkish feminists and others have raised questions about the AKP's agenda; Tunisian feminists have expressed reservations about an-Nahda—which won the largest number of seats in the October 2011 elections for a constituent assembly—although they are more worried about the new Salafist groups; and Egyptian democrats have voiced concerns about the attacks on Egyptian Copts (the Christian community that dates to pre-Islamic times) by Islamist extremists as well as by the repressive apparatus of the military.

The contemporary global women's movement has roots in first-wave feminism, with its focus on suffrage and justice for women, and in second-wave feminism, with its demands for equality and cultural change. First-wave feminism brought about international women's organizations around abolition, women's suffrage, opposition to trafficking in women, antimilitarism, and labor legislation for working women and mothers. In the United States, the 1840 Seneca Falls Convention comprised elite women familiar with the details of the French and American revolutions and supportive of the antislavery movement. First-wave feminism later grew to include women disappointed that the franchise was not extended to them when (male) slaves were emancipated and given the right to vote. Scholars have identified moderate, socialist, and militant strands of the early feminist movement. Among the social movement organizations (SMOs) of first-wave feminism was the International Woman Suffrage Alliance (IWSA), formed in 1904. Its methods included speaking tours and rallies, but militants were ready to be arrested, jailed, and force-fed for the cause. Militant suffragists in the United States and the United Kingdom deployed public agitation, civil disobedience, and sometimes violent tactics to draw attention to their cause; such methods were used by the Women's Social and Political Union in the United Kingdom and by Alice Paul and her associates in the United States.

The early twentieth century also saw the emergence of an international socialist women's movement. In 1900 the Socialist International passed its first resolution in favor of women's suffrage, and suffrage became a demand of socialist parties in 1907. Within the Second International, the women's organizations of France, Germany, and Russia mobilized thousands of working-class as well as middle-class women for socialism and women's emancipation. In Asian countries, as Kumari Jayawardena showed, many of the women's movements and organizations that emerged were associated with socialist or nationalist movements. Although feminists and leftists have not always agreed on priorities or strategies, there has been a long-standing affinity that helps to explain the involvement of feminists in the global justice movement today and in the World Social Forum. Examples of early international women's organizations are the Women's International League for Peace and Freedom (WILPF), the International Council of Women (ICW), the International Alliance of Women (IAW), the Women's International Democratic Federation (WIDF), and the Young Women's Christian Association (YWCA). In promoting women's rights, maternity legislation, and an end to child labor, they engaged with intergovernmental bodies such as the League of Nations and the International Labour Organization (ILO).[22]

THE WORLD-SYSTEM AND SOCIAL MOVEMENTS

World-system theory posits the existence of a hierarchical interstate system of unequal states and markets, with a hegemon (the dominant power, economically, politically, and militarily) and economic zones of core, periphery, and semiperiphery. In the 1950s, the United States supplanted the United Kingdom as the world-system's hegemon. Scholars have argued that American economic power declined relatively after the 1970s—that is, relative to the growing power of Europe, the newly industrializing countries, and, more recently, China. Beginning with the Reagan administration, so the argument goes, successive American administrations sought to maintain American hegemony through diplomacy and free trade, including the so-called Washington Consensus that resulted in the spread of neoliberalism throughout the world. Debates among scholars ensued, however, over whether we were observing a new phase of U.S. imperialism, the consolidation of an integrated system of global capitalism, or a combination of imperial and neoliberal projects.[23] Immanuel Wallerstein has argued that the current world-system is in crisis and in a stage of transition, the end product of which is unknown and cannot be predicted.[24] Certainly the global economic crisis of 2008 seemed to breathe new life into the global justice movement, with protests, rallies, and demonstrations encompassing most parts of the world by the end of 2011 and into 2012.

As the world-system is the primary unit of analysis, the position of a national state within one or another of the world-system's economic zones, and the relationship between the state in question and the hegemonic power, can shape the emergence, course, and consequences of social movements. Social movements in the democratic countries of the core may have more freedom to operate, mobilize resources, and express dissent, while those in peripheral or semiperipheral countries may lack adequate resources or face considerably more repression. Similarly, participation in the global justice movement may be shaped by world-systemic constraints: networks and organizations from richer countries are likely to be involved in a more sustained manner and in greater numbers than are those from poorer countries. The world-system also affects social movements in the way that it generates grievances. The global justice movement, for example, has emerged precisely to challenge the dominance of a neoliberal world order, to call for "another world," and to protest the excesses of corporate capitalism and its political allies. Islamist movements not only oppose aspects of what they see as a westernized and anti-Islamic modernity in their own countries but also take exception to the hegemonic power of the United States and its unwavering support for Israel's conduct with Palestinians and neighboring countries. The capitalist world-system generates various forms of inequalities, including gender inequality, while the behavior of corporations, banks, and many governments evinces the kind of hypermasculinity that feminists have long critiqued. In turn, these aspects of the world-system have galvanized sections of the world's female population to form transnational feminist networks or to join the global justice movement.

Social movement analysis has taken a clear theoretical shape within sociology. Scholars have long shown that the roots of social protest, organizing, and movement building are located in broad social change processes that destabilize existing power relations and increase the leverage of challenging groups. There is now an appreciation for the interconnection of political, organizational, and cultural processes in social movements, with scholars arguing that the three factors play roles of varying analytic importance over the course of the movement. Opportunities are critical to emergence, as they are tied to the relative openness or closure of the political system and the state, the stability of the elite, and the presence or absence of elite allies. Pertinent questions are, How does the national political system influence movements? How does movement strategy and structure change in response to political opportunities? How do movements act within, and help create, political opportunities? Mobilizing structures—networks, associations, and patterns of recruitment, leadership, and resource mobilization—

become more central as the movement develops. Much research has documented the formation and evolution of SMOs, but research also shows that these originate in small groups or informal networks. Framing processes—the meanings given to action, the formation of collective identities, the ways in which issues are presented—are always important, but they become more self-conscious and tactical over the course of the movement. Scholars also have identified an ongoing process of "frame alignment," whereby social movement actors link their claims to interested audiences, often to strategically construct more resonant and persuasive frames that will mobilize people.[25]

The three aspects of social movements are interrelated, inasmuch as the structure of political opportunities can affect resource mobilization; meanings, frames, and identities can be formed in connection with available opportunities, resources, and audiences; and the political context can be influenced or even changed by concerted collective action. In addition, scholars examine cycles and waves of protest, as well as "collective action repertoires" such as boycotts, mass petitioning, marches, rallies, barricading, and acts of civil disobedience. To this list we should add the meetings and conferences typical of feminist action, the suicide bombings deployed by radical Islamists, and the new forms of cyberactivism. Theorists continue to view social movements as a collective response to deprivation, the contradictions of late capitalism, or the availability of resources, but a consensus emerged in the 1990s that stresses political processes while also viewing cultural and structural processes alike as key to understanding the cycles and strategies of social protest.

All movements have some structure, but not all movements have major formal organizations that dominate and direct movement activity. According to Luther Gerlach, social movements are "segmentary, polycentric, and reticulate [SPR]." Illustrating his SPR thesis by way of the environmental movement, he shows that social movements have many, sometimes competing, organizations and groups (segmentary); they have multiple and sometimes competing leaders (polycentric); and they are loose networks that link to each other (reticulate). Despite the segmentation, however, there is a shared opposition and ideology. In the environmental movement, for example, SMOs have ranged from the very radical Earth First! to Greenpeace and Germany's Greens (who later evolved into the Green Party). Gerlach argues that the SPR nature of SMOs is very effective, allowing them to be flexible and adaptive and to resonate with larger constituencies through different tactics (for example, direct action versus lobbying and legal strategies). It also "promotes striving, innovation, and entrepreneurial experimentation in generating and implementing sociocultural change."[26] This argument is consistent with more recent scholarship in political science and sociology—such as works by Keck and Sikkink on transnational advocacy networks, myself on transnational feminist networks, and Jackie Smith, Marina Karides, and their colleagues on the World Social Forum—which underscores the openness, fluidity, and flexibility of contemporary network-based movements. The argument is also relevant to all three of the movements that we examine in this book. Indeed, the type of mobilizing structures found in the global Islamist, feminist, and justice movements include formal organizations but more typically fluid networks—and in the case of the Islamist movement, militant cells that act independently of any larger or more formal organization.

Combining world-system, Marxist, and social movement conceptual frameworks helps us to better grasp the factors behind the emergence of the transnational social movements under consideration in this book, their characteristics, and their prospects. And integrating feminist insights allows us to discern the role of gender, and especially of hypermasculinities, in social movement dynamics and in specific tactics and strategies.

In this book, we discuss the opportunities, mobilizing structures, and frames pertinent to the global justice, Islamist, and feminist movements. (See table 1.2 for an elaboration.) But the role of emotions is important too, as a growing body of literature points out.[27] Commitment, zeal, moral outrage, solidarity, ethics—these are aspects of social movement building and participation that scholars oriented toward rational choice theorizing have neglected. No one who examines Islamist movements can deny that there are strong emotional undercurrents and motivations among participants. When Muslim-owned media such as Al Jazeera and Al Arabiyya dwell on bombings in Afghanistan, Iraq, Lebanon, and Palestine, this can be regarded as a movement event that is also an emotion-producing ritual. Similarly, emotions play a role in the feminist and global justice movements. Violence against women is certainly addressed analytically by feminists but is often confronted in

Table 1.2. Social Movement Features of Feminist, Islamist, and Global Justice Movements

	Opportunities and Resources	Mobilizing Structures: Networks and SMOs	Frames
Feminist	Sociodemographics: women's educational attainment and labor force participation UN Decade for Women (1976–1985) and 1990s UN conferences Resources: women's organizations, donor agencies, European foundations	DAWN, WIDE, WLUML, WEDO, WILPF, World March of Women, MADRE, WLP, Code Pink[a]	Women's rights are human rights; end feminization of poverty; end violence against women; empowerment; gender justice; gender mainstreaming
Islamist			
Parliamentarian	Local support; resources from Muslim states; publicity and support via Arab media such as Al Jazeera	Hamas, Hezbollah, Muslim Brotherhood; an-Nahda	Islam is the solution; establish sharia law; end repression; justice for Palestine
Extremist	U.S.-sponsored Afghan war, 1980–1992; resources from Muslim states; personal wealth; publicity via Al Jazeera	Al-Qaeda and affiliates; various salafist or jihadist groupings	Get "Crusaders" out of Muslim lands; liberate Palestine, Afghanistan, Iraq; jihad against "near enemy" and "far enemy"; global caliphate
Global Justice	UN conferences of 1990s; occasional support from EU and social democratic governments; *Le Monde Diplomatique*; Workers' Party government of Brazil; rise of left-wing governments in Latin America; information and communication technologies	Third World Network; ENDA; Focus on the Global South; Oxfam; Jubilee 2000; ATTAC; World Social Forum; Occupy Wall Street	Against neoliberal globalization; for biodiversity and cultural diversity (*altérmondialisation*), economic justice; ending Third World debt, making poverty history, environmental protection, human rights, antiwar, ending corporate greed and power, "another world is possible," "we are the 99%!"

[a]Development Alternatives with Women for a New Era (DAWN); Women in Development Europe (WIDE); Women Living under Muslim Laws (WLUML); Women's Environment and Development Organization (WEDO); Women's International League for Peace and Freedom (WILPF); Women's Learning Partnership for Rights, Development and Peace (WLP).

emotive terms. Activists within the global justice movement frequently articulate their opposition to neoliberal capitalism and the international financial institutions in moral economy terms. Social movement actors do not simply engage in coolheaded cost-benefit calculations but also express strong feelings about injustices and entitlements. Nor are these expressions limited to anger, alienation, and moral outrage. Kum-Kum Bhavnani, John Foran, and Molly Talcott write of the Zapatista movement, "Love of life, love of people, love of justice—all play a role in the core values of Zapatismo."[28] At the antiglobalization protests and demonstrations of the early part of the century, during the anti-austerity protests in Europe in 2010 and 2011, and at the Occupy Wall Street protests of fall 2011, one observed laughter, music, satire, parody, puppetry—indeed, a festival-like atmosphere. Strong feelings of social solidarity, unity of purpose, and hope were evident in the Tunisian and Egyptian antigovernment protests of early 2011, which also saw poetry, song, and candlelight vigils. Emotions such as joy, anger, commitment, and solidarity are as important in the social movement experience as are the "entrepreneurial" dimensions.

For these reasons, elements of the older explanatory frameworks that focused on sociopsychological factors in protest mobilizations cannot be entirely ruled out as anachronistic or unhelpful. Indeed, the concept of cultural framing is rooted in social psychology. Moreover, the presence of emotions such as humiliation, anger, and frustration has been widely noted in connection with Muslim militants, by observers as well as by Islamists themselves. Osama bin Laden, for example, once declared that for over eighty years Islam had been "tasting . . . humiliation and contempt . . . its sons . . . killed, its blood . . . shed, its holy places . . . attacked."[29] In Tunisia, when the street vendor Mohammed Bouazizi ignited himself in December 2010 out of frustration at his inability to make a living, this seemed to express the frustration of a large segment of the Tunisian population, which had seen its once-vaunted welfare state deteriorate in the wake of neoliberal reforms as well as the global economic crisis. Anger and frustration also could be seen in Greece, Spain, Italy, Chile, Britain, and other countries where street protests and strikes targeted governments, corporations, and banks as the architects of the hated neoliberalism that had done away with the once strong social economy model. In the United States, Occupy Wall Street protesters expressed frustration with the inability of the world's largest economy to provide decent jobs and decent wages, as well as anger at bank bailouts and gross income inequalities. As noted above, however, expressions of anger and frustration are balanced—and in many democratic social movements, overridden or eclipsed—by more positive sentiments and energy. In Tunisia and Egypt these were fearlessness in the face of police repression, along with a fierce determination to end authoritarianism and bring about democracy, dignity, and social justice. The anti-austerity and Occupy Wall Street protests evoked similar emotions of bravery, determination, and solidarity.

ON STUDYING TRANSNATIONAL SOCIAL MOVEMENTS

Globalization continues to present challenges for scholars of social change and for theory building. One issue pertains to the permanence of some of the new institutions and processes that are observed, including institutions of global governance and the rules of free trade. Is "globalization-from-above" a fait accompli or a transitional phase that can be supplanted by new social relations and forms of governance? Are the responses known as "globalization-from-below" likely to be institutionalized? Answers to these questions require time and analysis. In the meantime, scholars continue to study globalization and transnational social movements, as well as to introduce methodological issues. Salvatore Babones, for example, elucidates the scope of global research, distinguishing it from cross-national, international, or comparative research. He stresses the distinctive nature of "global as a level of analysis," which presupposes systemic factors in the explanatory framework or causal model. "Data sources and research strategies for conducting global social research depend on the units of analysis used in answering the research questions posed," he writes, explaining that the unit of analysis can be an individual, a region, a country, an area, or the world. Global social research, he concludes, "is designed to answer questions about social phenomena that operate at a global level."[30]

While the study of globalization includes poring over international data sets to discern patterns of economic and political governance, the study of transnational social movements, including the three examined in this book, requires a mix of methods, both qualitative and quantitative:

participant observation, surveys, in-depth interviews with key figures, analysis of network publications and websites, and the use of secondary sources. Some scholars have tried to test empirically the relationship between globalization—whether measured by world trade, growing inequalities, or state integration in the world polity—and the rise and spread of global contentious politics and transnational social movements. Jackie Smith and Dawn Wiest, for example, have analyzed the impact of world culture and world polity on the spread of progressive, nonviolent social movements. They have found a positive relationship between state integration into world polity and civil society integration into transnational networks or global civil society. Omar Lizardo looked at the relationship between economic globalization or world culture and less salutary forms of global contentious politics, including violent militancy. In studying Islamist movements, scholars have visited offices, mosques, seminaries, and other institutions; conducted interviews (sometimes in prisons); utilized memoirs by former Islamists; and analyzed Islamist websites and publications. Edna Reid and Hsinchen Chen used hyperlink and content-analysis methodology to analyze extremist groups' websites. The study of transnational feminist networks requires similar methods: attendance at feminist conferences, observation at protest events or UN conferences, reading of websites and publications, and interviews with key figures. With respect to analyses of the global justice movement, researchers have attended the World Social Forum, where they have conducted surveys and in-depth interviews; they have closely followed the writings and publications of scholar-activists and other GJM leaders; and they have quantified protest events. The research products of the Institute for Research on World-Systems (IROWS), based at the University of California, Riverside, are especially prodigious. Sociologist Christopher Chase-Dunn and his students and colleagues have attended various World Social Forums, conducted surveys, and posted their findings on the IROWS website. Studies on the global justice movement by Italian sociologist Donatella della Porta and her associates are based on extensive and intensive observation of European movements and networks. Catherine Eschle, Jane Conway, and other feminist scholars who have attended the WSF analyze the place of, and reception to, feminism in the forum. Participant observation at the WSF and the United States Social Forum has produced a number of important studies.[31]

The present book synthesizes previous research, including my own fieldwork and published results over the years. I have consulted the relevant secondary sources on globalization, social movements, the Arab Spring, and the global Islamist, feminist, and justice movements. In addition, I have examined movement websites and publications. The chapter on transnational feminist networks draws on my previous research but now also covers feminist activism against militarism and war. The explanatory framework establishes a relationship between globalization-from-above and globalization-from-below; shows how political processes, resources, networks, and framings are used by contenders to build their movements and advance their causes; identifies key features of Islamism, feminism, and global justice; and highlights the role of gender and masculinities. As a scholar of the Middle East and North Africa, as well as of globalization and transnational social movements, I aim to show how the mass protests in the region are related to globalization and to elucidate the democratizing potential of the movements, in particular those of Egypt, Iran, Morocco, and Tunisia.

The assumptions, main arguments, and key concepts presented in this book may be summarized as follows:

1. Globalization is a multifaceted process of social change with economic, political, and cultural dimensions that reflect homogeneity and heterogeneity, new forms of inequality and competition, and transnational forms of organizing and mobilizing.
2. What is called globalization-from-above is the latest stage of capitalism on a world scale, involving the spread of neoliberal capitalism through investment, trade, and war.
3. Given the capitalist bases of globalization, the inequalities of class, gender, and race are maintained through processes of accumulation and patterns of distribution in the productive, reproductive, and virtual economies within and across the core, periphery, and semiperiphery of the world-system.[32]
4. Social movements—sustained contentious politics by mobilized groups that target states—have been affected by globalization in at least two ways: (a) they are increasingly influenced by forces and factors beyond national borders, and (b) they have been expanding their scope above and across borders.

5. Transnational social movements are related to globalization in three ways: (a) they are responses to the downside of globalization, specifically, neoliberal capitalism; (b) they reflect the global expansion of civil society, the transnational public sphere, and world culture; and (c) they benefit from opportunities and resources associated with the new information and communication technologies.

6. Transnationalization is a deliberate strategy to increase the global reach of social movements and expand movement diversity, representation, and influence. In some cases, as with transnational feminist networks and the World Social Forum, it is a way of transmitting democratization.

7. The transnational public sphere and global civil society are constituted by social movements, advocacy networks, militant opposition groups, diverse publics, and media networks in contentious interactions and with different conceptions of "the good society." Not all participating networks, representations, and discourses, however, are emancipatory or democratic. It may be more useful, therefore, to refer to multiple and sometimes overlapping transnational public spheres.

8. While social movement theory has emphasized the importance of organizations, the network form—with its flexibility and fluidity—appears to be most conducive to an era of globalization. The network structure is most characteristic of transnational social movements, including the three studied here.[33]

9. Globalization presents the social sciences with analytical challenges: how to theorize the links between local and global, national and transnational; the capacity of states, social movements, and networks in a world of global capital; and the future of the world-system.

10. The study of social movements in a global era calls for an integrated framework drawing on world-system theory and world polity theory for a macrosociological and global perspective; employing feminism for an understanding of the gendered nature of institutions and movements; referring to Marxism for an elucidation of the class-based nature of the neoliberal project and of the propensity of capitalism toward both expansion and crisis; and invoking social movement concepts such as griev-

ances, political opportunities, resources, mobilizing structures, and cultural frames. Such a holistic framework would help accomplish the goal of "globalizing social movement theory."[34]

This book is situated within critical globalization studies[35] while also seeking to globalize social movement theorizing. Conceptually, it establishes connections between globalization-from-above and globalization-from-below; politically it seeks to build a bridge between globalization studies and progressive global movements. This book is therefore intended for students, scholars, and activists alike.

CHAPTER 2

GLOBALIZATION AND COLLECTIVE ACTION

Another world is possible!

    —World Social Forum

Ben Ali, dégage!

    —Tunisian protest, 2011

We are the 99%!

—Occupy Wall Street slogan, 2011

Globalization has been approached from different disciplinary vantage points, and debates have addressed such issues as whether globalization is at heart an economic or cultural process, the implications for state capacity, the social and gender impacts, and the effects of trade liberalization, direct foreign investment, and capital markets on growth, poverty, and inequality. The issue of periodization has also been debated: is globalization new or cyclical? I argue that globalization is the latest stage of capitalism, and its features have given rise to transnational movements of protest and resistance. Although capitalism has had other internationalizing stages, contemporary globalization has distinct features that enable forms of collective action rather broader in scale and scope than those that prevailed in the nineteenth or early twentieth centuries. And while the communist movement of the twentieth century was transnational and global in scope, it was more centralized than the transnational social movements found today. As noted in chapter 1, Luther Gerlach's characterization of social movements as segmentary, polycentric, and reticulate is especially relevant to today's global movements. Collective action is organized at local, national, and transnational levels in fluid and flexible ways; it is directed at states, corporations, and institutions of global governance; it calls for alternative values, institutions, and relations that are democratic and driven by people's needs and rights rather than by market imperatives or state interests; and it often appears leaderless. Because of the Internet, frames and tactics can be widely transmitted and diffused more rapidly than before, enabling networks to intersect and interact both virtually and physically. With the global justice movement and transnational feminist networks, tactics and strategies are deliberately nonviolent and intensely concerned with the strengthening of democracy and citizen rights. This is not the case, however, with many Islamist movements and certainly not with militant Islamist movements.

This chapter provides an overview of discussions about globalization, considering its origins, dimensions, mechanisms, agents, and social implications. In addition, it examines the relationship between globalization and contemporary forms of collective action. Last but not least, it explores the status of the state in an era of globalization and in relation to social movements, including transnational social movements.

FROM DEVELOPMENT TO GLOBALIZATION

Globalization became a buzzword in the mid-1990s, but before then scholars and activists had been focused on the social and economic development prospects of Third World countries and the damage that had been done by structural adjustment policies in the 1980s. Critiques of the "lost development decade"—which is what the 1980s era of structural adjustments, Reaganomics, and Thatcherism came to be called—intersected with earlier criticisms of the growing power of multinational corporations.[1] Meanwhile, veterans of Third World socialist or solidarity movements, left-wing groups, student movements, anti-Vietnam protests, and peace and antimilitarist causes—some of whom were also active in international development circles—networked at various conferences to exchange ideas and plan strategies.

The 1970s had been a time of both horror and hope. The 1973 coup d'état against the democratically elected socialist president of Chile, Dr. Salvadore Allende, which had the support of the U.S. government, ushered in both a reign of terror and the Global South's first experiment with a neoliberal economic policy framework. In her book *Shock Doctrine: The Rise of Disaster Capitalism*, Naomi Klein highlights this event as the harbinger of the more expansive scope of neoliberalism at century's end and into the new millennium. David Harvey, in his book on neoliberalism, states that "neoliberalization" was accomplished in 1970s Chile and Argentina in a manner that was "as simple as it was swift, brutal, and sure: a military coup backed by the traditional upper classes (as well as by the U.S. government), followed by the fierce repression of all solidarities created within the labour and the urban social movements which had so threatened their power."[2] At the same time, the 1975 defeat of the United States in Indochina and the unification of the Socialist Republic of Vietnam suggested a more hopeful era. The Cold War between the United States and the Soviet Union was in full swing, but the presence of a powerful communist bloc checked further aggression by the United States while also providing moral and financial support to various Third World movements and institutions.[3]

The 1970s also saw the emergence of new international organizations supportive of Third World development, including the United Nations Conference on Trade and Development (UNCTAD), the South Center, and the Center on Transnational Corporations. The Society for International Development had been formed earlier, but in the 1970s it became an important forum for the discussion of development theories and strategies. The United Nations Educational, Scientific and Cultural Organization (UNESCO) promoted literacy and schooling, higher education, scientific networks, intellectual and cultural production, and research on and in developing countries. The International Labour Office, the Geneva-based secretariat of the International Labour Organization (ILO), produced many studies on labor and employment, often from a leftist perspective, as well as conventions and declarations. What is more, the UN General Assembly issued a Declaration on the Establishment of a New International Economic Order (NIEO), which targeted "the remaining vestiges of alien domination, colonialism, foreign occupation, racial discrimination, apartheid, and neo-colonialism." The declaration called for the "establishment of a just and equitable relationship" in the terms of trade between developed and developing countries, the "establishment of a new international monetary system" for the promotion of development in the Third World, and "securing favorable conditions for the transfer of financial resources to developing countries." It emphasized the need to "promote the transfer of technology and the creation of indigenous technology for the benefit of the developing countries in forms and in accordance with procedures which are suited to their economies" and the "necessity for all States to put an end to the waste of natural resources, including food products." The NIEO would continue to inspire scholar-activists in Third World solidarity movements and development studies for at least ten years and was the topic of discussion at many meetings of the global Left. For example, in the 1980s, the Communist Party of Yugoslavia was organizing the Cavtat Roundtable, which brought together Marxist theorists, socialists, and communists from across the globe in an annual dialogue that was also an important arena for networking and strategizing. Although discussions covered a range of issues, prospects for a new international economic order were debated at several of the meetings.[4]

By the latter part of the 1980s, however, the NIEO had become a dead letter. Third World countries had borrowed heavily during the hopeful years of 1970s developmentalism. International banks were only too eager to lend, and the developing countries needed the loans to offset the effects of the oil price hikes of 1973 and 1979 as they continued to implement their development strategies.[5] When interest rates suddenly soared in 1980–1982, the Third World was plunged into what Cheryl Payer presciently had called "the debt trap." The situation was exacerbated by the collapse of world market prices for Third World commodities such as copper, coffee, and oil. When developing countries turned to the World Bank and the International

Monetary Fund (IMF) for new loans to service their debts, to carry out their development plans, or to guarantee their creditworthiness, the international financial institutions insisted on policy changes as a condition for additional loans. In the name of efficiency and balancing budgets, the new "structural adjustment policies" called for austerity measures such as cuts in social spending, public-sector restructuring, denationalization, and the promotion of private capital. These were, indeed, "conditionalities" placed on indebted developing countries in return for new loans that would enable them to repay the outstanding debts. The immediate results of the structural adjustment programs and the various conditions on new loans were perverse financial transfers from South to North as a result of debt servicing; deterioration of health, education, and welfare in many developing countries; falling real wages and incomes; a heavy household burden on women to compensate for income loss and social service cutbacks; and the collapse of governments and emergence of conflicts. Within the women-in-development (WID) community, feminist scholars described the gender bias of these policies and the social hardships they created. A U.S.-focused study described the "structural embeddedness" (rather than highlighting mere greed or calling the perpetrators "bad apples") of the junk bond scandal of the 1980s, which normalized manipulations of the financial markets.[6]

The political economy was changing. Markets were becoming more integrated and less regulated, and labor practices were growing more "flexible" (that is, easier on employers, with fewer rights for workers); production sites in the United States were moving to nonunion or cheap-labor locations, first in the American South and then in the Global South; financial products were becoming more complex and widespread, taking over pension and retirement plans. In the process of this global restructuring, more women and migrants were integrated as flexible low-paid labor into increasingly segmented labor markets. Public services, basic provisions, and public goods were increasingly privatized and subjected to market principles. Dramatic reductions in transportation and communication costs, combined with the breakdown of Fordist/Keynesian regimes in the core countries, made it possible for firms to coordinate production on a truly global scale. In the United States, neoliberal capitalism entailed deindustrialization and loss of job security; in the United Kingdom, it meant attacking the trade unions first, then slowly chipping away at the welfare state. The shift from the post–World War II era of full employment and welfare creation through government spending and industrial policy to the pre-eminence of big business and the operations of "the market" was now complete. The institutionalization of economic liberalism—free trade, free markets, and capitalist globalization—came to herald the end of the "global age of capitalism." What is more, in the 1980s the United States and United Kingdom withdrew from one multilateral UN agency that they felt had become improperly radical: UNESCO.[7]

In concert with the World Bank and the IMF, the governments of Ronald Reagan in the United States and Margaret Thatcher in Great Britain became the proponents of the doctrine of neoliberal capitalism, which earlier had been implemented in Chile under the auspices of the "Chicago boys"—economist Milton Friedman and his associates from the University of Chicago. Along with the U.S. government, the World Bank and the IMF became the prime agents of not only structural adjustment policies in the Third World and neoliberalism in the rich capitalist countries but also the transformation of formerly socialist economies into capitalist economies in the 1990s. As the communist world weakened and then collapsed in the latter part of the 1980s, Prime Minister Thatcher's declaration that "there is no alternative" to global free market capitalism seemed to ring true.

By the 1990s, the so-called Washington Consensus (the term was coined by economist John Williamson) became the global framework for economic growth and debt reduction and entailed the following elements:

- A guarantee of fiscal discipline and a curb to budget deficit
- A reduction of public expenditure, particularly in the military and public administration
- Tax reform, aiming at the creation of a system with a broad base and effective enforcement
- Financial liberalization, with interest rates determined by the market
- Competitive exchange rates to assist export-led growth
- Trade liberalization, coupled with the abolition of import licensing and a reduction of tariffs
- Promotion of foreign direct investment

- Privatization of state enterprises, leading to efficient management and improved performance
- Deregulation of the economy
- Protection of property rights.[8]

How would the Washington Consensus, or agreement on what came to be known as neoliberal globalization, affect the world's regions and social groups? Economist Paul Streeten's globalization balance sheet suggested who the winners and losers would be. It is prescient in its insights, but as we know, neoliberal globalization would eventually adversely affect even the richest economies (see table 2.1).

Economists such as Jagdish Bhagwati, Jeffrey Sachs, and Dani Rodrik, or those who produced the United Nations Development Programme's *Human Development Report 1999*, saw globalization as "Janus-faced," with some capacity to reduce poverty and increase growth but also with a dark side. Rodrik pointed out, "The fact that 'workers' can be more easily substituted for each other across national boundaries undermines what many conceive to be a postwar social bargain between workers and

Table 2.1. Balance Sheet of Globalization

Good for	Bad for
Japan, Europe, North America	Many developing countries
East and Southeast Asia	Africa and Latin America
Output	Employment
People with assets	People without assets
Profits	Wages
People with high skills	People with few skills
The educated	The uneducated
Professional, managerial, and technical people	Workers
Flexible adjusters	Rigid adjusters
Creditors	Debtors
Those independent of public services	Those dependent on public services
Large firms	Small firms
Men	Women, children
The strong and risk takers	The weak and vulnerable
Global markets	Local communities
Sellers of technically sophisticated products	Sellers of primary and standard manufactured products
Global culture	Local cultures
Global peace	Local troubles (Russia, Mexico, Turkey, former Yugoslavia)

Source: Streeten 1997.

employers, under which the former would receive a steady increase in wages and benefits in return for labor peace." Joseph Stiglitz, formerly chief economist of the World Bank, was more critical, warning against the "unfair trade agenda" and the absence of democratic accountability in global governance. Guy Standing of the ILO wrote extensively about the challenges for developing countries of global labor market flexibility. In a 2002 report, Oxfam–U.K. argued that trade liberalization could benefit developing countries, but not invariably so. The multilateral trade system, it was noted, is weighted against the interests of developing countries because core countries practice double standards by urging developing countries to liberalize while keeping their own markets closed to imports such as agricultural products and textiles. Policy recommendations, therefore, were that investment and trade between advanced and less developed countries should proceed equitably, and development assistance from North to South should increase. The International Labour Organization called for a "fair globalization" that would include decent jobs and decent wages. And in 2000, concerned about the persistence of poverty, governments and multilateral organizations joined forces to adopt the Millennium Development Goals (MDGs), a set of eight objectives to be reached by 2015 that pertained to ending poverty and hunger; universal education; gender equality; child health; maternal health; combating HIV/AIDS; environmental sustainability; and global partnerships.[9] But the logic of neoliberal capitalism was not questioned, and by the second decade of the new century, it was clear that many countries would not be able to meet the goals, while others would be able to achieve some but not all the MDGs.

GLOBALIZATION: THE LATEST STAGE OF CAPITALISM

On the left, scholars have analyzed these developments in at least two ways, with some emphasizing the role of class conflict and others stressing structural processes. David Harvey argues that neoliberalism, headed by the United States, has aimed for the restoration of class power to a small elite of financiers and corporate leaders, accomplished through forced privatization, or "accumulation by dispossession," as well as by the "virtual economy" of finance capital. In her feminist political economy, Spike Peterson also draws attention to financialization as well as to the different ways in which women and men are situated in what she identifies as the virtual, productive, and reproductive economies. William I. Robinson maintains that the reorganization of world production through new technologies and organizational innovations has given rise to a transnational capitalist class (TCC) and the making of a transnational state apparatus (TSA). For Harvey, globalization is the "new imperialism," while for Robinson it is a historic stage in the maturation of capitalism as a driving economic force. Another structuralist position is taken by world-system theorists Immanuel Wallerstein and Christopher Chase-Dunn, who understand "globalization" as another word for the processes that they have always referred to as world-systemic: integration into the economic zones of core, periphery, and semiperiphery, with their attendant hierarchies of states and forms of resistance, known as antisystemic movements. Moreover, the capitalist world-economy has experienced cyclical processes and secular trends for hundreds of years, with various "waves of globalization."[10]

Globalization is certainly the result of forces such as technology, management innovations, and the market, but it does not just "happen." It is, rather, engineered and promoted by identifiable groups of people within identifiable organizations and states. Behzad Yaghmaian points out that the emergence of the neoliberal model of capitalism is part of a systematic effort to lower the social value of labor power and provide the flexibility demanded for global accumulation by removing all national restrictions on the full mobility of capital and by imposing a restructuring of the labor market centered on the creation of flexible labor regimes. Leslie Sklair, who like Robinson has theorized the making of a transnational capitalist class and state apparatus, adds to Marxian class theory by arguing that the TCC comprises not only those who own or control major corporations but also other groups whose resources and actions are deemed vital to the process of globalization: neoliberal bureaucrats and politicians, assorted professionals and technocrats, advertisers, and the mass media. These would be among the "globalizers," or those who have carefully promoted and disseminated the culture of consumer capitalism, as Sklair has demonstrated, or free market ideology, as discussed by Manfred Steger.[11] Globalization, therefore, is not an inevitable stage but the result of conscious neoliberal policy making by globalizers (the agents of globalization), including multinational corporations and international financial institutions. What is more, neoliberal global capitalism has produced social polarization—that is, widening inequalities and new categories of poor. (See table 2.2 for an elaboration of globalization's features, agents, and challengers.)

For progressives like Walden Bello, Martin Khor, David Korten, Jerry Mander, Samir Amin, and others, globalization reproduces great and growing inequalities of wealth and incomes within and across countries. As such, globalization should be vigorously opposed by organized movements starting at the grassroots, local, and community levels. Many in the labor movement across the globe espouse a similar view. Trade union leaders have decried the social costs of globalization, such as unemployment, job insecurity, and continued poverty—the so-called race to the bottom—and they have called for the establishment of core labor standards, fair trade, democratization of global economic management, a shift of focus from markets to people, and a tax on speculative financial flows (the so-called Tobin tax). Bello in particular has called for deglobalization.[12]

Global justice activists similarly refer to growing worldwide inequalities as the reason for their antiglobalization stance, citing research by economists such as Angus Maddison, Anthony Atkinson, Lance Taylor, and Branko Milanovic, as well as their own observations. Maddison's study of inequalities between nations since the nineteenth century showed rising cross-national inequalities since the 1970s, while Atkinson documented rising inequalities in the industrialized countries (except in France). Taylor found that globalization and liberalization have not been uniformly favorable in terms of effects on growth and income distribution. Among the eighteen countries studied, only Chile after 1990 managed to combine high growth with decreasing inequality—in contrast to that country's increasing inequality over the preceding fifteen years. In a 2005 book on measures of global inequality, Milanovic found a complex situation including greater inequality within nations, greater differences between countries' mean incomes, and the "catching up" of large, poor countries such as India and China. Still, he concluded that, with adjustments for price levels (purchasing power parity, or PPP, income), the bottom 90 percent of the world's population had half of world income, and the top 10 percent had the other half. In simple dollar terms (not adjusted for price levels), the top 10 percent earned two-thirds of the world's income.

Table 2.2. Globalization: Features, Agents, and Challengers

	Features	Agents	Challengers
Economic	Neoliberal/free market capitalism; accumulation via investment, trade, aid	Multinational corporations and banks, the World Bank, IMF, WTO, OECD; the transnational capitalist class	Global justice movement, transnational feminist networks
Political	Multilateralism, international solidarity, humanitarian operations	Intergovernmental organizations, transnational advocacy networks, international NGOs	[a]
	Humanitarian intervention and preventive war	NATO, United States, United Kingdom, Israel	Global justice movement, transnational feminist networks
Cultural	Consumer capitalism, free market ideology, electoral democracy	Multinational corporations, U.S. government, transnational capitalist class, corporate media	Global justice movement, Islamist movements
	Human rights, women's rights, environmental protection, human security, social justice, peace	Transnational feminist networks, global justice movement, civil society groups, some INGOs and UN agencies	[a]

[a]Occasionally, local nonstate actors, authoritarian states, and U.S. preference for bilateralism or unilateralism.

As the decade progressed, inequalities worsened in countries such as China, Chile, Iran, Egypt, and India. The United Nations Development Programme's (UNDP) *Human Development Report 2005* showcased India as an example of a "globalization success," but one with a "mixed record on human development" because of the persistence of pervasive gender inequalities, inadequate public health, and growing income-based inequalities. Among the richest countries, income inequality has been especially severe in the United States, but the *Human Development Report 2005* highlighted American health inequalities too. In an extensively documented book, Richard Wilkinson and Kate Pickett showed how U.S. income inequality had grown, absolutely and in comparison with Europe, and demonstrated convincingly that many modern social problems—such as the breakdown of community relations, drug use, obesity, lower life expectancy, poor education outcomes, teen birth, violence, imprisonment, and low social mobility—are tied to inequality. Rana Foroohar provided comparative data to show how the United States had become "the land of less opportunity," with less upward social mobility, compared with other rich Organisation for Economic Cooperation and Development (OECD) countries. This problem had been captured by sociologist Katherine Newman as early as the 1990s, when she wrote of the U.S. phenomenon of "downward mobility in the age of affluence."[13] George Monbiot summarized the root of the problem:

> What has happened over the past 30 years is the capture of the world's common treasury by a handful of people, assisted by neoliberal policies that were first imposed on rich nations by Margaret Thatcher and Ronald Reagan. Between 1947 and 1979, productivity in the U.S. rose by 119%, while the income of the bottom fifth of the population rose by 122 percent. But from 1979 to 2009, productivity rose by 80 percent, while the income of the bottom fifth fell by 4 percent. In roughly the same period, the income of the top 1 percent rose by 270 percent.[14]

The economic crisis that engulfed the world in 2008 laid bare the excesses of neoliberal globalization, especially its feature of financialization, which had brought about not only gaping income inequalities but also higher prices for many commodities—including food and fuel—and increased market volatility. The crisis also exposed what Marxists call the intrinsic "contradictions" of capitalism. What are those contradictions? There is no doubt that capitalism innovates, but it is also beset by crises, which occur periodically but invariably. Since the onset of globalization, the world has experienced recessions in 1979 to 1982, 1991, 1997 to 1998, and 2001. Because each recession was followed by a growth period, policy makers seemed to learn no lessons, even though the crises in Asia, Argentina, and Russia had been caused by volatility and speculation in financial markets. Financialization proceeded, especially in the form of Anglo-Saxon "casino capitalism," with its increasingly complex, and ultimately corrupt, financial instruments. This variety of capitalism produced hedge funds, derivatives, bundled mortgages, mortgage-backed securities, and leveraged buyouts; these were prioritized over the production of goods and investments in infrastructure, giving rise to cheap and easy credit and loans tied up in exotic, and toxic, financial instruments. Because short-term gains were rewarded with huge bonuses on top of huge salaries, traders and investors were encouraged to engage in risky and reckless speculation that eventually led to the bursting of the housing market bubble. In turn, businesses stopped growing or stopped hiring, unemployment rose, prices increased, and household budgets shrank. This is the context in which the Arab Spring, the European mass protests, and Occupy Wall Street (OWS) took place, and it is evidence of capitalism's contradictions and its crisis-prone nature. The power, privilege, and arrogance of the top economic elites constitute the context in which the OWS slogan "We are the 99 percent" took shape.[15]

GLOBALIZATION AND THE STATE

In such a context, what recourse do states have? One debate about globalization that is relevant to both the global economic crisis and social movements concerns the extent to which the sovereignty of nation-states and the autonomy of national economies have been weakened. In the early days of globalization, some argued that inasmuch as globalization entails "deterritorialization" through supranational economic, political, and cultural processes and institutions, the nation-state as a power apparatus would be superseded. Capital flows and the growing power of institutions of global governance, such as international financial institutions, leave states with greatly diminished options. In one version of this argument, Jessica Mathews held that "the absolutes of the Westphalian system," including "territorially fixed states," were all dissolving. According to Susan Strange, "Where states were once the masters of markets, now it is the markets which, on many crucial issues, are the masters over the governments of states." In another version, fixed and strong state systems had been replaced by networks and flows. For Ulrich Beck, rather than the state as such, "we are living in an age of flows—flows of capital, cultural flows, flows of information and risks."[16]

For Manuel Castells,

> Power . . . is no longer concentrated in institutions (the state), organizations (capitalist firms), or symbolic controllers (corporate media, churches). It is diffused in global networks of wealth, power, information, and images which circulate and transmute in a system of variable geometry and dematerialized geography. . . . The new power lies in the codes of information and in the images of representation around which societies organize their institutions, and people live their lives, and decide their behavior.[17]

Others did not go as far as Castells but argued that the activities of transnational corporations, global cities, and the transnational capitalist class rendered state-centered analysis outdated. Thus, Sklair's theory of the global system proposes taking the whole world as the starting point—that is, viewing the world not as an aggregate of nation-states but as a single unit and object of analysis. Sklair, Robinson, and others have theorized the emergence of a deterritorialized transnational capitalist class, with its attendant institutions. In contrast, Paul Hirst and Grahame Thompson asserted that the nation-state remains the dominant form of governance by comparison with more global or subnational levels. Similarly, Suzanne Berger, Ronald Dore, and their collaborators showed that national governments were still able to pursue different policies and maintain distinctive institutions, and they urged caution in generalizing about the extent of economic globalization.[18]

Empirically, states do seem to have lost power and control to markets; the financial crisis of 2008, which began in the United States, quickly engulfed many European countries and others that were integrated into the circuits of global finance capital. Even the U.S. economy, which had led globalization and financialization, found itself facing a collapsed housing market, rising unemployment, growing poverty, and widening income and social inequalities unseen since the early twentieth century. In 2011, Europe's "eurozone" was in crisis, as countries such as Portugal, Spain, Ireland, and especially Greece struggled with huge debts and budget deficits. While some pundits argued that individual governments or political cultures were responsible for reckless spending and unbalanced budgets, others insisted that the affected countries actually were the victims of a badly mismanaged and misguided global economic system.

The debate about globalization and the state has implications for our study of globalization and social movements. As we saw in chapter 1, social movement theory posits a central role for the state in movement formation and evolution, captured in the wide-ranging concept of the "political opportunity structure." Sidney Tarrow defines social movements as mobilized groups engaged in sustained contentious interaction with power holders in which at least one state is either a target or a participant. Hank Johnston sees social movements as constituting contentious politics, or a broad range of claims against the state that sets the stage for popular pressures through noninstitutional channels (protests and social movements) and possibly institutional ones (party politics and legislation).[19] What, then, do we make of a transnational social movement that targets institutions of global governance such as the World Bank, the International Monetary Fund, and the World Trade Organization? Does this reality mean that states have no effect on transnational movement prospects? Are transnational social movements ignoring states?

In fact, the state remains an important institution and the target of many social movement actions, as we saw with the mass protests of 2011 in the Middle East and North Africa, as well as with the anti-austerity protests in Greece. Transnational social movements also often target particular states in their critiques and protests. The state continues to matter for at least four reasons. First, neoliberal capitalism requires state regulation in order to function. As Tarak Barkawi observes, "States are not victims of economic globalization so much as they are agents of it."[20] The world-system is, after all, an *interstate* system. And while neoliberalism posits a less interventionist role of the state in general, it does require that states provide the legal and regulatory framework necessary for the functioning of markets and the private sector.

Second, the state matters because international law confers obligations on states for the implementation of treaties, conventions, resolutions, and norms. The state also remains the body primarily responsible for guaranteeing the rights of citizens and human rights more broadly. For feminists, the state is the most relevant institution on matters of reproductive health and rights, social policies for women in the work force, and family law for women's personal status and rights within the family. Pro-democracy social movement activists may protest authoritarian or laissez-faire states, but they expect the state to provide citizens with civil and political rights, as well as the material conditions and means to realize those rights (that is, social/economic rights).

Third, the world-system functions as an unequal hierarchy of states. Capital accumulation on a world scale relies on disparities in resource endowments, levels of industrialization, wealth, and power. It is precisely such structural inequalities and the ways in which powerful states may bully weaker states that motivate much transnational protest.

The capacity of states to implement human rights may be compromised by poor resource endowments, by the power of foreign investors, or by foreign intervention, occupation, or conflict. There also are states with the means and the capacity to provide civil, political, and social rights of citizenship but choose not to; instead, they repress any attempts at independent organizing or protest, or they allocate resources to militarism. Across the world-system's economic zones, we can see that state capacity is variable. This has implications not only for economic development but also for relations with civil society and social movements and for movement prospects. Margaret Keck and Kathryn Sikkink have suggested that globalization provides social movements with the opportunity of the "boomerang effect," in which advocacy networks are able to bypass their target states and rely on international pressure from other states or from transnational advocacy networks to accomplish their goals at home. And yet the boomerang effect is not always realized; some very strong semiperipheral states may be in a position to ignore or withstand pressure from stronger states or the pleas and demands of transnational social movements and networks. Examples include the Chinese government's repression of the pro-democracy movement in Tiananmen Square in 1989 and its continued refusal to consider the demands of the people of Tibet, the Iranian government's repression of the Green Protests in the summer of 2009, and the Israeli government's constant dismissal of international criticism of its policies toward the Palestinians. The boomerang effect could be irrelevant for strong states in the world-system's core, especially for the hegemon. For example, although massive street demonstrations took place across the globe in early 2003 to protest U.S. plans to invade Iraq, the George W. Bush administration ignored them and ordered military action nonetheless. Celebration of the "justice cascade"—as evidenced by trials for perpetrators of human rights violations within newly democratic states, legal cases brought by governments or NGOs against foreign perpetrators, and the number of special tribunals and cases brought to the International Criminal Court—ignores the fact that malfeasance by the largest or most powerful states, especially the hegemon, will almost always escape prosecution. Thus, although states do have obligations under international law, and it could be argued that they have moral obligations as well, it is usually the strongest states in the world-system that are able to ignore or withstand international pressures.[21]

As we saw in chapter 1, the Internet can play an important mobilizing role as well as bypass state secrecy or even reveal state crimes. But the Internet has not been able to supplant state security and intelligence services, which continue to monitor and sometimes disrupt dissident websites. In Iran, where the Revolutionary Guard controls the nation's main Internet provider, the regime used social media sites and Facebook pages during the Green Protests of June 2009 to identify opponents, post their photos, solicit denunciations, and trace connections to Western supporters, thus enabling the government to blame foreigners for stirring up the trouble. During the protests in Egypt, President Hosni Mubarak tried to unplug the Internet, though this did not help him. The Chinese government regularly monitors and shuts down dissident sites. In the United States, the WikiLeaks release of embarrassing U.S. diplomatic cables enraged the government of President Barack Obama and set in motion a blockade by credit companies. In November 2011, a U.S. judge ruled that Twitter must release details of the accounts of an Icelandic woman and two others linked to WikiLeaks. Evgeny Morozov points out that state security services use the Internet and cybertools such as Twitter as effectively as young dissenters, hacktivists, and would-be democratic revolutionaries.[22]

A fourth reason why the state continues to matter is that the presence or absence of elite allies and coalitions with state entities can be critical to a movement's formation and growth. In some cases, states have provided protest groups with needed leverage for their collective action. For example, the global justice movement found an ally in the Brazilian government, as scholar-activist Boaventura de Sousa Santos noted. In particular, the Workers' Party and the city of Porto Alegre were crucial to the making of the World Social Forum (WSF).[23] In the past, Islamist movements received funding and moral support from the United States, Saudi Arabia, Kuwait, and other state entities. In 2011, Libyan rebels opposed to longtime strongman Muammar Ghaddafi received diplomatic and military assistance from a number of Western states, notably France, the United Kingdom, and the United States, as well as U.S. ally Qatar. In early 2012, Western powers and their regional allies (notably Saudi Arabia and Qatar) demanded regime change in Syria and extended support to the opposition, while China and Russia vetoed a UN Security Council resolution that would have forced the change. Thus, attention needs to be directed toward sub- and suprastate processes, and the significance of processes of multilevel governance has to be recognized.

Nor has the concept of the nation-state disappeared. In the Middle East, proponents of Islamic fundamentalism and supporters of revolutionary Iranian Islam initially saw their movements as supranational and railed against "artificial colonialist borders" that divided the *umma*, or the community of Muslim believers. But the activities and objectives of many political movements have largely remained within national borders. Territorial state nationalism has deep roots in the region, as demonstrated all too vividly by the Iran-Iraq war of 1980–1988, the overlong Israeli-Palestinian conflict, and the Kurdish struggle for autonomy or independence. Moreover, many Islamist groups have explicitly targeted what they have regarded as illegitimate state systems: such Islamist groups include the late Ayatollah Khomeini and his movement in Iran, the mujahideen in Afghanistan, the Front Islamique du Salut (FIS) in Algeria, and Gama'a Islamiyya in Egypt. Others seize the political opportunities available to mobilize resources, recruit supporters, strengthen their networks, and expand their power and influence through both electoral and noninstitutional politics, including militancy; examples are Hezbollah in Lebanon and Hamas in Palestine. Indeed, research shows that many Islamist movements are focused on national-level problems and have national-level goals, even while they may be in close contact with other Islamist movements and governments.

On the other hand, the emergence of Osama bin Laden's al-Qaeda network in the 1990s would suggest, or confirm, that globalization facilitates the formation of loosely organized, deterritorialized transnational groups; in al-Qaeda's case, this has included al-Qaeda on the Arabian Peninsula, al-Qaeda in the Islamic Maghreb, and elements fighting in Iraq, Afghanistan, and Pakistan. Thus far, as the latest stage of capitalism, globalization has not supplanted the international system of states, even though it has generated powerful new global institutions that have weakened state sovereignty and engendered protest movements on a world scale. We may conclude that while states still matter, globalization provides a new opportunity structure for social movements—one that enables them to take on a transnational form with a global reach or to draw on transnational networks to strengthen their cause at home.

GLOBALIZATION, EMPIRE, AND HEGEMONIC MASCULINITIES

The various aspects of globalization have promoted growing contacts between different cultures, leading partly to greater understanding and cooperation and partly to the emergence of transnational communities and hybrid identities. But globalization has also hardened the opposition of different identities. This is one way of understanding the emergence of reactive movements such as fundamentalism and communalism, which seek to recuperate traditional patterns, including patriarchal gender relations, in reaction to the "westernizing" trends of globalization. Various forms of identity politics are the paradoxical outgrowth of globalization, which Benjamin Barber aptly summarizes as "jihad vs. McWorld." He uses the term "jihad" as shorthand to describe religious fundamentalism, disintegrative tribalism, ethnic nationalisms, and similar kinds of identity politics carried out by local peoples "to sustain solidarity and tradition against the nation-state's legalistic and pluralistic abstractions as well as against the new commercial imperialism of McWorld." Jihad struggles against modernity and cultural imperialism alike and "answers the complaints of those mired in poverty and despair as a result of unregulated global markets and of capitalism uprooted from the humanizing constraints of the democratic nation-state."[24] It is not surprising, then, that Islamist movements have gained strength in many authoritarian countries. The question that arises is whether Islamist movements are able to contribute to, and help consolidate, democratization that is also women friendly.

"Jihad" is perhaps best known for its struggle against "empire," also known as imperialism, colonialism, or neocolonialism. Technically speaking, empires no longer exist, though the term was revived in one sense through the writings of Antonio Negri and Michael Hardt, and in a different sense altogether in the wake of the U.S. invasion of Afghanistan in 2001 and Iraq in 2003. Thus, "empire" has been used as shorthand for hegemonic militarism and expansion.[25] In particular, many Islamist groups look beyond the "near enemy" (their own rulers or states) and target the hegemonic behavior of the United States (the "far enemy"), even though they were once supported by the United States. In world-historical terms, the U.S.-supported war in Afghanistan in the 1980s was especially significant. Its immediate outcomes were the collapse of the Soviet Union and world communism, the expansion of a militarized Islamist movement, and the emergence of a unipolar world and single economic system dominated by the United States.[26]

Although the United States had been the world-system's hegemon since the 1950s, its power had been checked periodically by the Soviet Union. The end of the Cold War and the collapse of the Soviet Union left the United States in a position of unparalleled military predominance. In the 1990s the U.S. ruling elite began using this strategic asset to redraw the imperial map of the world, first in the Gulf War and then in the Kosovo war. It should be noted that this development encompassed the administrations of President George H. W. Bush and President Bill Clinton, with the cooperation of both political parties. The new imperial design did not become fully realized, however, until the rise of the neoconservative wing of the ruling elite and the victory of George W. Bush in the presidential election of 2000. Even then, this scheme awaited the conditions in which it could be implemented. The attack on the World Trade Center in 2001 created those conditions.

For a while, following the invasion of Afghanistan in late 2001 and the routing of the Taliban, it appeared that the neoconservative "Project for the New American Century" was being successfully implemented. However, the invasion of Iraq in 2003 served to underline the limits of U.S. power. These limits had at least three sources. First, there was the relative economic weakness of the United States. Unlike during the golden age following World War II—when the dollar was supreme and the United States enjoyed economic growth, rising wages and prosperity, and high rates of employment—the rise of other advanced economies and the strength of the euro began to make the world-system a much more competitive environment. The combination of relative economic decline and overwhelming military strength propelled the Bush administration to rely on its military capacity to discipline both its allies and its competitors on the world stage. Second, the limits of U.S. power came to be seen in the intense factionalism within the ruling elite, including in the disagreements between Democrats and Republicans over the conduct, costs, and morality of the wars in Iraq and Afghanistan and in the standoff, during the administration of President Barack Obama, over health-care reform and government spending.[27] Third, there was the concerted resistance to the U.S. government's designs in Iraq and Afghanistan —invasion, occupation, and privatization of the countries' resources and security apparatuses. The resistance was both homegrown and transnational, and it was fierce. It consisted of some nationalists but largely of Islamists with sophisticated weapons, a transnational reach, and patriarchal agendas. The resurgence of the Afghan Taliban was aided and abetted by Pakistani Islamists and, apparently, by rogue elements of the Pakistani state security apparatus. These developments have served to complicate the initial U.S. designs and expectations.[28]

The NATO intervention in Libya—in which France and the United Kingdom took the lead and the United States "led from behind"—may be interpreted as a way of compensating for the foreign policy failures in Iraq and Afghanistan, maintaining a foothold in the Middle East and North Africa, and guaranteeing oil supplies. The longer-term outcome of the Libyan rebellion and intervention is as yet unknown, but the extreme violence of all parties—the Ghaddafi government, the rebels, and the NATO air strikes—cannot be denied.

Here we must pause to take into account competing hegemonic or hypermasculinities, such as those of al-Qaeda and the Bush administration or of the Ghaddafi regime and the armed opposition. Hegemonic masculinity has become a key concept in gender analysis since R. W. Connell identified it as a particular culture's standards and ideal of real manhood, at a particular time in history.[29] In countries such as the United States and Australia, hegemonic masculinity is defined by physical strength and bravado, exclusive heterosexuality, suppression of "vulnerable" emotions such as remorse and uncertainty, economic independence, authority over women and other men, and intense interest in sexual "conquest." What Connell has defined as "emphasized femininity" is constructed around adaptation to male power. Its central feature is attractiveness to men, which includes physical appearance, ego massaging, suppression of "power" emotions such as anger, nurturance of children, exclusive heterosexuality, sexual availability without sexual assertiveness, and sociability. Both standards and ideals may be observed in many cultures, albeit with variations in the sexual element. (For example, in Muslim cultures, female modesty is valued much more than sexual availability. And rather than intense interest in sexual conquest, hegemonic masculinity in, for example, a typical Middle Eastern context might consist of the capacity to protect family or personal honor by controlling the comportment of the women in the family, the community, or the nation.) Hegemonic masculinity, in particular, is reproduced in various social institutions, including the media, the sports arena, the family, the military, the corporate sector, and sometimes religious institutions. In turn, it can be expressed at the level of an individual or a collective: a frat house, a military unit, a street gang, a movement, a political regime.

Lauren Langman and Douglas Morris advance a similar analysis in their discussion of "heroic masculinities." As they point out, civilizations and cultures based on conquest or expansion, societies where politics and militarism are fused, and countries where the military is a central and valorized institution all exhibit discourses, images, and practices of heroic masculinity. In considering American society and the role of its military in both economic growth and empire building, and in considering the foundational narratives of heroic masculinity in Islam, one can easily imagine a "clash of heroic masculinities" (as Langman and Morris put it) between the American security state and a transnational Islamist network such as al-Qaeda or between Ghaddafi's forces and the armed rebels. From a feminist perspective, hegemonic, heroic, or hyper masculinity is a causal factor in war, as well as in women's oppression. As Anne Sisson Runyan has aptly noted, "The world is awash with contending masculinities that vie to reduce women to symbols of either fundamentalism or Western hypermodernity."[29]

In a way, contemporary rivalries in hypermasculinity mirror the intercapitalist rivalries of the early part of the twentieth century—which led to World Wars I and II. They underlie many of the factors that have been attributed to the "new conflicts" of the post–Cold War era, such as the emergence of a global weapons market, the decreasing capacity of states to uphold the monopoly of violence, interethnic competition, and Barber's "jihad vs. McWorld."[30] Indeed, rival masculinities constitute a key factor in the conflicts that emerge over natural resources, such as oil or diamonds; in aggressive nationalism and ethnic rivalries; and in politicized religious projects. Hegemonic masculinity is a central ideological pillar of both empire and some forms of resistance, notably militant Islam.

Hypermasculinity similarly was in evidence during the financial meltdown of 2008. The crisis has been analyzed in many ways, but attention should be directed to the hypermasculinity that lies beneath the capitalist relations of production and the behavior of the (predominantly male) transnational capitalist class. The masculinist institution par excellence may be the military (as feminist political scientist Cynthia Enloe has argued), but hypermasculinity is also a defining feature of the corporate domain—with its risk takers, rogue traders, reckless speculators, and manipulative financiers. In chapter 31 of volume 1 of *Capital*, Marx has some rather pithy things to say about the emergence of the "modern bankocracy," along with the international credit system, the modern system of taxation, "stock-exchange gambling," and "the class of lazy annuitants thus created." In rereading those passages, one is struck by how insightful, prescient, and true they are. The economic crisis was the product at least in part of the overwrought masculinity of this "bankocracy" on trading floors and in bank boardrooms.[31]

Would the situation be better if there were a critical mass of women in the corporate world? Some argue that women in the corporate domain would be less likely to promote casino-style capitalism. Others retort that corporate women would have to conform to the corporate culture and imperatives. And yet, when one thinks of women like Sherron Watkins, who tried to blow the whistle on Enron; Brooksley Born of the Commodities Futures Trading Commission (CFTC) during the Clinton administration, who tried to warn against deregulation and the emerging toxic assets until she was forced to resign; Gretchen Morgenson of the *New York Times*, with her sober and critical analyses of the financial crisis; and Harvard professor Elizabeth Warren, who led the Obama administration's credit card company oversight, chaired the Troubled Assets Relief Program (TARP) oversight panel, and then was overlooked by the Obama administration in its appointment of a head of the oversight agency that she had created—it would appear that there might indeed be less recklessness. There may be an argument for including more women on corporate boards, as first Norway did, with its law mandating a minimum 40 percent female share, followed more recently by France. Even so, having a critical mass of women on corporate boards might not save ordinary citizens from what is a crisis-prone system of economic governance. For that, alternatives and a new vision are needed.

ON GLOBAL SOCIAL MOVEMENTS AND TRANSNATIONAL COLLECTIVE ACTION

The capitalist world-system has often produced antisystemic movements that cross borders and boundaries, while national-level class conflicts and political contradictions similarly have generated forms of collective action and social protest, including social movements. For example, sociologists Susan Eckstein and Timothy Wickham-Crowley identified several arenas of rights that were at risk in Latin America as a result of the spread of neoliberal economic policies and categorized the relevant social movements that emerged: protests against cuts in urban services, strikes and labor struggles, gender-based movements, and rural movements.[32] Some of those movements have come to be connected to the global justice movement or to global feminism. In turn, the global feminist, Islamist, and justice movements are part of the world-system, constitute products of globalization, and target both states and the global order. They also reflect the growth of what has been called global civil society and the transnational public sphere.

The UN conferences of the 1990s were important to the making of global civil society and the growth of transnational social movements and their organizations/networks: the UN Conference on Environment and Development (UNCED), held in Rio de Janeiro in June 1992; the World Conference on Human Rights, held in Vienna in June 1993; the International Conference on Population and Development (ICPD), held in Cairo in September 1994; the World Summit on Social Development, held in Copenhagen in March 1995; and the Fourth World Conference on Women, held in Beijing in September 1995. As more and more governments signed on to the international treaties associated with these and related conferences, their agreements created a conducive global opportunity structure for social movements and civil society actors. State integration into the world polity enabled cross-border networking and mobilizations and facilitated cross-cultural framings. The making of a global social movement is illustrated in figure 2.1.

It may be helpful to pause here to reiterate a working definition of transnational or global social movements. If a social movement is "a sustained campaign of claims-making, using repeated performances that advertise the claim, based on organizations, networks, traditions, and solidarities that sustain these activities," then transnational social movements are "socially mobilized groups with constituents in at least two states, engaged in sustained contentious interactions with power-holders in at least one state other than their own, or against an international institution, or a multinational economic actor."[33] As

Global Opportunity Structure
- Intergovernmental and governance structure
- Elite allies at international level
- International law
- Computer technologies

Cross-border Mobilizations
- Use of organizational infrastructure
- New networks, cells, associations
- Recruitment and financial drives

Cross-cultural Framings
- Shared identities
- Moral outrage
- Diffusion of tactics
- Website activism

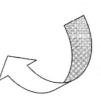

Global Social Movement

Figure 2.1. The Making of a Global Social Movement

discussed in chapter 1, transnational social movements often consist of domestically based or transnational networks, including transnational advocacy networks. What makes transnational activists different from domestic activists is their ability to shift their activities among levels and across borders, coordinating with groups outside their own countries. As noted, this has been made possible by the new information and communication technologies, including mobile phones, YouTube, and social-networking sites.

What is it that transnational social movements do? Chadwick Alger's observation of a decade ago remains apt, at least with respect to the nonviolent transnational movements studied here: they create and activate global networks to mobilize pressure outside states, they participate in multilateral and intergovernmental political arenas, they act and agitate within states, and they enhance public awareness and participation. Time and space compression through the Internet has made all this easier to accomplish. Thus activists are able to organize structures above the national level, uniting adherents across borders with similar identities and goals around a common agenda. In the process, they contribute to the making of global civil society or a transnational public sphere. As John Guidry, Michael Kennedy, and Mayer Zald have noted, "Globalization has in fact brought social movements together across borders in a 'transnational public sphere,' a real as well as conceptual space in which movement organizations interact, contest each other, and learn from each other."[34]

In their study of the global justice movement, Mario Pianta and Raffaele Marchetti highlight the link between global civil society and global social movements. Global civil society is "the sphere of cross-border relationships and activities carried out by collective actors—social movements, networks, and civil society organizations—that are independent from governments and private firms and operate outside the international reach of states and markets." Global social movements are "cross-border, sustained, and collective social mobilizations on global issues, based on permanent and/or occasional groups, networks, and campaigns with a transnational organizational dimension moving from shared values and identities that challenge and protest economic or political power and campaign for change in global issues. They share a global frame of the problems to be addressed, have a global scope of action, and might target supranational or national targets."[35]

Are all transnational movements actors within global civil society? Here we must draw attention to the normative dimension of certain social science concepts and categories. Many scholars have viewed social movements and civil society (as well as revolutions and liberation movements) through a progressive lens. Mary Kaldor has noted that civil society tends to be defined as "the medium through which one or many social contracts between individuals, both women and men, and the political and economic centers of power are negotiated and reproduced." This is a "rights-based definition of civil society . . . about politics from below and about the possibility for human emancipation." However, the rise of nonstate and anticorporate movements, organizations, and networks that appear to eschew values of equality, democracy, and human rights has called such a view into question. Are all nonstate actors that engage in negotiated interactions with state actors, whether at the local or global levels, constituent elements of civil society? What of a network such as al-Qaeda? Or the cells created by disaffected young Muslim men in Europe that planned and executed terrorist bombings? Or neo-Nazi groups in Europe? Kaldor concedes that some of the most vital forms of global civil society to emerge are found in religious and nationalist social movements, many of which are profoundly antidemocratic, and that this has tempered the initial enthusiasm for civil society among many activists. To avoid subjectivity, she and the other editors of the *Global Civil Society Yearbook* have stated, "We believe that the normative content is too contested to be able to form the basis for any operationalization of the concept."[36]

Conversely, Rupert Taylor takes a strong position in favor of the normative content and offers a subjective as well as objective analysis of global civil society. There is little to be gained analytically, he argues, in including any and all nonstate actors in the definition of (global) civil society. This is also the position of the transnational feminist network Women Living under Muslim Laws, which has issued statements decrying violations of women's human rights by nonstate actors and published a manual on the subject. Taylor maintains that "at an objective level, global civil society structurally relates to a multi-organizational field that encompasses both those organizations that tend to work within the INGO and nation-state system, follow professionalized advocacy styles and agendas, and are involved in complex multilateralism, and those movements—anti-neoliberal and anti-corporate alike—committed to street protest and other forms of direct action." At a subjective level, he continues, "the intent of global civil society activism is to confront neoliberal globalization and create a better world through advocating a fairer, freer, and more just global order." Global civil society, then, should be taken to be "a complex multi-organizational field that explicitly excludes reactionary—racist, fascist, or fundamentalist—organizations and movements."[37]

Viewed in normative terms, therefore, global civil society is the site of democratic, nonviolent, and emancipatory associational interaction. Viewed in a strictly empirical way, however, (global) civil society is not a necessarily emancipatory sphere of action and identity, and not all (global) social movements are progressive or democratic. Certainly, the segmentary, polycentric, and reticulate nature of social movements guarantees the presence of different tendencies within a movement, including radical, militant, or even terrorist wings. Thus we can distinguish between progressive and reactionary social movements and civil society (or nonstate) actors. Progressive social movements and civil society actors seek to negotiate new relationships and arrangements with states and institutions of global governance—including the building or deepening of democratic practices and institutions—through popular support and respect for human rights. Terrorist factions generally are not interested in building or enhancing democracy; they neither work to cultivate popular support nor respect human rights. This book, therefore, recognizes that globalization has enabled the formation of all manner of nonstate organizing and collective action and that not all of these may be viewed as emancipatory or transformative. In much the same way that globalization itself is complex and contradictory, the transnational social movements associated with it or resulting from it are also complex and contradictory. That is, globalization has produced life-affirming, nonviolent, and democratic social movements but also deadly rebellions, martyrdom operations, and transnational networks of violent extremists.

All transnational collective action takes place within, and is shaped by, the capitalist world-system and its current phase of globalization. In turn, globalization has given rise to criticisms and grievances, as well as opportunities for collective action. It has created a global opportunity structure and enabled cross-border framings and mobilizations. These framings and mobilizations may be driven by proximate causes but, as was discussed in chapter 1, are rooted in preexisting discourses, collective memories, and organizational infrastructures. Islamist activism has been motivated by corrupt, authoritarian, or pro-Western regimes in their own Muslim-majority countries; by solidarity with their confrères in Palestine, Iraq, and Afghanistan; and by opposition to secularizing and westernizing tendencies. The transnational Islamist movement consists of groups and networks ranging from moderate to extremist, using methods that range from participation in the political process to spectacular violence. Transnational feminist activism is motivated by concern for women's participation and rights in an era of neoliberal globalization, militarism, war, and patriarchal fundamentalisms. Transnational feminist networks—the principal mobilizing structure of global feminism—consist of women from three or more countries who mobilize for research, lobbying, advocacy, and civil disobedience to protest gender injustice and promote women's human rights, equality, and peace. The global justice movement consists of loosely organized mobilized groups that protest the downside of globalization and call for economic and social justice. A key institution is the World Social Forum, a gathering place for democratic deliberation by the numerous transnational networks and nationally based advocacy groups that have grown exponentially since the mid-1990s. Initially organized by the Brazilian Workers' Party and the landless peasant movement, the WSF was intended to be a forum for the participants and supporters of grassroots movements across the globe and a counterpart to forums of representatives of governments, political parties, and corporations, most notably the World Economic Forum (WEF). More recently, manifestations of the global justice movement were seen in the anti-austerity protests of Europe and in Occupy Wall Street.

The three movements examined in this book are interconnected, inasmuch as feminists and moderate Islamists have taken part in the WSF, and the global justice movement includes individuals and groups active in transnational feminist networks. Transnational feminist groups are also present on the International Council of the WSF. All three movements are counterhegemonic in that they are opposed to globalization's hegemonic tendencies of neoliberalism, expansion, and war. Each movement itself is transnational, inasmuch as it targets states and international institutions and is a coalition of local grassroots groups as well as transborder groups. But the three differ in significant ways. For Islamists, the solution to current problems is the widespread application of Islamic laws and norms; global justice activists present a variety of alternatives to neoliberalism, from deglobalization to cosmopolitan social democracy or democratic socialism; transnational feminists insist on the application of international conventions on women's human rights and call for greater attention to feminist values. The similarities and differences, as well as the connections to globalization, will be elucidated in the subsequent chapters.

CONCLUSION

Globalization remains a contested subject for scholars, policy makers, and activists. Its enthusiasts try to show the promises of free trade, deregulation, and flexibility, while its detractors emphasize the problems of inequalities, unfair trade relations, political domination, and militarism. Meanwhile, many organized groups and networks—some associated with Islamism and others with the global justice movement, including feminist networks—have taken a stance against the adverse effects of globalization. In this they have been joined by concerned social scientists and intellectuals.

Globalization has created grievances that motivate protest as well as opportunities for mobilization. The contemporary era of globalization is marked by a distinct set of economic policies, the worldwide dissemination of cultural products, and a political-military project of domination. It has engendered competition and contestation—even among its main agents and supporters—and grievances and resistance from its detractors. Among its detractors are transnational activists who promote an alternative vision of global interactions.

This chapter has shown that a key characteristic of the era of late capitalism, or neoliberal globalization, is the proliferation of networks of activists within transnational social movements. Guidry, Kennedy, and Zald have correctly regarded globalization as a new opportunity structure for social movements. Globalization brings important new resources to mobilization efforts, and movements can frame their claims in terms that resonate beyond territorial borders. I have noted the paradoxes of globalization: while its economic, political-military, and cultural aspects have engendered grievances and opposition, it has also provided the means for rapid cross-border communication, coordination, mobilization, and action. The next chapters explore in more detail how movements of Islamists, feminists, and global justice activists address globalization. But first, we turn attention to the democratizing aspects of social movements at both national and global levels.

CHAPTER 3

SOCIAL MOVEMENTS
AND DEMOCRATIZATION

The democratization of the world beyond the states has yet to begin.

—John Markoff 1999: 301

The year 2011 will go down in history for at least two seminal events. First, it will be remembered as the year of mass social protests for democratization and justice that led to the collapse of authoritarian governments in the Middle East and North Africa (MENA), most notably in Tunisia and Egypt. In Morocco, a slower, less dramatic democratic transition had been taking place since 1998, but the regional protests spread there too, with the consequence that the king agreed to constitutional amendments to restrict his vast powers. Protests also took place in Libya, Bahrain, Yemen, and Syria, but they differed significantly from those in Tunisia, Egypt, and Morocco in that they entailed more violence as well as foreign intervention. Second, 2011 will be remembered for Occupy Wall Street (OWS), a protest movement that began in New York City to highlight financial-sector malfeasance and draw attention to the interests and aspirations of ordinary citizens. Occupy Wall Street spread across the United States, and in a show of global solidarity, cities across the world held Occupy protests on October 15, 2011, one month after the movement's emergence in New York. This chapter examines both sets of protest movements by elucidating their relationship to globalization processes and by demonstrating how they are pro-democracy movements with the potential to bring about genuine democratization at societal and global levels. It also reviews the strengths and weaknesses of different models of democracy, the gender dynamics and effects on women's rights of various waves of democratization, and how the world-system affects democracy movements and governments.

SOCIAL MOVEMENTS AND DEMOCRACY

Social movements are critical for advancing inclusion and democracy, but the literature examining the democratic nature of social movements is relatively sparse. Although studies do exist, to some extent, for North America and Europe, they are scarce for developing countries. The literature on democratization or democratic transitions rarely analyzes the role of social movements or revolutions, though a notable exception is Barrington Moore's *Social Origins of Dictatorship and Democracy*. John Guidry, Michael Kennedy, and Mayer Zald point out that until relatively recently, most academic social movement theory was being developed in the United States. The movement analysis was dominated by an implicit metatheory of movements as a variation on the voluntary organization sector, and the mobilization of resources was the key to success or failure in movement activity. Social movements were not theorized as antisystemic but rather as alternative means of expressing a democratic pluralism or, as in the case of the U.S. civil rights movement, helping to deepen democracy through full citizenship for a previously excluded and marginalized population. Even so, the pluralist supposition underlying movement theory was largely implicit. In recent years, however, scholars have more explicitly examined the contributions of social movements to democratic transitions in authoritarian settings or the deepening of democracy in mature democratic societies. Laurel Weldon, for example, examines how women's movements in the United States brought to public and government attention women's policy issues related to the family, work, and violence, and she shows how women's movement organizations helped to increase women's representation in the public sphere through their role as powerful policy advocates. Such action on behalf of marginalized groups, Weldon argues, deepens *representative democracy*. Graciela Di Marco emphasizes the significance of social movements to *radical democracy*, such as in the case of Argentinian workers who took over factories abandoned by their owners following the financial crisis of 1998. For Di Marco, Argentinean democracy deepened and was radicalized as a result of the social movements of the period, including the coalitions of workers, students, intellectuals, and feminists that brought to power the left-wing government of Nestor Kirchner. This was, in fact, part of a broader regional wave of anti-neoliberal popular mobilization.[1]

Hank Johnston asserts that in democratic societies, social movements are actually a part of regular politics; they derive from civil society organizations, draw on or create public opinion, and challenge elites using democratic expectations; and their goals are to extend state openness or capacity for citizenship, equality, responsiveness, and protection. As such, he agrees with the postulate of the social movement society, as discussed by David Meyer and Sidney Tarrow, to the effect that social movements are a part of normal politics in democratic society, with tactics such as e-petitioning, advocacy and lobbying, the spread of professional social movement organizations, and checkbook memberships.[2] Such a view may (inadvertently) dovetail with the perspective of civil society as co-opted by the state and an instrument for legitimation. But can one conclude that Occupy Wall Street represented "normal politics" when the official response, in many cities, was police brutality?

Studies on democratic transitions in authoritarian contexts have looked most closely at the relationship between social movements and political change. In South Africa, the antiapartheid movement and demands for full enfranchisement of the country's black majority brought about a democratic polity and one of the most egalitarian constitutions in the world. In the 1980s in South Korea, protest groups consisting of militant industrial workers, Christian groups, students, and intellectuals formed a pro-democracy movement that ended authoritarian military rule and in 1987 ushered in a remarkable period of democratic consolidation that entailed a growing civil society with the capacity for considerable reform from below. Social movement organizations such as the Citizens Coalition for Economic Justice and the Citizens' Coalition for Participatory Democratic Society have continued to actively promote democratic practices and policy making. Argentina's democratic transition vastly opened up political spaces for workers, feminists, students, and other social groups, though it was not until after the economic crisis of 1998 that the full extent of citizen direct action could be seen. Even the practices of trade unions changed, with more female participation and leadership and considerable internal discussion and debate on "women's issues" as well as economic rights issues.[3]

DEMOCRACY MOVEMENTS: WAVES, LOCATIONS, CONDITIONS

According to Guillermo O'Donnell and Philippe Schmitter, democracy's guiding principle is citizenship:

> This involves both the right to be treated by fellow human beings as equal with respect to the making of collective choices and the obligation of those implementing such choices to be equally accountable and accessible to all members of the polity. . . . Given the existence of certain prominent "models" and international diffusion, there is likely to exist a sort of "procedural minimum" which contemporary actors would agree upon as necessary elements of political democracy. Secret balloting, universal adult suffrage, regular elections, partisan competition, association recognition and access, and executive accountability all seem to be elements of such a consensus in the contemporary world.

This definition, however, is not inclusive of notions of social rights and economic citizenship. Indeed, democracy in the neoliberal era often is associated with competitive elections (political democracy) and free markets (liberal capitalist democracy) and not with egalitarian relations within workplaces (economic democracy) or within the family, which many feminists have called for.[4]

Benjamin Barber has noted that different types of democracies and their varied practices produce similarly varied effects. In a liberal democracy, a high degree of political legitimacy is necessary, as is an independent judiciary and a constitution that clearly sets out the relationship between state and society, as well as citizen rights and obligations. Written constitutions serve as a guarantee to citizens that the government is required to act in a certain way and to uphold certain rights. However, as noted by Philippe Schmitter and Terry Lynn Karl, "the liberal conception of democracy advocates circumscribing the public realm as narrowly as possible, while the socialist or social-democratic approach would extend that realm though regulation, subsidization, and, in some cases, collective ownership of property." This observation points to the difference between formal and substantive democracy as well as the difference between formal political rights and the material means to enjoy or exercise them—or what T. H. Marshall called social and economic rights of citizenship. In this connection, a key question is how to reconcile the demand for democracy with the need to advance people's welfare and well-being. How can pro-democracy movements connect civil and political participation and rights with social/economic participation and rights?[5]

When communism collapsed and Eastern Europe transitioned away from socialism, Francis Fukuyama declared this development "the end of history" and the triumph of liberal democracy and free market capitalism across the world. Samuel Huntington's response was to theorize waves of democratization and to argue that the history of democracy should be viewed as a succession of waves that have advanced and receded, then rolled in and crested again. Huntington's definition of democracy, democracy waves, and democratic transitions was limited to successful outcomes of liberal democracy.[6] Hence he left out many movements that aimed for popular sovereignty or more expansive concepts of democracy: populist, anarchist, socialist, communist, and nationalist.

In Huntington's account, the first wave occurred with the democratic revolutions of Europe and North America in the late eighteenth and early nineteenth centuries. Some of these democratic revolutions lost momentum in the period between World Wars I and II, when authoritarian regimes arose; Huntington cited the democratic breakdowns in Italy in the early 1920s and in Germany a decade later. The second wave occurred after World War II, notably in Germany, Italy, and Japan, but petered out in the 1960s. The third wave began in the mid-1970s in southern Europe, with the democratic transitions in Greece, Portugal, and Spain, followed by South Korea, the

Philippines, and Latin America in the latter part of the 1980s and the former communist countries of Eastern Europe in 1989 to 1990. Huntington had the third wave ending in 1990, but the trend continued with the peaceful transition in South Africa (1990–1994) and Indonesia (1998). What is more, democratic openings occurred during this period in countries of the Middle East and North Africa, such as Algeria, Jordan, Morocco, Turkey, and Tunisia, though they were mostly partial or aborted. But what of the movements of the twenty-first century, such as the wave of antiglobalization protests that took place in the early part of the new century and the emergence of the World Social Forum (WSF)? What of Latin America's "pink tide"—with the election of left-wing governments in Brazil, Argentina, Venezuela, Uruguay, Bolivia, and Ecuador—and, more recently, the pro-democracy movements in Iran, Tunisia, and Egypt? A case can be made that they constitute a fourth wave. Although many democratic transitions have typically taken place in the semiperiphery of the world-system, what is distinctive about the fourth wave is (1) the left-wing turn, or "pink tide," in Latin America; (2) pro-democracy movements, some successful, others unsuccessful, in a part of the world that had been viewed as almost permanently authoritarian, the Middle East and North Africa; and (3) the occurrence of pro-democracy movements in the context of neoliberal globalization. An examination of the fourth wave confirms Huntington's observation about the uneven history of democracy, but it also shows the connection between social protests and democratic transitions, on the one hand, and world-system dynamics—including globalization—on the other.

World-system analysis contributes to our understanding of where democratic transitions take place and when. Democratic transitions have been concentrated in semiperipheral countries. Indeed, a country's core, semiperipheral, or peripheral position in the world-system may shape the rate and quality of democratic growth. Democratic movements and polities are less likely to be found in peripheral countries that are disadvantaged economically, unable to access global resources, and devoid of large middle classes or a modern working class. What is more, external intervention or control may undermine efforts by social movements or their leaders to effect positive social change. This occurred time and again in the semiperiphery and especially in peripheral countries throughout the history of the modern world-system, or since the earliest democracy wave.

Political scientists point out that processes through which international actors bring pressure to bear for democratization include "contagion, consent, control, and conditionality."[7] Contagion—or what world polity analysts call diffusion—may occur in relation to tactics and frames, but norms, institutional models, and bureaucratic procedures also spread. Consent refers to the voluntary adoption of norms, models, or procedures. In contrast, control has come about through colonialism, neocolonialism, military intervention, or unequal terms of trade and is closely related to conditionality. Indeed, control and conditionality on the part of the core have been the primary means of undermining democracy movements in the periphery, including movements that Huntington did not include in his framework of democratic waves. As became evident in 2011, however, even core countries—such as the southern European countries that consented to the European Union's terms upon ascension—may be subject to control and conditionality when debts and deficits are perceived as threatening economic stability.

Conditionality commonly refers to terms set by lenders and creditors, or more powerful allies, for any assistance provided. In the 1980s, semiperipheral and peripheral countries facing enormous debts were forced to accept economic conditionalities—known as structural adjustment policies—in return for new loans or debt restructuring. In addition to austerity measures to bring down government spending, other policies included de-nationalization, contraction of the public-sector wage bill, privatization, flexibilization of labor markets, and liberalization of prices and trade. These were the principal means by which countries were forced to shift from state-led growth toward the neoliberal model advocated by the World Bank, the International Monetary Fund (IMF), and the U.S. government. Structural adjustment policies became very controversial in international development circles, defended by the international financial institutions but adamantly opposed by transnational feminist networks and transnational advocacy networks such as Jubilee 2000, Christian Aid, Oxfam, Association for the Taxation of Financial Transactions and for Citizens' Action (ATTAC), and other groups that helped form the global justice movement.

Some scholars noted that structural adjustment policies in Africa coincided with a wave of democratization in the region in two ways: by diminishing the power and maneuverability of authoritarian regimes and by directly or indirectly broadening opposition to the regimes. Others argued, however, that the adjustment regime was a critical factor in bringing down more benign regimes. Gambia's democratic regime, for example, "had a record of stability, respect for human rights, and the rule of law for nearly three decades. As a result of the 50 percent devaluation of the CFA franc in 1994, the Gambia's vital re-export trade was crippled. Essential imports plummeted, and economic hardship became widespread. These effects cost the Jawara regime much of its legitimacy, and paved the way for widespread public acceptance of the July 1994 military coup."[8] What is more, the growth of "civil society" promoted by outside agencies was less the site of associational groups that provide a buffer between citizens and the state and generate a public sphere than an organized alternative economy to meet basic needs in peripheral countries.

In very rare cases, countries manage to withstand core pressure and reject conditionalities. This was the position taken by Argentina, which chose in 2001 to default on its debt and came out in very good shape. Most countries, however, are unable to do so. Thus, in 2011, the European Union's monetary union, the Eurozone, faced crisis due to high levels of debt and deficits on the part of the several southern European countries. Greece, for example, had to accept conditionalities similar to those that peripheral countries endured in an earlier era, only this time the conditions were demanded by fellow Europeans in Germany and France. The austerity measures in Greece were accompanied by rising unemployment and loss of incomes, but they also generated massive protests in Syntagma (the central square in Athens opposite the parliament and thus analogous to Cairo's Tahrir Square) and in public spaces in other major cities. Calling themselves the "outraged," the people attacked what they viewed as the pauperization of working Greeks, the loss of sovereignty, and the destruction of democracy.[9] The mass protests eventually forced the collapse of the government of Andreas Papandreou. Earlier, the *indignados* in Spain waged mass protests against high unemployment and the hated austerity measures, and new elections led to the defeat of the government. Students and public-sector employees held protests in the United Kingdom against tuition hikes, pension cuts, and rising costs of living; similar protests occurred in Chile. As in the European and Chilean cases, the mass protests in Tunisia and Egypt occurred in the context of a global economic crisis— one that the core and the hegemon seemed unable to attenuate. Following from world-system theorizing, therefore, the third and especially the fourth wave of democratization coincide with the global B-phase downturn of the Kondratieff wave and the decline of the hegemon.

PROPITIOUS CONDITIONS

Social movements may help bring about democracy, but what conditions bring about pro-democracy social movements and enable democratic consolidation? Scholars have identified a number of causes or contributing factors: a society's wealth, socioeconomic development, capitalism, an educated population, a large middle class, civil society, civic culture, human empowerment and emancipative values, a homogeneous population, and foreign intervention. Barrington Moore famously identified a modernizing bourgeoisie as key to democratic development. In classic democratic theory, socioeconomic development is key to the making of a democratic polity and culture; likewise, sociologist Kenneth Bollen found "a positive relationship between economic development and political development."[10] In other words, structural conditions essential for the formation of a sustained pro-democracy movement include socioeconomic development, modern social classes, and resources for coalition building and mobilization. Whether or not a pro-democracy movement succeeds depends on a complex of factors, including the capacity of the state and its responses to the movement, the strength of the coalition, and the movement's ability to resonate with the population at large as well as with world society.

Barbara Wejnert identifies two broad sets of factors that contribute to the making of democracy: (1) endogenous or internal features, that is, socioeconomic development broadly defined, and (2) exogenous variables that influence democratization via forces that work globally and within a region. This second set of factors may be referred to as diffusion processes (or what others term contagion). Diffusion processes come through media, international organizations, and connections to transnational advocacy networks.[11] In an era of globalization, with its feature of "time-space compression," such diffusion processes are especially rapid and arguably more effective than in earlier periods or waves of democratization. Thus, whole countries may be influenced through diffusion processes. Movements and processes in one country can inspire citizens in other countries. The spread of the "pink tide" in Latin America may have reflected that process, when one country after another elected left-wing governments. Another example is the Arab Spring of early 2011, which was launched in Tunisia and then spread to Egypt and elsewhere. Of course, earlier inspirations may have been the Kefaya (Enough) movement in Egypt in 2005 and the larger Green Protests in Iran in June 2009, the first time in the new century that citizens boldly took to the streets to challenge authoritarian rule. At the same time, connections between the Egyptian April 6 Youth Movement and the Serbian youth organization Otpor, which had hoped to topple Slobodan Milošević, provide another example of diffusion as well as the salience of international linkages.[12]

Diffusion of frames and tactics includes the widespread adoption of the frames of human rights, dignity, democracy, women's human rights, and environmental protection, as well as the spread of movement tactics such as the sit-in or the protest encampment. Mala Htun and Laurel Weldon argue that there has been norm diffusion regarding violence against women as well as family law reform. Kathryn Sikkink argues that there has been a "justice cascade," whereby perpetrators of human rights violations have been brought to justice, whether in their own countries or through the International Criminal Court.[13] Understanding how norm diffusion works requires identifying the actors who facilitate diffusion; the role of institutions, organizations, and networks in diffusion processes; how globalized diffusion may be localized; and the ways that diffusion might be resisted. With democracy movements, American foundations and democracy-promoting institutes (such as the National Endowment for Democracy, National Democracy Institute, National Republican Institute, and Open Society Institute), as well as other transnational advocacy agencies (e.g., International IDEA, based in Stockholm), play an important role in this respect.[14] Also pertinent is that the most powerful countries in the world-system, including the hegemon, are able to deflect the "justice cascade."

We may conclude that the social transformations accompanying semiperipheral development, along with diffusion processes, have provided the conditions for democracy movements in the Global South. In the fourth wave, neoliberalism's adverse effects—financial crisis, high unemployment, rising costs, widening income inequality—generated the grievances that led to protests and alternative governments in many parts of the Global South.

Tables 3.1 and 3.2 illustrate the various waves of democratization. They draw on but go beyond the Huntington framework by including movements missing in the latter, highlighting failures and imperialist interventions, identifying a fourth wave, and underscoring the salience of world-system dynamics. The tables draw attention to what could be a key difference between the third and fourth waves; the latter includes transnational or global as well as national movements for democracy. Or can we expect setbacks and reversals?

WOMEN'S MOVEMENTS AND DEMOCRATIZATION

Political philosopher Nancy Fraser has differentiated social movements that call for recognition and representation from those that focus on issues of redistribution. This is one way of distinguishing "old" and "new" social movements, but one may argue that the women's movement entails redistribution of economic resources (across women and men more broadly), recognition of women's roles and contributions, and demands for representation in the political process as well as other domains.

Significantly, pro-democracy social movements have opened up political space for women and other historically marginalized or disadvantaged groups. Of course, socialist revolutions had similar outcomes, as evidenced by the discourses of women's emancipation in revolutionary Russia, China, Cuba, Vietnam, South Yemen (1967), and Afghanistan (1978). Here we focus on the third and fourth waves of democratization. In the Philippines, women played important roles in the labor and liberation movements. The feminist coalition GABRIELA was formed in 1984 and challenged the 1985 presidential elections that Ferdinand Marcos won. Such groups, along with women in general, were a visible presence in the "people power" revolution that overthrew the Marcos regime. In Latin America, women's movements and organizations played an important role in the opposition to authoritarianism and made a significant contribution to the "end of fear" and the

Table 3.1. Four Waves of Democratization: Successes, Failures, and External Impositions

	First Wave: 1770s–1880s	Second Wave: 1900–post-WWII	Third Wave: 1968–1990	Fourth Wave: 1990–Present
Successes	American Revolution; French revolutions (1789 and 1848); Chartist movement (United Kingdom, 1838–1850)	Germany, Italy, Japan; India; U.S. civil rights movement	Student revolts, 1968; Greece, Portugal, Spain; South Korea, Taiwan, Philippines; Chile, Argentina, Brazil; Eastern Europe	South Africa, 1990–1994; Ghana, 1993–2001; Liberia, 2003; Northern Ireland, 1998; Latin American "pink tide," 2001–2011; Morocco, 1998–present; Ukraine, 2004; Tunisia, 2011–2012
Failures	Haiti (antislavery revolt, 1794)[a]	German uprising 1918[b]; Iran's Constitutional Revolution, 1906–1911[c]; nationalist movement, 1951–1953; Guatemala, 1954; Dominican Republic, 1963[d]	Burma 1988; China 1989; Algeria 1990[e]	Haiti, 2004 (Aristede and Fanmi Lavalas); Iran, 2009
External control or imposition				Serbia, Bosnia, Kosovo, 2000; Afghanistan, 2001; Iraq, 2003; Libya, 2011
Ongoing			Feminist movements; youth/student movements	Zapatista indigenous movement (Mexico, since 1994); World Social Forum (since February 2011); Egypt (since February 2011); Occupy Wall Street (since September 2011)

[a] Led by Toussaint-Louverture, the revolt did not lead to democracy but did overthrow slavery and the plantation system.

[b] Revolutions in Mexico and Russia brought about progressive sociopolitical change but did not lead to democracy.

[c] Iran's Constitutional Revolution of 1906 to 1911 introduced a constitution and brought down the Qajar dynasty but failed to bring about a democracy or a republic.

[d] The pro-democracy movements in Iran, Guatemala, and the Dominican Republic were defeated by U.S. intervention.

[e] The failure in Algeria was caused by the violent extremism of the Islamist opposition as well as by the ruling party's cancellation of the 1991 election results.

Table 3.2. "Third Wave and Fourth Wave" Pro-Democracy Sociopolitical Movements: World-System Location, Frames, and Outcomes

Semiperiphery	Frames	Outcomes
1970s: Greece, Spain, Portugal	Against dictatorship; for democracy, constitutionalism, and/or socialism	Successful transition and consolidation; shift from socialism to social democracy in Portugal; entrance of all into EU in new century
1980s: Argentina, Brazil, Chile	Against dictatorship; for democracy, human rights, and women's rights	Successful transition and consolidation; "pink revolutions" in new century; women leaders in all three countries
South Korea, Taiwan, the Philippines	Against dictatorship; for worker rights 'South Korea), "people power" (Philippines)	Successful transitions and consolidation
Eastern Europe	Against communism; for democracy and human rights	Successful transitions and consolidation; contention over women's rights; entry of various countries into EU in new century
1990s: South Africa	Against apartheid; for democracy, civil rights, and/or socialism	Black majority government; rights-based constitution and laws; truth and reconciliation process; shift to neoliberalism in new century
Mexico: Zapatistas	Against neoliberal globalization; for indigenous rights in Chiapas	Truce between state and Chiapas; autonomy
Indonesia	Against Suharto dictatorship and economic hardships	Multiparty elections; rise of Islamic parties and movements; marginalization of religious minorities
2001–present: World Social Forum	Against neoliberal globalization; for democratic spaces and deliberation	Annual meetings held in semiperipheral sites; regional forums that include core countries; mobilization of democrats, feminists, socialists, youth, and labor, environmental, and indigenous rights activists
2005: Egypt's Kefaya movement	Enough of Mubarak; for change, no to succession/ inheritance of power	Charges of election fraud levied against presidential contender Ayman Nour; Mubarak's "election" to a fifth term
2009: Iran's Green Protests	"Where is my vote?"; against dictatorship; for genuine electoral democracy	State repression of 2009 and 2010 protests
2011: Tunisia and Egypt	Against personalist and authoritarian rule; for dignity and economic, civil, and political rights	In progress; military rule and rise of Islamists in Egypt; success of an-Nahda Islamic party in Tunisia but with coalition building

inauguration of the transition. Here women organized as feminists and as democrats, often allying themselves with left-wing parties.[15] Where women were not key actors in the negotiated transitions, they nonetheless received institutional rewards when democratic governments were set up and their presence in the new parliaments increased. In addition to the quotas that enhanced their parliamentary representation, women were rewarded with well-resourced policy agencies and legislation on violence against women. As Jane Jaquette observes,[16]

> Feminist issues were positively associated with democratization, human rights, and expanded notions of citizenship that included indigenous rights as well as women's rights. This positive association opened the way for electoral quotas and increased the credibility of women candidates, who were considered more likely to care about welfare issues and less corrupt than their male counterparts.

The examples above would confirm that women's rights movements are not "identity movements" but rather democratizing movements that entail redistribution as well as recognition and representation. Many studies show that women's organizing tends to be inclusive, and women's movement activism often involves the explicit practice of democracy.[17] What is more, women's movement activism and advocacy—whether in the form of social movements, transnational networks, or professional organizations—contribute to the making of vibrant civil societies and public spheres, which are themselves critical to sustaining and deepening democracy. John Keane, for example, finds democracy and civility in public discourse dependent upon a vibrant civil society/public sphere. This is perhaps why Tunisia's democratic transition has been smoother than Egypt's—it has had a longer tradition of secular republicanism and a well-organized and well-coordinated civil society, including feminist, human rights, and left-wing organizations staffed by activists who have acquired strong civic skills[18] (see further discussion below).

Democratic transitions can create a window of opportunity for legal and policy reforms for women's rights, but this is not always guaranteed. For example, Chile returned to democracy in 1990 but waited until 2004 to legalize abortion; the eventual legalization of divorce depended on the assumption of power by the Socialist Party.[19] In some cases, democratic transitions actually close political participation for some groups, including women and minorities, or they do not narrow the huge social inequalities, including income inequalities, in society. We refer to these as the paradoxes of democracy, or democracy's deficits, to which we now turn.

DEMOCRACY'S DEFICITS: THE PROBLEM WITH GLOBALIZATION

In its 2002 study of globalization and democracy, the United Nations Development Programme asserted that "economically, politically, and technologically, the world has never seemed more free—or more unjust." The statement pointed to the paradox of democracy and almost anticipated the global protests of 2010–2011. John Markoff identifies the following issues: the meaningfulness of electoral accountability to citizens, the nature of citizenship, the reinvigoration of exclusionary politics, and the continued effectiveness of social movements as a force for democratization.[20] In this section, we focus on the following deficits: (1) displacement of decision making from the local or national domain, (2) huge income inequalities and the concentration of wealth among an ever-smaller proportion of the population, (3) the capture of government by the business sector and other moneyed concerns, and (4) the tendency of some democratic transitions to marginalize women and minorities.

As noted, the third wave of democratization opened up political systems and expanded civil and political rights, but this took place during the expansion of neoliberal capitalist globalization, which also saw the sphere of citizen social/economic rights shrinking. While not all models of democracy guarantee the material means for the enjoyment of civil and political rights, the "golden age of capitalism" had afforded citizens a modicum of social rights and economic prosperity, and with that, governments ruled with a high degree of legitimacy and consent. This began to change in the era of neoliberal globalization and especially with the onset of the world economic crisis. In the welfare states of the core, the global economic crisis required governments to look for ways to cut social spending. Neoliberal economic policies, particularly financialization, allowed for growing wealth in the hands of a tiny proportion of the population, leading to gaping income inequalities, especially in the United States but increasingly in the United

Kingdom as well. South Africa, Russia, India, Brazil, and China saw similar trends: the opening up of political space (to a certain extent) at the same time that income inequalities increased. When citizens in the core began to protest income disparities, high unemployment, and rising costs of health care, education, and food, they were calling into question the system's legitimacy. In the semiperiphery and periphery, the persistence of social inequalities, poverty, and various forms of violence and conflict raised questions about the efficacy of democratic governance. For these reasons, transnational feminist networks and the global justice movement—including the Occupy Wall Street protests—have focused on alternatives to social and economic inequalities and injustices. And they have interrogated models of democracy that reduce rather than enhance citizen participation, rights, and welfare. For perhaps the first time in its existence, the U.S. model of democracy is not a beacon of hope or source of inspiration for at least four reasons: the adverse effects of neoliberal globalization have hit the U.S. middle and working classes hard, income inequality in the United States is the highest in the developed world, social mobility has slowed considerably, and the pervasive role of money in U.S. politics is seen as corrupting and corrosive of democracy.[21]

The role of mass media is relevant to the discussion of democracy and democratic movements. In the mature democracies, the media are typically outside of state influence, but their corporate ownership tends to make them biased toward "business as usual" and against movements that might challenge the status quo. As such, social movement events might face limited or no coverage at all. For example, the United States Social Forum in Atlanta in 2007 and Detroit in 2010, while attended by thousands, was ignored by the mass media. In contrast, the right-wing Tea Party Convention, which was much smaller, received extensive media coverage. In authoritarian settings, state ownership or control of media often has similar effects. Fortunately for social movements, the Internet affords rapid and extensive coverage and diffusion through alternative media.

In the late 1990s and into the new century, European citizen groups as well as scholars used the term "democracy deficit" to refer to the displacement of local or national decision making onto the new bureaucratic centers in Brussels. In late 1999, the so-called Battle of Seattle—a mass demonstration that effectively shut down the World

Trade Organization (WTO) ministerial summit—was a protest against neoliberalism and democracy's deficits, challenging economic and political elites with the slogan "This is what democracy looks like!" In 2011, Greek protesters were especially vociferous in their denunciation of the EU's democracy deficit. They demanded a say in how their country's huge debt burden should be tackled, arguing that the Greek government's simply accepting the conditionalities emanating from the EU's Brussels headquarters, not to mention Berlin and Paris, was undemocratic. Spain, Italy, and the United Kingdom all saw protests as their governments implemented austerity measures or announced plans to do so. Occupy Wall Street, which spread throughout the United States, objected to the rising cost of living, high youth unemployment, income inequality, and the cozy relationship between business and government. These developments confirm that even in the core countries, globalization exerts an indirect impact on democracy in two ways: (1) by undermining national sovereignty through control by institutions of global or regional governance, as in the EU, or through the power of money and rich lobbyists, as in the United States; and (2) by generating opposition to such forces, in the form of massive protests and transnational social movements.

If there is limited democracy in regional governance, there is none in global governance. Moreover, one deficit in the current model is that some international organizations are more influential and powerful than others. Jackie Smith includes the United Nations in what she identifies as the global pro-democracy network. But, as I have argued in a paper with Dilek Elveren, the era of globalization has seen a hierarchy among the major international organizations such that the international financial institutions and the WTO have much more power, influence, and enforceability than do UN agencies, such as the International Labour Organization (ILO), United Nations Children's Fund (UNICEF), United Nations Educational, Scientific and Cultural Organization (UNESCO), or the United Nations High Commissioner for Refugees (UNHCR).[22]

The persistence or heightening of income inequality at the national level is one of democracy's paradoxes, but scholars have identified other aspects of democracy's dark side. In *Setting the People Free: The Story of Democracy*, John Dunn provides a sweeping history of the origins and evolution of democratic theory and governance. He maintains that as early as the late eighteenth and early nineteenth centuries, the ideals of democracy had been co-opted and distorted by advocates of a competitive market economy. This notion is echoed in a study by Adam Przeworski and colleagues: "Today, modernization means liberal democracy, consumption-oriented culture, and capitalism." It also points to concerns raised by Benjamin Barber and German political philosopher Jurgen Habermas, who maintain that the public sphere—so critical to the functioning of a democracy—has been taken over by private or market interests.[23] Perhaps nowhere is this more obvious than in the United States, with its array of paid lobbyists and the revolving door between government and business.

Many social movements in semiperipheral countries push for democracy, and since at least the 1980s, the democracy frame has been diffused throughout the world by movements and advocacy networks as well as by international organizations and governments in the core. In some cases, however, the democratic opening can have highly problematic consequences, bringing fringe elements to power, putting minorities in jeopardy, or unleashing violence. In *World on Fire,* Amy Chua argues that markets and elections often pull societies in opposite directions. Indonesia's democracy movement was accompanied by attacks on ethnic minorities, notably the Chinese, who had held a prominent position in the country's economy. Attacks on Christian churches followed. Similarly, John Lukacs, in *Democracy and Populism: Fear and Hatred,* maintains that unchecked popular sovereignty often unleashes a host of evils, targeting minorities but also degrading democracy itself.[24] This echoes Huntington's observation that democracy can rise and fall, as it did with the collapse of the Weimar Republic and the coming to power of the Nazi Party, which then set about targeting communists, Jews, and other "undesirables." Beyond that observation, it also points to the perils as well as the promises of electoral democracy.

The historical record shows that women can pay a high price when a democratic process that is institutionally weak, or is not founded on principles of equality and the rights of all citizens, or lacks a well-organized civil society allows a political party bound by patriarchal norms to come to power and immediately institute laws relegating women to second-class citizenship and imposing controls over their mobility. This was the Algerian feminist nightmare, which is why so many educated Algerian women opposed the Front Islamique du Salut (FIS) after its expansion in 1989. The quick transition unsupported by strong institutions did not serve women well. Algeria had long been ruled by a single-party system in the "Arab socialist" style. The death of President Houari Boumedienne in December 1978 brought about political and economic changes, including the growth of an Islamist movement that intimidated unveiled women, and a new government intent on economic restructuring. Urban riots in 1988 were followed quickly by a new constitution and elections, without a longer period of democracy building. The electoral victory of the FIS—which promised (or threatened) to institute sharia law, enforce veiling, and end competitive elections—alarmed not only Algeria's educated female population but also the ruling party and the military, which stepped in to annul the election results. That the FIS went on to initiate an armed rebellion when it was not allowed to assume power only confirms the violent nature of that party. The even more extreme Group Islamique Armée committed numerous atrocities (for details, see chapter 4). In contrast, a similar case in Turkey had a far different outcome. When the Turkish military banned the Islamic Refah Party, which was in fact more "modern" and moderate than Algeria's FIS, Refah chose to reorganize itself rather than take up arms.[25]

Mark Tessler makes the interesting observation that Algerian respondents to the fourth wave of the World Values Survey (WVS), conducted between 2000 and 2002, show less attachment to religiosity than inhabitants of some other Muslim-majority countries. Only one-third of respondents agreed or strongly agreed that it would be better for the country if people with strong religious beliefs held political office.[26] This could be the legacy of their experience with Islamist intégrisme and terrorism, although it remains to be seen how rooted the more secular and democratic segments of Algerian society are able to become.

The Algerian experience of the 1990s is highly instructive; it compels us to acknowledge the perils as well as the promises of democracy and to appreciate the importance of strong institutions and a civic culture to promote and protect civil liberties, participation, inclusion, and social welfare. The Algerian experience, or, at the very least, the Indonesian case, may be the specter that haunts Egypt.

MENA PROTESTS, GLOBALIZATION, AND DEMOCRATIZATION

As the Algerian case shows, not all protest movements are pro-democracy movements. At this writing, it is not clear that the 2011–2012 protests and rebellions in Libya, Yemen, and Syria were democratic movements. Moreover, not all pro-democracy movements necessarily result in stable democratic institutions and cultures. It is difficult to predict outcomes of ongoing social movements and especially of more controversial forms of violent contention. In this section we focus on four cases: the pro-democracy Green Protests in Iran in 2009 and the ongoing democratic transitions in Egypt, Morocco, and Tunisia. National, regional, and global dynamics will be highlighted.

The pro-democracy movements in MENA occurred in a region long assumed to be impervious to democracy. In much the same way that adherents of the "totalitarian thesis" argued that political change was impossible in the communist world, many political scientists examining MENA wrote at length about the "robust" nature of authoritarian institutions in the region. As Larry Diamond once wrote, "The continuing absence of even a single democratic regime in the Arab world is a striking anomaly—the principal exception to the globalization of democracy."[27] Other scholars of the Middle East and North Africa focused on the severity of social problems and the likelihood of popular unrest. The *Arab Human Development Report*, a series of reports on the state of Arab countries produced by a group of Arab social scientists, identified three deficits in the Arab region: the absence of democracy, the absence of women's equality, and deficiencies in knowledge production and information dissemination. In previous work, I examined widening inequalities and income gaps, high rates of youth unemployment, deteriorating infrastructure and public services, and rising prices attenuated only by subsidies. I also analyzed the growth of women's movements in the region and the demands they made on states. Asef Bayat wrote about "street politics" and "quiet encroachments" as informal politics in authoritarian settings. Joel Beinin followed labor actions, while Jillian Schwedler and others examined the growing influence of moderate Islamic parties. This literature was, in fact, attentive to forms of popular mobilizations, civil society formation, and attempts at reform and liberalization.[28]

MENA democracy movements took place in the context of the global economic crisis, which itself was a consequence of neoliberal economic policies on a world scale. In the 1990s, MENA countries joined the rest of the world in the move away from a statist economic strategy, in which large public sectors held sway, toward one that prioritized denationalization, privatization, the adoption of "flexible" labor markets, and recruitment of foreign direct investment. In many MENA countries, oil wealth helped to attenuate some of the adverse effects of this policy shift, and governments continued to provide citizens with cheap oil (for heating, cooking, and transportation) as well as other subsidies. Even so, unemployment kept rising, making the region's double-digit unemployment rates—especially among youth—possibly the highest in the world and the subject of many academic and policy studies. In more recent years, various social policy "reforms" were enacted, in line with neoliberal prescriptions, such as the withdrawal of state subsidies for food, public utilities, and social services. Then came the financial meltdown of 2008 and ensuing global economic crisis, which led to rising food prices in MENA countries. Egypt in particular saw strikes and street protests over rising prices, but elsewhere in the region, the combination of high unemployment, high costs of living, and authoritarian rule heightened popular dissatisfaction.

In short, factors common to the rise of pro-democracy movements in Iran, Egypt, Tunisia, and Morocco include the unraveling of the old social contract in the context of neoliberal globalization, authoritarian rule, a youth bulge, and rising expectations and aspirations on the part of the growing middle and working classes. In all four countries, citizens have demanded more participation and rights. This has been the case most explicitly for civil society organizations focused on women's rights and human rights, but some Islamic groups have also called for free elections to replace the authoritarian regimes in power. As such, the protest movements are connected to globalization in two ways: (1) through the adoption and localization of global cultural and norm diffusion, and (2) in terms of popular responses to neoliberalism's effects on income inequalities, unemployment, and high commodity prices. Sociodemographic factors are important, too, especially for what Doug McAdam termed "biographical availability," that is, "the absence of personal constraints that may increase costs and risks of movement participation."[29] In Iran, Tunisia, Egypt, and Morocco, young people launched the uprisings, and their use of social-networking media for cyberactivism was a critical factor in the success of the mobilizations.

MENA democracy movements may be in part products of the global diffusion of norms, frames, and tactics, but they are also the heirs of earlier popular movements (see table 3.2). The democracy movements of MENA have at least two antecedents: (1) the third wave of democratization and earlier manifestations of the fourth wave, and (2) specific movements for national independence and dignity. The latter include Iran's 1905–1911 constitutional movement and the 1977–1979 revolution against the shah; Egypt's nationalist movement of the early 1900s and the Nasser revolution of the 1950s; Tunisia's liberation movement and postcolonial state-building project of the 1950s, along with a period of political liberalization in the late 1980s and early 1990s; and Morocco's political opening of 1998. Mention also should be made of the 2002 launch of the *Arab Human Development Report*, authored entirely by Arab social scientists and intellectuals, which identified three major deficits in the region: authoritarian rule, restrictions on knowledge, and gender inequality. Since then, successive reports have focused on the three deficits, as well as on the conceptualization of, and need for, human security in the region.

Pro-Democracy Movements: Iran, Morocco, Tunisia, Egypt

While Iran, as a non-Arab country, is not included in the *Arab Human Development Reports*, it shares the deficits identified by the reports: women are legally second-class citizens subjected to an array of discriminatory laws and policies; knowledge production is surveilled, libraries are poorly stocked, and access to international research products is limited; and while elections take place regularly, they are controlled, and the candidates are vetted by an unelected body called the Guardian Council. Independent organizing is not permitted, with the effect that trade unionists who try to organize workers face harassment or worse. Mansour Osanloo, a prominent workers' rights activist and trade union leader for the Syndicate of Workers' of Tehran and Suburbs Bus Company, endured years of harassment and beatings before being sentenced to five years' imprisonment. His years in jail took a toll on his health. As a member of the ILO, Iran is obligated to respect and institute basic workers' rights standards;

tellingly, however, it has not ratified the core conventions relating to freedom of association and the right to organize. Dissent is not tolerated in the Islamic Republic of Iran; the student movement that had sought to expand the political and cultural opening under former president Mohammad Khatami was repressed in the summer of 1999, and several student leaders were forced into exile.[30] Similarly, a number of the "new religious intellectuals," who question authoritarian Islam and seek to reconcile Islamic norms with a democratic polity, have been harassed, arrested, or compelled to leave the country. Even feminists have been charged with undermining national security, arrested, and imprisoned. The women of the One Million Signatures Campaign—launched in 2007 as a door-to-door grassroots movement for the repeal of discriminatory laws and a call for women's equality through constitutional change—have been harassed and arrested, and a number of feminist leaders have been forced into exile.

Meanwhile, rising educational attainment among women as well as men, the high rate of youth unemployment, and access to world society and global norms through satellite television, social-networking media, and travel have generated aspirations for more freedoms as well as dissatisfaction with the status quo. This is the broad sociopolitical and demographic context in which Iranians protested the results of the June 2009 elections. What began as a protest framed as "Where is my vote?" became a more direct challenge to the authority of the state, including that of the unelected leader, Ayatollah Khamenei.[31] The protest movement was repressed, however, when the state put the presidential challengers under house arrest, a sniper killed a woman protest participant, and hundreds were arrested and jailed. As noted, many dissidents have had to leave Iran and find refuge abroad, including a number of the new religious intellectuals (see table 4.1), freethinking university professors, and feminist activists.

In February 2011, Morocco saw the formation of the 2nd February Youth Movement, as part of the diffusion of the protests in neighboring Tunisia and in Egypt, which forced King Mohammed VI to agree to constitutional changes that would limit his powers. But in Morocco's case, this was part of a more gradual democratization process that began in 1998, with the formation of a progressive government, and included a twelve-year feminist campaign for family law reform that succeeded in 2003. The growth of civil society, as well as international factors such as the emerging discourse of democratization with the end of the Cold War and an embarrassing book about the king and political repression that appeared in France, helped pave the way for the country's transition from authoritarian and personalist monarchical rule to political liberalization through constitutional changes in 1996. For women's groups, the political opening came with multiparty elections in 1997 and the appointment in the following year of a new prime minister.[32]

Abdelrahman Youssefi was a socialist and former political prisoner as well as leader of the Union Socialiste des Forces Populaires (USFP) whose new cabinet would include progressives such as Mohammad Said Saadi, an economics professor and Communist Party member, as minister of family affairs and Aicha Belarbi, a sociology professor and long-standing socialist, as minister for social affairs. The new coalition government—*le gouvernement d'altérnance*—announced its support for human rights and women's rights and quickly endorsed the Action Plan for the Integration of Women in Development (Plan d'Action pour l'Intégration des Femmes au Développement), which women's groups had produced.[33] An ambitious document aiming to extend education, employment, and political participation to Moroccan women, the plan included a chapter on the need to reform the *moudawana*. As described by Latifa Jbabdi, one of the feminist leaders, "Youssefi held a meeting with us and asked, 'Are you still socialists? Because if you are, I will help you.' So we worked together."[34] Women's groups formed an umbrella group called Chabaka (literally, "network" in Arabic) and allied themselves with the government with the goal of promoting women's rights, a democratic polity, and national development. Their communications strategy included narratives about the devastating effects of polygamy and unilateral male divorce on women, children, and the family.[35]

The strategy of Moroccan women's rights activists was to build consensus for the action plan and family law reform through various research, advocacy, and awareness-raising activities. These included publications, press releases, flyers, and advertisements and articles in the national dailies explaining the discriminatory provisions of legal texts in matters of repudiation, divorce, child support, and domestic violence. Their allies in government instituted a series of "social dialogues" to promote the plan. But women's groups also took to the streets in support of the plan and women's rights. Huge rallies for and against the plan and family law reform took place in March 2000. In the face of sustained hostility from Islamist forces, the government felt compelled to withdraw the plan.

The women's organizations, however, pressed ahead, with a shift in strategy and framing. In an overwhelmingly Muslim and pious country, women's groups formulated arguments rooted in an egalitarian interpretation of Islam, thus exercising *ijtihad* (reinterpretation of sharia-based jurisprudence to accommodate new conditions). Other frames were the imperatives of social development and poverty alleviation in Morocco and the rights of women and children. At the same time, women's groups in Morocco continued to work domestically and with their Algerian and Tunisian partners in the Collectif Maghreb Egalité 95 on surveys and reports pertaining to women's conditions and the legal frameworks. Law professor Farida Bennani of the Association Démocratique des Femmes du Maroc (ADFM) was the chief Moroccan contributor to a 2003 Collectif publication, *Dalil pour l'égalité dans la famille au Maghreb*, which laid out arguments against existing family laws from theological, sociological, and international law perspectives.[36] In a move away from the exclusively secular socialist or feminist discourses, women's groups deliberately developed arguments that could tread safely between tradition and reform and that drew on religious as well as nationalist frames.

A series of terrorist bombings in Casablanca on May 17, 2003, put the Islamist movement on the defensive, compelling it to halt its public opposition to the family law reform. The Islamist opposition thus held no street protests when the king announced in October 2003 that the Royal Commission had recommended the formulation of a new family law. In his capacity as commander of the faithful, the king announced that the proposed new family code was consistent with the egalitarian and emancipatory spirit of the sharia. On January 25, 2004, after a decade of feminist action and several years of intense debate and consultation, the Moroccan parliament passed a series of sweeping revisions to the *moudawana*.

Dissatisfaction with the political environment remained, especially in connection with the vast powers of the king. Former cabinet minister Mohammad Said Saadi emphasized that Morocco's political opening had been thwarted. The main problem, he said, was that the monarch retained excessive powers, preventing both political democratization and egalitarian economic measures.[37] At the time, Dr. Saadi was part of a loose coalition of progressives, including socialists and nationalists, who aspired to a transition to the "Spanish model." Following the street protests of February 2011 and a referendum to approve changes to the constitution, they have come closer to the Spanish model of a constitutional monarchical democracy.

Next door, Tunisians similarly grappled with authoritarianism, with occasional manifestations of opposition by the leading trade union, feminist associations, and human rights groups. Research shows that organizational resources may counterbalance the dampening effects of a closed political context, and Tunisia's civil society grew across the decades. For example, since the late 1980s, women's groups have decried fundamentalism and called for women's equality, and since 1999 the Association Tunisienne des Femmes Démocrates (ATFD) and the Association des Femmes Tunisiennes pour la Recherche et le Développement (AFTURD) have militated for gender equality in matters of inheritance. In addition to helping form the Collectif Maghreb Egalité 95, Tunisian women's groups have worked together and with other civil society associations on matters such as human rights, social welfare, and fair elections. Tunisia's social and economic development, a well-organized social provisioning system, and friendly ties with Europe as well as the Arab world and Africa ensured stability. But the economic crisis took its toll on employment and the cost of living, while WikiLeaks' revelation in 2010 of the corruption and self-enrichment of the family of the president's wife enraged Tunisians. When a street vendor ordered to stop his trade resorted to self-immolation in December 2010 after being denied justice, his act seemed to symbolize a protest against the collective loss of dignity. The tragedy triggered massive street protests the following January with slogans such as "Ben Ali, d'égage!" ([President] Ben Ali, leave!) and "L'emploi, notre droit" (employment is our right). Leftists, secularists, feminists, trade unionists, and supporters of the long-banned Islamic movement all took to the streets, while young people maintained the momentum through social-networking media.

Larbi Sadiki, writing for Al Jazeera online, notes that in the October 2011 elections, an-Nahda may have won, but it did so in a context whereby 3 million eligible citizens did not register to vote, and of the 4 million who did register, few voted, giving an-Nahda a plurality (40 percent of votes cast) rather than a sweeping majority of the electorate. Sadiki argues that coalition building and partnership are needed in such a context.[38] In fact, an-Nahda wisely did this by offering prominent posts to leaders of secular and leftist political parties. This bodes well for Tunisia's democratic transition and for women's groups, who want Tunisia's legal frameworks to reflect the prevailing reality of family relations and to establish parity between men and women. The transitional government ceded to the demands for parity, and the remaining reservations regarding the Convention on the Elimination of All Forms of Discrimination against Women (CEDAW)—the United Nation's bill of rights for women—were lifted after the downfall of Zine El Abidine Ben Ali.

Turning to Egypt, Hosni Mubarak, a former military officer, had been president since the assassination of Anwar Sadat in 1981. His presidency increasingly came to be equated with cronyism, rigged elections, and repression of any and all dissent. The government's crackdown on Islamist terrorism in the 1990s was perhaps appreciated by many, but sweeping or arbitrary arrests were not. Among the most notorious cases were those of Nawal Saadawi, the feminist author and activist, whose organization was ordered shut down because she criticized Egypt's role in the 1991 Gulf War; Saad Eddin Ibrahim, sociology professor and advocate of democracy, who was imprisoned on charges of accepting foreign funds; and Ayman Nour, a leader of the Ghad Party and participant in the 2005 Kefaya movement, who had the temerity to run against Mubarak in a presidential election and was imprisoned on charges of election fraud. Meanwhile, adoption of the neoliberal model entailed privatization of previously state-owned assets, with the result that wealth came to be concentrated among a small segment of the population while the middle and working classes faced unemployment and high costs of living. Urban overpopulation stretched public services, including schooling and health care, to their limits, while housing was in such short supply that the poor erected a shantytown in a vast cemetery just outside the city. Neoliberal social policy reforms were set to end subsidies on consumer goods. A series of labor actions, including that in the industrial town of Mahalla el-Kubra in 2008, constituted a call for economic justice and led to a coalition that came to be known as the April 6 Youth Movement. Indeed, between 2004 and 2010, nearly 2 million workers voiced grievances through strikes, sit-ins, and other forms of protest against poor living conditions caused by the erosion of wages, rising inflation, and precarious employment. Demands were initially to increase the minimum wage, combat poverty and unemployment, end the state of emergency, and remove the minister of the interior; soon it became a single demand: the departure of President Mubarak.

Throughout the years of the Mubarak presidency, and despite the fact that it was officially banned, the Muslim Brotherhood engaged in its own "quiet encroachment": recruiting supporters and sympathizers; fielding "independent" candidates in parliamentary elections, winning an astonishing 20 percent of seats in the controlled elections of 2005; and extending its influence across an array of societal institutions, including the education system, the media, and associations of lawyers and journalists. It therefore came as no surprise when the Muslim Brotherhood won nearly two-thirds of seats in the November 2011 parliamentary elections. The surprise, however, was that self-described Salafists won seats as well. The combination of conservative Islamists and the power of the military establishment does not bode well for Egypt's democratic transition. What is more, Egypt's transition thus far seems not to have allayed fears that women and Egyptian Christians will not obtain equality in participation and rights.[39]

SOCIAL MEDIA AND SOCIAL MOVEMENTS IN MENA

The revolutions in Tunisia and Egypt have been called "Facebook revolutions," organized by a technologically savvy, albeit leaderless, youth generation. Web-based social networks have proved critical for users in alerting activists, gaining momentum, and informing the world as events unfold on the ground. The role of the new information and communication technologies in the MENA social movements cannot be underestimated. For too long, authoritarian states have had a monopoly not only on the means of violence but also on the means of communication, especially with monopolized television, radio, and print journalism. New media technologies have increasingly undermined the regimes' censorship efforts. Some examples follow.

Following the contested elections in Iran, the government of Mahmoud Ahmadinejad clamped down on protesters, who then turned to Twitter, YouTube, and Facebook; citizen journalism in Iran helped make the Green Protests a worldwide cause célèbre. Ahmadinejad shut down the Internet in Iran for around twenty hours. After the ban was lifted, the government continued to filter the Internet heavily, blocking sites such as Facebook and BBC News. Iranian activists used whatever means they could to get their message out. People in other countries began setting up their computers as proxies so that citizens could access the Internet through them, circumventing the security set up by the Iranian government. The cyber-based hacking group Anonymous began a website titled Anonymous Iran that provided tools to get around Iran's security measures. Citizens themselves began using the newly popular Twitter to post blurbs about the protests and the unjustness of the election; they also used photo sites such as Flickr and Tehran24, as well as YouTube and Facebook, to post images of protests and violence against protesters. The sniper's murder of Neda Agha-Soltani was captured on a mobile phone, uploaded to the Internet, and distributed across the globe. Immediately, the dying young woman's beautiful face became the symbol of a pro-democracy movement facing the ugliness of state repression.[40]

The cyberjournalism of WikiLeaks damaged the legitimacy of Tunisian president Ben Ali beyond repair. The Internet generally opened up space for Tunisian dissidents through blogs, discussion forums, and music. The street demonstrations were captured on cell phone cameras and then uploaded as videos to known opposition sites and blogs, such as ATunisianGirl.blogspot.com (created by blogger Lina Ben Mhenni), Nawaat.org, and Les Révolutionaires de la Dignité, whose contents served as news feeds for satellite networks like Al Jazeera.

In Egypt in 2008, "Facebook girl" Israa Abdel Rattah, a young woman in her twenties, used Facebook to organize a campaign of civil disobedience to protest the deteriorating conditions of the average citizen. On the morning of a planned general strike by workers, April 6, 2008, she was arrested and detained for eighteen days. The violent suppression of the workers' strike resulted in the formation of the April 6 Youth Movement. On January 18, 2011, Asma Mahfouz uploaded a short video to YouTube and Facebook in which she announced, "Whoever says women shouldn't go to the protests because they will get beaten, let him have some honor and manhood and come with me on January 25." The same day, Wael Ghonim created a Facebook page in honor of Khaled Said, a young Egyptian blogger killed by police. The

Mahfouz video went viral, countless Egyptians learned about Khaled Said, and the planned one-day demonstration became a popular revolution. The temporary Internet shutdown that marked the first week of revolt highlighted the significance of new and alternative media.

Another useful tool to Egyptian protesters was "Speak to Tweet." The work of a Zurich-based activist, this tool emerged to allow Egyptians to leave voice recordings by calling an international phone number. The recordings were automatically transcribed as Twitter messages, which were then picked up by a separate group of volunteers and translated into various languages on a website called Alive in Egypt. Camera cell phones, social media, opposition blogs, chat rooms, and Al Jazeera's "continuous coverage" and advocacy journalism all served to form a feedback loop for information, keeping the story alive and transmitting it to other Arab countries and to Western publics. The growth of Internet use in Egypt and especially in Tunisia illustrates the capacity of citizens to circumvent state censorship (see table 3.3).

All this suggests the important role of social-networking sites for social change, giving voice to a new dissident public. The Internet redefines the terms of civic engagement, protest, and the public sphere and enables transnational cyberactivism. Among other advantages, the Internet reduces the "transaction costs" for organizing, mobilizing, and participating in collective action.[41]

The brief discussion of the four democracy movements in MENA shows similarities but also differences across the movements. Of the four countries, Tunisia and Morocco appear best suited to effect successful democratic transitions, as activists there arguably have more of the civic skills needed to consolidate democracy; Morocco also seems to have a monarchy receptive to democratic reforms. On the other hand, Rachid Ghannouchi's promise to follow the "free market model" in Tunisia raises questions about the kind of democracy that would

Table 3.3.   Internet Usage in Egypt, Morocco, and Tunisia, circa 2011

Country	Total Population	Capital City Population	Internet Usage (percentage of total population)
Egypt	82 million	7.9 million	21.6 million (26.4)
Morocco	31.9 million	1.7 million	15.6 million (49.0)
Tunisia	10.6 million	740,000	3.8 million (36.3)

Sources: "Africa," Internet World Stats, http://www.internetworldstats.com/africa.htm.

address citizen concerns. Will Tunisians' social rights and economic citizenship be addressed? How will Tunisians' preference for a kind of social democracy be reconciled with the current model of neoliberalism? If Tunisia maintains a vibrant civil society—with its many human rights, women's rights, and other advocacy organizations, its professional associations and charities, and its strong labor movement—along with a well-functioning political society, it could become a model of a democratic polity and society—and not just for the Arab region.

Moroccan society continues to inch its way toward greater democracy and rights, although high unemployment plagues large sections of the population, and the contraction of available jobs in Europe makes labor migration less of an option. Citizens also are concerned about the wealth gap, as noted by economist Driss Benali: "What matters is the redistribution of riches. Morocco has the biggest poverty gap in the Maghreb." In an attempt to contain further protest, the government made concessions that included subsidies on essentials and a higher minimum wage.[42] Egypt's transition is more problematic, characterized by military government, the rise of Salafist Islamists and attacks on Egyptian Christians, no action on women's rights, and ambiguity about the next steps forward. In a country where Islamists and the military are the leading powers, the development of democratic institutions and culture remains a formidable challenge. Finally, Iran's recent history of collective action suggests that another wave of protest can be expected for at least three reasons: the regional diffusion of the democracy frame, domestic political and economic problems, and international pressures on the Iranian state. At the same time, the threat of international intervention—for example, over Iran's nuclear power program—could be exploited by the regime to harden its stance on dissent and collective action even further.

BUILDING GLOBAL DEMOCRACY: OCCUPY WALL STREET AND THE WORLD SOCIAL FORUM

The Universal Declaration of Human Rights asserts, "The will of the people shall be the basis of the authority of government." As shown by the above discussion of democracy's deficits, however, there are serious problems with the realization of people's democratic aspirations as well as with the models of democracy that are in place. People have less and less control over decisions that affect their daily lives. And they see far too much control in the hands of political and economic elites. Globalization has fundamentally altered the character of national states and the practice of democracy, affecting national policy making and the ways that popular groups can advance their interests. We have seen that the growing wealth and power of economic elites and the hegemony of the financial sector have coincided with rising unemployment and the cost of living. In Occupy Wall Street, as in the global justice movement more generally, many are angry that globalization has taken decision making away from citizens and placed it in the hands of lobbyists and those in institutions of global governance, bringing into sharp relief the deficiencies of a "representative" democracy that seems to represent the interests of Wall Street and the transnational capitalist class rather than the basic needs and rights of citizens.

On September 17, 2011, in response to an appeal by Adbusters, a Canadian-based free-information group, several hundred people gathered in New York's Zuccotti Park located in the Wall Street financial district. In the days that followed, the demonstrators quickly grew in number as their message about social inequality, corporate greed, and corporate power in government and their slogan, "We are the 99%," resonated with a wider population. An initial media blackout was followed by news accounts that dismissed OWS as comprising hippies and naïfs, but as the movement grew and its main tactic, encampment, spread across the country, the media began to take the movement more seriously. By October 2011, OWS encampments were seen in over one hundred major cities and six hundred communities across the United States, and on October 15 a global day of solidarity with OWS took the form of demonstrations in hundreds of cities across more than forty-five countries. The Occupy protests spread across the world because the problems they rail against are global in scope.[43]

From its inception, and in light of the media blackout and negative media criticism, OWS has relied heavily on cyberactivism and alternative media—Facebook, Twitter, Flickr, Buzz, MySpace, YouTube, and its own website—to mobilize supporters and disseminate information. OWS placed a high premium on democratic practices and deliberation, as was evident in both the way that decisions were made at the encampments (by consensus) and the features of their website. An examination of the OWS website in early 2012 found daily updates, meeting agendas, and video clips and media coverage. For example, the OWS website's "Forum" link took users to a blog-style page where they could log in to post material for discussion or to comment on others' posts. However, access required that visitors register with the site and read the rules for posting. Spamming, advertising, and posting of other people's personal information, election material, threats, or conspiracy theories were not allowed. There was a place to report any of these activities; when reported, such posts would be removed and the author barred from participating in the public online forum. At the same time, users were encouraged to comment on the rules. The "Chat" tab took users to a site where they could register to post comments and take part in a live chat on the "LiveStream" page. Emphasis on democratic deficits in the United States and the need to deepen democracy was evident across the OWS website and in its framing devices.

Such OWS frames as "We are the 99%," "Democracy not corporatocracy," and "This is what democracy looks like" are simple but effective. They draw attention to the concentration of wealth and the gaping income gap in the United States, the inordinate power of banks and corporations and their close ties to government, and the need for genuine democracy. The following is a representative expression of the movement's grievances and values:

> The participation of every person, and every organization, that has an interest in returning the U.S. back into the hands of its individual citizens is required. Our nation, our species and our world are in crisis. The U.S. has an important role to play in the solution, but we can no longer afford to let corporate greed and corrupt politics set the policies of our nation. We, the people of the United States of America, considering the crisis at hand, now reassert our sovereign control of our land. Solidarity Forever![44]

The above passage is interesting for the way it bridges two American master frames—democracy and patriotism—in an enactment of frame alignment and frame resonance. But OWS is clear about its goals, aspirations, and sources of inspiration:

> #ows is fighting back against the corrosive power of major banks and multinational corporations over the democratic process, and the role

of Wall Street in creating an economic collapse that has caused the greatest recession in generations. The movement is inspired by popular uprisings in Egypt and Tunisia, and aims to fight back against the richest 1% of people that are writing the rules of an unfair global economy that is foreclosing on our future.[45]

OWS's emergence in 2011 and spread across the globe were significant in at least two ways: the Occupy movement has reinvigorated the global justice movement and reinforced the transnational movement for global democracy. In her 2008 book *Social Movements for Global Democracy*, Jackie Smith identifies two contending global networks. The neoliberal globalization network includes agents and institutions such as the World Bank, the IMF, the WTO, transnational corporations and banks, and the transnational capitalist class (see also table 2.2 in this book). The pro-democracy or democratic globalization network includes the World Social Forum, nonhegemonic international organizations, and various civil society and social movement organizations. To this we would add Occupy Wall Street. The pro-democracy network has real and potential allies in the world of multilateral organizations. Drawing on Robert O'Brien and colleagues, Smith identifies complex multilateralism as constituting possibilities for different actors to articulate and advance their interests, build transnational alliances, and so on. Along with the ILO, one might point to such UN agencies as UNICEF, the United Nations Population Fund (UNFPA), and UN Women. Smith identifies the United Nations as providing "ideals and principles for organizing a transnational state that can challenge the neoliberal globalization project."[46] She contrasts the UN Charter—with its references to peace and human rights—with the financial and interstate system, which breeds war and violations of civil, political, and social/economic rights. Neoliberal globalizers, she writes, have used four major strategies to influence the world's political and economic life and to counteract the prodemocracy network: (1) redefining the functions of national governments and transforming the welfare state into a garrison state; (2) marginalizing international organizations oriented toward social welfare, such as the United Nations and specific agencies within it; (3) advancing international organizations that support neoliberal economic policies; and (4) promoting a culture/ideology that advances consumerist practices worldwide, justifies the activities of business, and delegitimizes opponents of neoliberalism. Indeed, during Kofi Annan's tenure, the United Nations was captured by neoliberal interests and became more corporate friendly.

In this connection, it is worth noting that the United Nations has been the subject of reform by both neoliberal and pro-democracy networks, though in different ways and for divergent ends. Whereas the neoliberal network has sought financial reform, management changes, and streamlining, the pro-democracy network has focused on democratizing decision making, updating the Security Council from its post–World War II configuration to make it more reflective of contemporary international politics, increasing financing for rights-based development, and shifting power from the Bretton Woods institutions to something like an Economic and Social Council.

Social movements' engagement with—and democratization of—multilateral institutions is essential in terms of both the efficacy of "elite allies" and the democratic potential of multilateral organizations. "Democratic globalizers" have advanced the cause of global democracy, Smith writes, "by expanding global agendas, promoting multilateral initiatives, encouraging national implementation of international law, reconciling competing visions of globalization, and generating alternatives to the programs of governments and corporations." The challenge is to "reclaim the UN and other global institutions for all the world's people." But such engagement comes with risks, which Smith identifies as co-option, fragmentation, disempowerment, and high opportunity costs for movements or civil society organizations with limited time and resources. Still, "social movement actors should be more self-conscious of their historic role as forces for democratizing both national and international political institutions, and they should be more purposeful in their efforts to come together around the cause of global democracy."[47]

Smith's democratic globalizers are located in civil society, social movements, and alternative media; they operate through dense horizontal webs, linked by shared values even though they represent a "diversity of identities, structures, and organizational logics." The shared values are an anticapitalist orientation and concern about the social and economic destruction of market processes. An example is the World Social Forum, a gathering of activists and progressive intellectuals, which, despite its diversity, enables participants to develop a common, global identity. The WSF, Smith writes, is a key site for amplifying the values of democracy, cooperation, and community over the neoliberal values of profit, competition, and individualism. She calls the WSF an "incubator" or "laboratory" for global democracy, comparing it favorably with the Latin American feminist *encuentros*. Similarly, Donatella della Porta asserts that democracy functions as a unifying theme and shared value for many in the global justice movement.[48]

One might add that another site for democratic practices, as well as economic citizenship, is the burgeoning solidarity economy, constituted by forms of cooperative and nonprofit economic relations and enterprises that may be found in Spain, Brazil, Quebec, Bolivia, and some parts of the United States. Walden Bello, a key figure in the World Social Forum who advocates for deglobalization, emphasizes "democratic forms of economic decision-making" in place of market governance (or what some have called free market fundamentalism and economic totalitarianism). Philosopher William McBride has written of the workers' self-management model in the former Yugoslavia as an appropriate alternative to neoliberal capitalist control. A similar model was found in Porto Alegre, Brazil, where participatory and gender-responsive budgeting was predicated on citizen participation in preparing municipal budgets; this helped reallocate spending toward human-development priorities. During the first seven years of the experiment, the share of households with access to water services increased, moving from 80 to 98 percent, and the percentage of the population with access to sanitation almost doubled, moving from 46 to 85 percent.[49]

What would economic democracy look like at a transnational or global level? Apart from the restructuring of the United Nations and redistribution of power and budgets across multilateral organizations, economies would be realigned to favor local producers. The global economy would see the reining in, and regulation of, transnational corporations and banks, with a cap on CEO earnings; implementation of the Tobin tax; a global social policy predicated on full employment, decent wages, decent work, and social provisioning; and a culture of human rights and international solidarity.[50] This form of "global Keynesianism" would best begin at national and regional levels, with full citizen participation in the making of a more expansive and robust democracy.

CONCLUSION: THIS IS WHAT
DEMOCRACY LOOKS LIKE

Liberal democracy refers to a system of government in which those who hold public political office are chosen through regularly held competitive elections in which all adult citizens possessing legal capacity may freely participate by casting equally weighted votes. The strength of this model of democracy is that citizens are constitutionally guaranteed their rights to acquire and disseminate information, organize for lawful purposes, express their views, receive due process of law, and participate in the political process. But this form of democracy does not require that the state be proactive in ensuring the participation and rights of citizens, providing economic rights, or guaranteeing social equality. The entrenchment of this model has allowed neoliberal globalization to shift the balance of power and oversight from citizens to financiers, corporate heads, and lobbyists—to whom elected representatives have become increasingly beholden. Moreover, "faceless bureaucrats" in institutions of global governance make many decisions with significant implications for the living standards and welfare of citizens.

In the perspective of this chapter, real democracy should be seen as a multifaceted and ongoing process at different levels of social existence: in the family, community, workplace, economy, civil society, and polity. In turn, global democracy reinforces national and local democracy through the efficacy of multilateralism, democratic decision making at the global level, and redistribution. Certainly an infrastructure exists for a global democracy in the form of international NGOs, transnational advocacy networks, transnational feminist networks, global civil society, transnational social movements, and the World Social Forum, all of which are carriers of a deliberative, participatory democracy. Social movement organizations in particular have a historic role to play in changing the status quo and deepening democracy at both national and global levels. In Egypt, Morocco, and Tunisia, civil society and social movements should press, at a minimum, for a social democracy that provides for the health, education, and welfare of citizens; guarantees the equality of women and men in the family and society; encourages workplace democracy through worker participation in decision making; protects small business owners; and promotes regional and global cooperation for peace and rights-based development. As Markoff has aptly stated, democracy has never been a finished thing but has been continually renewed, redefined, and reinvented. It remains to be seen if the Arab Spring and Occupy Wall Street will be able to contribute to the renewal and redefinition of democracy and to help consolidate a fourth wave of global democratization.

CHAPTER 4

ISLAMIST MOVEMENTS

The crisis exists precisely in the fact that the old is dying and the new is not yet born; in the interregnum a great variety of morbid symptoms appear.

—Antonio Gramsci, *Prison Notebooks*

Like the women's movement and the global justice movement (see chapters 5 and 6), Islamism may be seen as a "movement of movements." Its overarching common goal is the establishment or reinforcement of Islamic laws and norms as the solution to economic, political, and cultural crises. And yet Islamist movements are heterogeneous and diverse, evincing different tactics and strategies in achieving their goals. This structural feature is in keeping with the segmentary, polycentric, and reticulate character of social movements, as discussed in chapters 1 and 2. Distinctions have been made between "moderate" and "extremist" Islamists, and as we saw in chapter 3, Islamists can be involved in pro-democracy movements. Generally, moderates engage in nonviolent organizing and advocacy in civil society. They form or join political parties and field candidates in parliamentary elections, even though they may be critical of existing political arrangements. Such groups include the Muslim Brotherhood of Egypt and Jordan, Islah of Yemen, the Justice and Development Party (AKP) of Turkey, and the Parti de la Justice et du Développement (PJD) of Morocco. To this grouping I would add Tunisia's an-Nahda (Ennahda in the Tunisian spelling), which in October 2011 took part in the country's first democratic elections for a constituent assembly.

Extremists, on the other hand, call for the violent overthrow of political systems they regard as anti-Islamic, westernized, and dictatorial. They operate clandestinely, form networks and cells across countries, and may engage in spectacular forms of violence. They brand as un-Islamic any participation in electoral politics. Also known as jihadists (or Salafi jihadists), they may or may not have links to the transnational network of al-Qaeda, with its satellites in South Asia, North Africa, and Iraq. Salafists argue that Islam is at once political, economic, cultural, social, and religious. This view is shared by other Islamists, such as radical Islamists, who call for Islamization of their societies and often engage in fiery rhetoric (for example, calling for executions of apostates or infidels, jihad against oppressors, and so on), though they may not themselves engage in violent acts. These groups include Wahhabists influenced by Saudi Arabia, such as the United Kingdom–based Islamist groups Tablighi Jamaat and Hizb ul-Tahrir. Yet others, such as Palestine's Hamas, Lebanon's Hezbollah, and Iraq's Mahdi Army, have large social bases of support and are widely seen as patriots and national heroes engaged in legitimate resistance against foreign intervention.

This chapter examines the origins, activities, and discourses of Islamist movements, drawing attention to differentiation within the transnational Islamist movement, highlighting their relationship to globalization processes, and elucidating similarities and differences with other transnational social movements.

STUDYING ISLAMIST MOVEMENTS

Islamist groups have been studied by social scientists including Saad Eddin Ibrahim, Olivier Roy, Gilles Kepel, Fawaz Gerges, Mohammed Hafez, Jillian Schwedler, and Quintan Wiktorowicz, often through rigorous field research but also through the examination of Islamist websites. Their studies elucidate the common discourses but also the divergent strategies deployed by Islamists, as well as the factors that drive Islamist action. Jillian Schwedler examined the activities and goals of Islamist parties in Jordan and Yemen and their role in the political process, while Jenny B. White, Carrie Rosefsky Wickham, and Malika Zeghal studied Islamists in Turkey, Egypt, and Morocco, respectively. All four social scientists utilized ethnographic methods of research. Political scientist Fawaz Gerges conducted interviews with scores of jihadists during 1999 and 2000, stressing the importance of distinguishing between national jihad and transnational jihad and arguing that the latter arose from the failure of the former. Some national jihadists and other Islamists, he found, condemned the indiscriminate violence of global jihadists such as al-Qaeda. Sociologist Quintan Wiktorowicz's study of reformist and militant Salafi Islam showed how Salafi networks and organizations developed, changed, and helped drive political crises from Algeria to Afghanistan over the past three decades. Jordan's Salafists, he argued, now focused on spreading their ideas through study circles and publishing, and he concluded that "radicals respond rationally and strategically to structures of opportunity." Like Wiktorowicz, Mohammed Hafez has argued that Islamic radicals turn to violence when the state forecloses opportunities for participation and inclusion in the public sphere and resorts to repression.[1]

The Islamist groups mentioned above are quite conservative in their cultural and social worldviews, though in this respect they might not be so different from the general population. As such, they should be distinguished from a tendency that some scholars call liberal or democratic Islam, a tendency that has been associated with both individual scholars and collective groups. The late Pakistani scholar Fazlur Rahman was one such scholar and proponent of liberal Islam. Others have included Iranian scholars Seyyid Hossein Nasr and Abdolkarim

Soroush and Egyptians Hassan Hanafi and Nasr Hamed Abou Zeyd.[2] In the Islamic Republic of Iran, a generation of lay advocates and dissident clerics known as the "new religious intellectuals" emerged in the 1990s, calling for human rights and civil liberties informed by an emancipatory interpretation of Islam, along with the separation of the clerical establishment and religious law from the state apparatus.[3] The Turkey-originated Gulen movement promotes peaceful spirituality and does not challenge state systems.

Another version of liberal and democratic Islam is found in the global network of Islamic feminists who have taken issue with patriarchal and violent interpretations of Islam, seek legal reforms, and call for women's rights through their own rereadings of the Quran and early Islamic history. Among the most organized, vocal, and visible are Malaysia's Sisters in Islam (SIS), who work with feminist groups across the globe and are associated with the transnational feminist network Women Living under Muslim Laws. In the United States, a number of liberal Muslim groups and institutions exist, including Muslim Wake-Up; the Free Muslims; the Center for the Study of Islam and Democracy, based in Washington, DC; the Ahmadiyya Muslim Community, USA, which offers a strong message of peace and nonviolence; and the American Society for Muslim Advancement (ASMA), led by Imam Feisal Abdul Rauf and his wife, Daisy Khan, a Muslim feminist. Internationally, the Swiss-born intellectual Tariq Ramadan is known as a proponent of nonviolent and liberal Islam, although some feminist groups continue to view him with suspicion.[4] Many of the Muslim groups or scholars with liberal views on cultural and social issues should not be deemed "Islamist," but they also may not be highly representative of populations in the Muslim world, especially on such issues as homosexuality, gender equality in religious and family matters, and the equal legal status of all citizens (see table 4.1).

How might we define Islamism? Let us begin first with "Islamic fundamentalism," which motivated a great deal of research in the 1980s and 1990s, including the grand Fundamentalism Project. Syrian Marxist political philosopher Sadik al-Azm identified fundamentalism, whether Christian or Islamic, as the notion of inerrancy or infallibility of holy texts. Thus, "the Koran is absolutely infallible, without error in all matters pertaining to faith and practice, as well as in areas such as geography, science, history, etc." As such, fundamentalism may be

Table 4.1. Types of Islamist or Muslim Movements and Organizations, 1980s–Present

	Parliamentary	Liberal/Democratic	Radical	Jihadist
Afghanistan				Mujahideen; Taliban; Haqqani network
Algeria			Front Islamique du Salut	Armed Islamic Group
Egypt	Muslim Brotherhood		Nour Party	Islamic Jihad; Gama'a Islamiyya
Indonesia				Jemaah Islamiah[a]
Iraq			Mahdi Army	
Islamic Republic of Iran		New religious intellectuals		
Jordan	Muslim Brotherhood/Islamic Action Front			Salifiyya movement; Jaish Muhammad
Lebanon	Hezbollah		Hezbollah	Fatah al-Islam[b]
Morocco	Justice and Development Party (PJD)	PJD		
Malaysia	Islamic Party of Malaysia (PAS)	Sisters in Islam	PAS	
Nigeria				Boko Haram
Pakistan	Jamaat-i Islam		Jamaat-i Islam	Tahrik-i Taliban; Lashkar-i Taiba
Palestine	Hamas		Hamas	Islamic Jihad; Fatah al-Islam
Somalia				al-Shabab
Tunisia	an-Nahda	an-Nahda		
Turkey	Justice and Development Party (AKP)	AKP; Gulen movement		
United Kingdom			Tablighi Jamaat; Hizb ut-Tahrir	al-Muhajiroun
United States		American Society for Muslim Advancement/Cordoba Initiative (Feisal Abdul Rauf) Women's Islamic Initiative in Spirituality and Equity (Daisy Khan)		
Yemen	Islah Party			
Global				al-Qaeda

[a]Responsible for 2002 bombings in Bali and Jakarta.
[b]Responsible for summer 2007 uprising in Palestinian camps.

found in Christianity as well as Islam. Political Islam, however, refers to movements and ideas predicated on the spread of Islamic laws and norms, whether through parliamentary or violent means. Wiktorowicz prefers the term "Islamic activism," which he defines as "the mobilization of contention to support Muslim causes." His definition would include both moderate and radical tendencies of political Islam. Wiktorowicz maintains that "Islamists are Muslims who feel compelled to act on the belief that Islam demands social and political activism, either to establish an Islamic state, to proselytize to reinvigorate the faithful, or to create a separate union for Muslim communities." He argues, as does Mohammed Hafez, that Islamist rebellions arise from state repression.[5]

Sadik al-Azm provides a rather less sympathetic definition of Islamism:

> Islamism is a highly militant mobilizing ideology selectively developed out of Islam's scriptures, texts, legends, historical precedents, organizations, and present-day grievances, all as a defensive reaction against the long-term erosion of Islam's primacy over the public, institutional, economic, social, and cultural life of Muslim societies in the twentieth century. The ideology is put in practice by resurrecting the early concept of Islamic jihad in its most violent and aggressive forms against an environing world of paganism, polytheism, idolatry, godlessness, infidelity, atheism, apostasy, and unbelief known to that ideology as the Jahiliyya of the twentieth century.[6]

Similarly, Egyptian political economist Samir Amin, a key figure in the global justice movement and a longtime activist in Third World, anti-imperialist, and socialist movements, has penned harsh criticisms of Islamism, including a recent essay titled "Political Islam in the Service of Imperialism." He maintains that Islamist movements should be understood as politically and culturally right-wing, pointing out that the Muslim Brotherhood members of the Egyptian parliament "reinforce[d] the rights of property owners to the detriment of the rights of tenant farmers (the majority of the small peasantry)."[7]

As will become evident in this chapter, my understanding of Islamism combines elements of the perspectives mentioned above but moves beyond them. Like Wiktorowicz and Hafez, I believe that the concepts and categories of social movement theory can be applied to elucidate the dynamics of Islamist activism. However, I do not believe that Islamists are motivated exclusively by state repression; as discussed in chapters 1 and 2, sociopsychological and gendered explanations, including the role of masculine identities and religiously informed heroic masculinities, are pertinent. The violence perpetrated over Salman Rushdie's *The Satanic Verses* in 1989 and over the Danish cartoons caricaturing the Prophet Muhammad in 2006 was not related to state repression. Here my approach to Islamist politics is similar to that of Amin, and my definition of Islamism is more consistent with that of al-Azm: I see it as a politicized movement, network, or ideology selectively based on Islamic theology and history but motivated by contemporary developments. My analysis situates the rise and expansion of contemporary Islamism in world-systemic and globalization processes while also recognizing the gendered nature of Islamist politics and practices. In this book, the juxtaposition of Islamism with transnational feminism and the global justice movement reveals stark differences in their frames and strategies.

ORIGINS OF ISLAMIST MOVEMENTS

Contemporary Islamist movements have their origins in the history and theology of Islam, which are also inscribed in their cultural frames. Salafists and jihadists in particular emphasize the doctrinal obligation of Muslims to defend the faith when Islam is deemed to be under threat. They point out that the Prophet Muhammad and his companions engaged in battle to defend themselves and spread the faith, and they interpret Quranic verses in particular ways to justify attacks on "apostates" and "infidels."[8] In contrast, moderate and liberal Muslims emphasize the "inner struggle" that Muslims are called on to perform in order to strengthen their faith. Applying a historical perspective, they note that in early Islam, apostasy was equivalent to the modern concept of treason; hence, in an era of modern nation-states, changing one's religion cannot be considered a treasonous, capital offense.

As discussed in chapter 1, contemporary Islamists have been inspired by the writings of Islamic intellectuals such as Egypt's Rashid Rida, Hassan al-Banna, and Sayyid Qutb and Iran's Ayatollah Khomeini. Certainly these texts provide a theological and intellectual context for Islamism. And yet, national and global political factors constitute critical determinants of political Islam. The Cold War and the fervent anticommunism of the United States led to sustained efforts to eliminate left-wing movements and governments, as well as nationalist governments perceived to be soft on communism. Seminal events would include the 1953 coup d'état against Iranian prime minister Mohammad Mossadegh; the 1965 coup in Indonesia that eliminated the Communist Party and brought the military dictator Suharto to power; the support for military dictatorships in Pakistan and Bangladesh in the 1980s; and the support for Islamist rebels fighting a left-wing government in Afghanistan in the 1980s.

Many Muslim intellectuals and clerical leaders had long been opposed to the secularism and perceived atheism of communist movements. In this they converged with repressive regimes as well as with various U.S. governments. The growth of left-wing movements in the 1960s and 1970s led many regimes to encourage the Islamic tide in hopes of neutralizing the Left. This was the basic strategy of President Anwar Sadat, who released the members of the Muslim Brotherhood from prison in an attempt to counter the Egyptian Left in his campaign of de-Nasserization. Iran's Shah Mohammad Reza Pahlavi followed the same strategy in the early 1970s, as did the Turkish authorities after the 1980 military coup. Indeed, in the latter case, as the generals' overriding objective was to rid Turkish society of Marxist ideology and parties, they encouraged Islamic ideas and education as an antidote. Thus, in 1982 the military regime made the teaching of Islam compulsory in schools; since 1967 it had been optional. When Islamists in Iran were able to seize control of what had been a largely populist revolution against the shah in 1978–1979, the victory of the "Islamic revolution" inspired and encouraged Muslims and Islamists throughout the world. In 1981 Egyptian Islamists assassinated President Anwar Sadat.[9]

In Indonesia, Muslim militants had helped to track down and kill communists during the mass murders that accompanied the 1965 coup d'état, and in the 1980s elements of the state and military covertly funded and promoted Muslim groups, a policy that facilitated the growth of more extremist Islamist networks. Moreover, the state ignored the financial assistance that some of these organizations received from Saudi Arabia and other foreign sources. Throughout this period, the United States was in close alliance with Saudi Arabia, an oil-rich country that guaranteed the flow of oil to the West, used its wealth to help build Islamic institutions and networks across the globe, and participated in the fight against communism. Thomas Hegghammer has described how the Saudi state and its many religious institutions not only funded jihadist activities but were instrumental in igniting the jihadist movement—at least until al-Qaeda formed in the Arabian Peninsula and began to attack Saudi targets. Afghan specialist Barnett Rubin refers to the "arms pipeline" to the Afghan mujahideen and other militant Islamist groups, made possible by Saudi and Kuwaiti money. In 1992, the U.S.-supported Afghan mujahideen toppled the modernizing government of President Mohammad Najibullah. In Yemen, when the northern regime fought the southern socialists in a short civil war in 1994, the Islamists fought alongside them to defeat the socialists. By this time, Islamist networks existed across the globe, and they proliferated steadily.

The collapse of the Soviet Union may have been celebrated by some, notably conservative political theorist Francis Fukuyama, as the harbinger of the worldwide expansion of liberal democracy. But in the Muslim world, it meant the end of the reigning alternative ideology of socialism/communism. In his study of the "unholy wars," John Cooley refers to the "strange love affair which went disastrously wrong: the alliance, during the second half of the twentieth century, between the United States of America and some of the most conservative and fanatical followers of Islam." Mark Curtis has written of "Britain's collusion with radical Islam," tracking that country's role in the overthrow of Iranian premier Mohammad Mossadegh in 1953; its alliance with Saudi Arabia as a hedge against Egyptian president Gamal Abdel Nasser's secular pan-Arab vision; Margaret Thatcher's support for the anticommunist mujahideen of Afghanistan and her stated hope that Muslims would not "succumb to the fraudulent appeal of imported Marxism"; the creation of "Londonistan," where Islamist groups from Algeria, Libya, Egypt, and elsewhere were based; and the fallout from the British roles in Iraq and Afghanistan.[10]

Meanwhile, the global and epochal shift from Keynesianism to neoliberalism—along with the end of the Third World, the nonaligned movement, and emergent discussion of a new international economic order—created economic conditions that would generate grievances as well as opportunities for protest, recruitment, and mobilization, finally culminating in the Arab Spring of 2011 as well as rebellions in Libya, Yemen, and Syria. The shift in political economy from state-directed

development to privatization was accompanied by political liberalization, which occurred in some measure in Algeria, Egypt, Jordan, Morocco, and Turkey. This broad world-systemic perspective is critical
to an understanding of Islamist movements, because it contextualizes
the periodic protests that had arisen over structural adjustments and
unemployment since the 1980s; the spread of Islamic NGOs and their
social welfare activities; the political openings that allowed the "Islamic
alternative" to present itself, in some cases as moderate and parliamentarian and in others as radical and jihadist; and the successful electoral
outcomes of Tunisia's an-Nahda and Egypt's Muslim Brotherhood in
the two countries' first elections, in October and November 2011, respectively, following the collapse of their regimes.

Our analysis is not complete, however, without reference to sociode-
mographics and social psychology, including issues of urbanization,
anomie, class background, and education. As early research by Saad Eddin Ibrahim and John Entelis revealed, recruits to Islamist movements
were often first-generation educated urbanites from the lower middle
classes and conservative family backgrounds. Such sociodemographic
and class features have been widely theorized to evince status anxiety
and cultural discomfort, in a pattern that suggests parallels with recruits to right-wing or fascistic movements. At the same time, feminist
research has shown that women's growing social visibility and participation challenged men's dominance in public spaces, rendering recent
migrants and men of the lower middle classes and conservative backgrounds alienated and angry. As Moroccan feminist sociologist Fatima
Mernissi wrote, "If men are calling for the return of the veil, it must
be because women have been taking off the veil." These conditions
made such men highly vulnerable to an ideology whose grievances
and solutions resonated because it was anchored in religion. In the
case of Islamic fundamentalism and political Islam, therefore, a linkage
between structural strain and movement contention at a national level
could plausibly be made. In turn, global processes of which Muslim
societies were a part exacerbated structural strain. Whether in Europe
or in Muslim-majority countries, the Islamist message came to resonate
largely with young men confronting socioeconomic difficulties and cultural changes that provoked feelings of anxiety, alienation, and anger.
Islam became the source of a mobilizing ideology and organizational

resources used to combat domestic injustices, cultural imperialism, and changes to traditional notions of the family.[11]

To summarize the argument, I present a set of propositions regarding the causes and characteristics of Islamist movements.[12]

- Islamist movements emerged in the context of the worldwide shift from Keynesianism to neoliberalism. Rising indebtedness, unemployment, and problems stemming from austerity measures and economic restructuring in the 1980s added to tensions everywhere. These were linked to global restructuring and recession, or what world-system theorists refer to as the B-phase downturn of the Kondratieff wave; the falling price of oil on the world market had an adverse effect on development and on living standards.

- Politically, many Muslim-majority countries were characterized by authoritarian and neopatriarchal state systems that silenced left-wing and liberal forces while fostering religious institutions in their search for legitimacy. This created an ideological and political gap that could be filled by Islamist groups with substantial resources and a culturally resonant frame.

- Islamist movements also arose in the context of the demographic transition, the result of which was accelerated population growth and a social burden of a larger, more youthful, and more dependent population in Muslim-majority countries. Many young men found themselves without secure prospects and became willing recruits to Islamism. In turn, Islamist groups, whether moderate or extremist, mobilized among the growing population of university-educated youth who found themselves either unemployed or stuck in low-income jobs.

- In many parts of the Muslim world, capitalist and precapitalist modes of production coexisted, with corresponding social and ideological forms as well as types of consciousness. There was an uneasy coexistence of modern and traditional social classes, such as the westernized upper middle class on the one hand and the traditional petite bourgeoisie organized around the bazaar and the mosque on the other. The urban centers all had large numbers of people outside the formal wage market and among the ranks of the urban poor and uneducated. In poorer Muslim countries such as Afghanistan, Pakistan, and Yemen, recruits to Islamist extremism could be found within these populations as well as among the rural poor.[13]

- Female education and employment, while still limited, had been increasing, thanks to economic development and the expanding state apparatus. This trend challenged and slowly weakened the system of patriarchal gender relations, creating status inconsistency and anxiety on the part of the men of the petite bourgeoisie. Changes in gender relations, the structure of the family, and the position of women resulted in contestation between modern and traditional social groups over the nature and direction of cultural institutions and legal frameworks. A kind of gender conflict emerged, although this conflict had class dimensions as well.

- The nonresolution of the Israeli-Palestinian problem and a pervasive sense of injustice caused by Israeli and American actions helped to engender Islamist movements. The failure of the secular-democratic project of the Palestine Liberation Organization encouraged the Islamist alternative among Palestinians and throughout the region. The invasion and occupation of Iraq in 2003 fomented more Islamism, in Iraq and elsewhere.

- In the absence of fully developed and articulated movements, institutions, and discourses of liberalism or socialism, Islam became the discursive universe, and Islamist movements spread the message that "Islam is the solution." For some Muslims, the new Islamic ideology reduced anxiety because it was able to offer a new form of assurance, and the movement provided new forms of collective solidarity and support.

- In the context of economic, political, and ideological crisis—including unpopular state regimes and marginalized leftist movements—the vacuum came to be filled by Islamist leaders and discourses, whether fundamentalist, pietistic, or extremist.

- In the new ideological formation, tradition was both exalted and frequently invented. Despite traditional forms of modest dress throughout the Muslim world, often reflecting local cultures and histories, Islamists in the 1980s began to promote a uniform kind of veiling, consisting largely of all-encompassing dark clothing. A recurrent theme was that Islamic identity was in danger; Muslims had to return to a fixed tradition; identity was incumbent upon women's behavior, dress, and appearance; and Muslim personal laws were necessary at the level of the state (in the case of majority-Muslim societies) or in the community (in the case of minority-Muslim groups).

- Islamist movements were a product of the contradictions of transition and modernization; they also resulted from the North-South contention and hegemonic intrusions into the Muslim world and constituted political projects concerned with power in what they viewed as a repressive, unjust, and un-Islamic order. Culture, religion, and identity served as defense mechanisms and as means by which a new order was to be shaped.

GLOBALIZING ISLAMISM

We may refer to a global Islamist movement even though many movements and networks within it are locally or nationally based. The term "global" describes the scale, scope, and reach of Islamism and acknowledges that many Islamists engage in cross-border communication, coordination, solidarity, and direct action. Some scholars distinguish between local and transnational Islamism, demarcating al-Qaeda from, for example, Hamas or Hezbollah. Both forms, however, have roots in theology, history, and contemporary events.

The rise of transnational Islamism has been documented by Fawaz Gerges, among others, who writes that Islamists—steeped in Sayyid Qutb's revisions of the classical doctrine of jihad—aimed to target "apostate" Muslim rulers who were not enforcing sharia; these were the "near enemy." In the 1980s and early 1990s, the national jihad in Afghanistan took a global turn when thousands of young Muslims poured into Afghanistan to join it; they were allowed to do so by governments that either wished to rid themselves of unruly young men or genuinely desired the downfall of a left-wing state in a Muslim-majority country. When the "Afghan Arabs" returned home—for example, to Algeria, Egypt, and Jordan—they triggered bloody confrontations with the state. Al-Qaeda was formed in the years following Iraqi ruler Saddam Hussein's invasion of Kuwait in 1990 and the subsequent events. Osama bin Laden, a Saudi citizen from a rich family, was angry that the Saudi government had selected the U.S. Army rather than his own militia to rout Saddam Hussein in Kuwait, and he was especially provoked by the presence of U.S. troops on Saudi soil. Expelled in 1991, he went to Sudan until 1996, then to Afghanistan to be harbored by the Taliban, which by that time had replaced the U.S.-supported mujahideen. In Afghanistan, bin Laden and Ayman al-Zawahiri, his Egyptian-born deputy, shifted attention to the "far enemy": the United States. In 1998 they publicly declared the creation of a transnational network called the International Front for Jihad against Jews and Crusaders. The September 11, 2001, attacks on the United States were carried out by nineteen young men, fifteen of them Saudis. The repercussions for the United States of its support for the Afghan jihad in the 1980s have been termed "blowback."[14]

In distinguishing between transnational and local Islamists, Gerges points out that many national Islamists were angered by 9/11 because it compromised their position in Europe, where they had sought refuge from government repression in the 1990s. Gerges surveys a wide range of literature published by Islamists and national jihadists that is bitterly critical of the transnational jihad. Nonetheless, local and transnational Islamists have tended to articulate similar grievances.

Most Islamists have been inspired by Sayyid Qutb's writings, but transnational jihadists take special inspiration from his book *Jahiliyyat al-Qarn al-Ishrin* (the *jahiliyya* of the twentieth century), which implies that now that Western modernity has come full circle to the *jahili* condition, Arabs and the Muslims should lead humanity once more out of the *jahiliyya* created by Europe and defended by the West in general. Many Islamists blame the spread of Western values and practices for a wide variety of social and economic ills, including rising unemployment, stagnant economic development, soaring debt, housing shortages, and dwindling public social and welfare expenditures. Western values are also blamed for what Islamists see as the breakdown of the traditional Muslim family. Blaming Western influence for such developments is, as Wiktorowicz notes, "an important component of most Islamic movement diagnostic frames."[15] It follows that the solution is the return to or strengthening of Islamic values, norms, and laws.

For the moderate Islamist, the answer is peaceful "regime change" within the Muslim world through parliamentary means and the gradual Islamization of key social institutions. This includes a call for adherence to Muslim family laws and the sharia as the guide to personal and public behavior. This was the strategy of the Muslim Brotherhood in

Egypt during the 1990s. For the radical Islamist, it is a short step from viewing Islam as endangered by the West to taking up arms against Western targets and their domestic allies. Such is the motivation behind, inter alia, the Islamist revolution against the shah in Iran (and later against the Left in that country), the assassination of Egyptian president Anwar Sadat, the targeting of secular intellectuals in Egypt and Turkey, the violent revolt in Algeria in the 1990s, and the Red Mosque affair in Pakistan in 2007. The view of Islam as under threat also is behind the rise of transnational networks of militant Islamists, including but not limited to al-Qaeda. In these cases, violence becomes the principal form of contention.

Islamism has also been globalized through migration. The migration of large populations of Muslims to the West, largely for economic reasons, has created both an existential burden and an opportunity structure. One aspect of the burden is to try to live a meaningful life in the new countries of residence, which are secularized and evince values and practices deemed inimical to Muslim values. This has led to difficulties in integration and to antipathy on the part of the native population. In Europe, therefore, there has been much discussion of what is often framed as the problem of Muslim integration and sometimes as "Islamophobia." The opportunity structure of Western tolerance and pluralism, as well as explicit policies of multiculturalism in Europe, has meant that Muslim immigrants have been able to practice their faith openly, in highly visible ways, such as by building mosques and faith-based schools, wearing veils, spilling out onto the streets during prayers, establishing halal meat stores, building Islamic charities and other associations, demanding prayer rooms at universities, and proselytizing and seeking converts for the Islamic faith. In some countries, "Islamic courts" have provided informal rulings. Such practices, as noted, have not always been well received by natives or by liberal or secular Muslim immigrants, and this has created or reinforced a collective identity among a certain section of the immigrant population as self-defined "Muslims" or even as "fighters for Islam." (In the United Kingdom, for example, the category "British Muslim" was assumed by many citizens originally from South Asia but eschewed by Iranian-born Britons who left Iran because of Islamism.) The presence of radical youth who have engaged in terrorist actions on European soil eventually led to many debates about multiculturalism, self-segregation, discrimination, and social exclusion. More typically, the spread of veiling, the growth of mosques and other Muslim institutions in Europe, and the ability of radical preachers to recruit young people were blamed on "misguided multicultural policies" in Britain, the Netherlands, Finland, Germany, and elsewhere, countries that now reject those policies and insist on assimilation. Heavy veiling has been banned in France and Belgium, the Swiss voted in 2009 to disallow construction of any more tall minarets alongside mosques, and British prime minister David Cameron ended the local council funding to Islamic groups that he said had bred extremism and "home-grown terror."[16]

How have states or other elements of the opportunity structure contributed to the making of a globalized Islam? And what is the relationship between states and violent contention? Here we underscore the role of elites, state agencies, and state-managed media. To reiterate a point made earlier, Muslim elites in some cases become involved in or encourage Islamist contention to enhance their own credentials, undermine the organized Left, or distract the public from pressing socioeconomic issues. As noted, states and political elites in Muslim-majority Middle Eastern and South Asian countries deployed this strategy in the 1970s and 1980s. The fatwa, or religious edict, issued against Indian-British writer Salman Rushdie in early 1989 by Ayatollah Khomeini, leader of Iran's Islamic revolution, helped to globalize Islam by mobilizing militants across the world to protest what Khomeini claimed to be an affront to the Quran and the Prophet. The Rushdie affair showed how the mass media and elite complicity helped to galvanize violent contention. In his study of the 2006 Danish cartoons conflict, Thomas Olesen argues that elites and the mass media were the prime movers in the transnational escalation of the controversy. Street manifestations such as riots and demonstrations took place first in Palestine and Kuwait, then in Yemen, Indonesia, Turkey, Syria, Lebanon, Afghanistan, Iran, Egypt, and the Philippines. Danish embassies in Damascus and Beirut were set on fire. Egyptian state-owned newspapers called for a boycott of Danish goods, decrying the cartoons as "a crime against the Muslim world." In Pakistan, the emergence of a military dictatorship in the 1980s that also assisted the United States in its battle against the left-wing government in Afghanistan led to the gradual radicalization of Pakistani society and the growing power of Islamists. Thus, by 2011, a leading politician could be assassinated—by an Islamist policeman, no less—because he had defended an impoverished Christian woman falsely accused of insulting Islam. The murder of Salmaan Taseer followed a campaign of vilification by the clergy and sections of the press. What is more, the assassin's cause received support in Pakistan, with lawyers outside the court showering him with rose petals. As one report stated, "The Pakistani state has given succor to violent, extremist organizations."[17]

The literature on social movements suggests that state repression could have a preemptive or dampening effect on collective action. Conversely, state repression could force contenders to turn to violent methods. John Entelis, a scholar of North African politics, views Algeria's Front Islamique du Salut (FIS) as a "quintessential . . . Islamist reformist movement" and sees the Algerian regime as conforming to a widespread practice of confrontation that "unleashed a much more virulent form of Islamic radicalism." In their joint work and separate writings on Islamic activism and Muslim rebellions, Wiktorowicz and Hafez argue that the use of violence by groups as varied as the Armed Islamic Group (GIA) in Algeria, the Gama'a Islamiyya (Islamic Group) in Egypt, the Palestinian Hamas, and Shiites who revolted during the 1990s in Bahrain "was, to a large extent, a tactical response to shifting opportunity structures and emerged under particular conditions and circumstances." Hafez shows how the Algerian GIA moved toward "a growing belief in total war" when the Islamist movement was excluded from institutional politics and suffered indiscriminate state repression. Here he refers to the events of 1992, in which the ruling party, supported by the military, annulled the results of elections that favored the FIS and subsequently banned it. A similar argument has been made regarding Egypt's Gama'a Islamiyya. Hafez and Wiktorowicz maintain that "the cycle of violence in Egypt began largely in response to a broad crackdown on the Islamic movement that targeted moderates, radicals, and a number of tangential bystanders. The crackdown included arrests, hostage taking, torture, executions, and other forms of state violence." There and elsewhere, it is argued, Islamist insurgencies are provoked by state-sponsored exclusion, marginalization, and repression.[18]

But there is more to the cycle of Islamist contentious politics than state repression, and a rather complex and almost symbiotic relationship exists between states and Islamist movements. Efforts by political elites to incorporate or co-opt Islamist institutions between the 1950s and 1980s were only partially or temporarily successful, for radical elements that saw the society or state as insufficiently Islamic would periodically assert themselves. Islamists in Algeria, after all, had been encouraged by their experience in Afghanistan and were allowed to operate openly in the 1980s. Algerian feminists were alarmed when Islamists began to bully unveiled women in the districts where they predominated. Feminists began to mobilize when the new government of Chadli Bendjedid acquiesced to Islamist pressure and pushed through a very conservative family law. Even Hafez admits that the Algerian GIA—whose revolt against the state in the 1990s featured wanton and breathtaking brutality against civilians and foreigners—did not resort to violence due to the cancellation of the election results and the banning of the FIS. "On the contrary, it viewed its 'jihad' as a broader struggle to rid the Muslim world of un-Islamic rulers and establish the 'rule of God.'" In the GIA's own words, expressed in a 1993 communiqué, "Our struggle is with infidelism and its supporters beginning with France and ending with the leader of international terrorism, 'the United States of Terrorism,' its ally Israel, and among them the apostate ruling regime in our land." Four years later, the group expressed the following views in a London-based Islamist paper:

> The infidelism and apostasy of this hypocrite nation that turned away from backing and supporting the mujahideen will not bend our determination and will not hurt us at all, God willing. . . . All the killing and slaughter, the massacres, the displacement [of people], the burnings, the kidnappings . . . are an offering to God.[19]

While Algerian state repression clearly played a role in exacerbating societal strains and political grievances, the GIA's extreme violence, including sexual violence against women, suggests a kind of pathology and misogyny that is rather far removed from rational, cost-benefit calculations, much less a justified defense.

Similarly, Egyptian Islamists not only targeted symbols of the state, such as financial centers and the tourism industry; they also killed tourists, Egyptian Christians (Copts), and secular intellectuals. Sociologist Jeff Goodwin makes an elegant argument that identifies "categorical terrorism," or forms of extreme violence that deliberately target civilians, as a strategy taken up in a context of "indiscriminate state repression" and "civilian complicity." Terrorism thus becomes a way of punishing mass passivity or complicity with the state. Goodwin applies this framework to the actions of militants in French Algeria, the West Bank and Gaza, and Chechnya. Also, to a certain extent, he employs this conceptual lens in looking at al-Qaeda's September 11 attacks. While persuasive on one level, Goodwin's thesis basically posits that extremists—like repressive states or occupying powers—can and do engage in collective punishment to achieve their goals and assert their authority.[20]

It is true that many liberation movements and social revolutions have entailed armed struggle as a key tactic. Research on revolutions shows that the more accessible the state, the less likely it is to unify opposition behind a violent strategy.[21] And yet the hyperaggressive language and actions of the GIA and similar groups help analysts and progressives alike to clarify the distinction between the legitimate actions of a liberation movement and the illegitimate actions of terrorists.

At the same time, the brazen actions and self-confident language of the GIA suggest that the struggle in Algeria should be viewed in the larger context of the growth of transnational Islamism. After all, the 1990s were the decade of transition on a world scale, defined by the end of the Soviet Union and the collapse of communist ideology; the assumption of power in 1992 by the Afghan mujahideen (who had been supported by the United States for over a decade); the attacks on U.S. marines in Lebanon and the withdrawal of American troops; the breakup of formerly socialist Yugoslavia; the Islamist revolt in Chechnya; spectacular terrorist assaults in various parts of the world, including Tanzania and Kenya; and the emergence of the Taliban in Afghanistan following its 1996 overthrow of the mujahideen. The Taliban, it will be recalled, harbored Osama bin Laden following his expulsion from Sudan.

Transnational Islam was made possible by the post–Cold War world order, along with the opportunities afforded by the new information and communication technologies. Geographic reordering and collapsed states allowed for the distribution of arms and militants across porous borders. Meanwhile, Muslim grievances were diffused across the Muslim world via the Internet and Arabic-language media. The grievances included the dire effects of the UN sanctions against Iraq following Saddam Hussein's invasion of Kuwait; the presence of U.S. troops in Muslim lands (Kuwait, Saudi Arabia, Lebanon); the continuing injustices suffered by Palestinians at the hands of Israel; the killing of Chechens,

Bosnians, and Kosovars; and the U.S. bombing of what turned out to be a pharmaceutical factory in Khartoum, conducted during the search for bin Laden. In the new millennium, nineteen young Arab men plotted to attack symbols of American power in the United States. This was GIA on a transnational, global scale.

Mobilizing structures thus developed from nationally based to transnational and often coordinated networks. If the language, goals, and methods of Algeria's GIA have strong parallels with those of al-Qaeda, it is likely that some GIA activists went on to join al-Qaeda's transnational network in the new century. Islamists from Egypt, Jordan, Morocco, Tunisia, Pakistan, and elsewhere also joined the al-Qaeda network, while radicalized youth among second-generation Muslim immigrants in Europe undertook terrorist acts there. Violence became the tactic of choice of transnational jihadist Islamism, as evidenced by the bombings of commuters in London and Madrid and assaults and bombings in Baghdad, Casablanca, and Algiers (the latter by the shadowy al-Qaeda in the Islamic Maghreb). In Indonesia, bombings by extremist Muslim groups affiliated with al-Qaeda struck a Bali nightclub, the Marriott hotel in Jakarta, the Australian embassy, churches, and gatherings of religious minorities such as the Ahmadiyya sect.

MODERATE AND PARLIAMENTARY ISLAMIST MOVEMENTS: WHAT OF THE GRAY ZONES?

The preceding narrative pertains to the emergence, resources, frames, collective action repertoires, and other defining features of militant Islamist networks. What of moderate or parliamentary Islamism? Frame alignment among moderate Islamists is distinctive and diverges from that of militant Islamists as the two groupings address different audiences, whether domestic or international. In general, moderate Islamists eschew violence as a tactic to gain political or state power; they take part in electoral politics and field candidates, sometimes openly and other times through independents; and they take an active part in civil society associations or build new ones. In Turkey, for example, moderate Islamists claim to accept the secular and republican ideals of modern Turkey's founder Kemal Ataturk. In Egypt, the Muslim Brotherhood maintains that it favors democracy and civil rights for all citizens. Rachid Ghannouchi, head of Tunisia's an-Nahda party and its spiritual guide, has said, "We want an-Nahda as an open space: open to religious people, non-religious, male, female, open to all Tunisians."[22] In Europe, moderates draw on human rights and antidiscrimination frames to claim the right to veil and to build mosques. Some scholars have therefore pondered the possibility that moderate, reformist Islam evinces similarities either to Christian liberation theology or to the Christian-democratic (conservative) political parties of Europe.

Does Turkey's ruling Islamist party fall within the radical or the liberal category? And is there any connection between liberal Islamists and the Christian groups that have espoused liberation theology, with its pro-poor activism and anticapitalist critique? Writing about the now defunct Refah (Welfare) Party that made electoral headway in the 1990s before it was banned by the Turkish military, Turkish sociologist Haldun Gulalp points out,

> While liberation theology constitutes a novel interpretation of Christianity from a socialist perspective, Welfare's Islamism focused on the question of cultural superiority or inferiority. . . . Turkey's political Islam . . . was concerned with a cultural project and attempted to mobilize people by addressing their class interests in order to effect that project. . . . Welfare used class-related issues as a vehicle to promote a project of change in lifestyle and to establish its own version of an "Islam" society.[23]

Gulalp goes on to argue that moderate Islamist movements are part of the phenomenon of postmodernist "new social movements" in that they are focused on issues of culture, identity, and lifestyle rather than class and ideology.

In discussing the social bases of Turkey's Islamism, Gulalp links mobilization and recruitment to broad structural changes. He notes, correctly, that the rise of Islamism coincided with the decline of the Keynesian economic project, Fordist industrialization, and the welfare state, with its attendant focus on the working class. Islamism gained prominence concurrently with the economic trends of privatization, subcontracting, and entrepreneurship, which favor property owners and small businesspeople. In Turkey, while political power remained in the hands of bureaucratic, military, and political elites, economic power was shifting to the growing private sector. The Islamist movement claimed to be the voice of the owners of small and medium-sized businesses, who complained of inadequate financial support by the state. Gradually this movement nudged its way from the fringes to the centers of political power. Thus, in contrast to Latin American–style liberation theology, with its focus on the poor and its demand for redistribution, Turkey's Islamists created a new capitalist culture. Their vision esteemed both business and Islamic lifestyle norms such as the wearing of the veil, the prohibition against alcohol, and attention to religious schooling. Gulalp notes that the Islamist party's discourse of "justice" appealed to working-class voters, even though the party was in reality an extension of the neoliberal project. Written from a left-wing perspective, Gulalp's analysis elucidates the compatibility of Islamism with neoliberalism—even if Islamists may oppose other aspects of globalization. Likewise, Cihan Tugal states that Turkey's AKP actually shuns the label "moderate Islamist" and prefers to be known as "conservative democratic." This is partly to emphasize the party's affinity with the Western conservative tradition (rather than the Islamist tradition), to escape possible legal complications in Turkey, and to avoid the implication that it represents just another interpretation of Islam.[24]

With the Arab Spring and the electoral successes of Islamic parties in Tunisia, Egypt, and Morocco, moderate Islamists are gaining more visibility, and in time their political practices and policies will be better defined. Thus far, analysts have drawn attention to ambivalences, ambiguities, or inconsistencies in the discourses and practices of moderate Islamists. Nathan Brown, Amr Hamzawy, and Marina Ottaway refer to these ambiguities as the "gray zones," which they attribute to

> the character of these movements as political and religious organizations, the rise of a new generation of activists, and the contradictions of the broader sociopolitical context of the countries where they operate. As a result, there is no guarantee that time will automatically lead to the elimination of the gray zones and that non-violent Islamic organizations will continue to evolve in a liberal direction. Rather, the outcome is still uncertain, and it will be determined by how the political situation evolves.[25]

They are referring in part to Egypt's Muslim Brotherhood (Ikhwan), considered the world's largest, oldest, and most influential Islamist organization. Founded by Hassan al-Banna, the brotherhood was for decades a radical movement bent on overthrowing the secular Egyptian regime and replacing it with an Islamic state. As noted, an early leading figure, Sayyid Qutb, became even more radicalized after a trip to the United States and, upon his return, wrote fiery pamphlets and books. For his role in fomenting violent resistance, the government of Gamal Abdel Nasser executed him; the brotherhood was banned from 1954 until the political revolution of 2011. Sympathizers have portrayed Egypt's Muslim groups as pressure groups oriented toward specific political interests and operating within and upon a regime whose mix of repression, acculturation, and semi-toleration effectively limited their room for maneuver. Others point out that the brotherhood has maintained its societal and political presence through a sympathetic judiciary, Al-Azhar University and theological seminary, adherents in professional syndicates, and parliamentary candidates running as independents. As well as having influential branches around the world, the brotherhood was Egypt's strongest opposition to President Hosni Mubarak, who had ruled as an autocrat since 1981 and was a key U.S. ally. Estimates of the brotherhood's Egyptian membership range from one hundred thousand to four hundred thousand.[26]

The metamorphosis of the Egyptian Muslim Brotherhood from a religious mass movement into a modern political party has its roots in the changing political economy of the 1980s, with the deterioration of public services, declining real wages, and rising unemployment. Although the brotherhood distanced itself from some of the more rigid doctrines of its founder, it continued to proffer the slogan "Islam is the solution" and to call for adherence to the sharia. Shrewd political maneuvers, including extensive participation in local councils, grassroots associations, and syndicates, assured electoral gains by moderate Islamists associated with the Muslim Brotherhood. The brotherhood shocked the ruling National Democratic Party and Western observers in 2005 by winning one-fifth of seats in the Egyptian parliament through independent proxies. The Muslim Brotherhood's association with Al-Azhar, a site of fundamentalist Islam as well as a university, provided the movement with both legitimacy and an important mobilizing structure.

In the new century the brotherhood began to issue statements in support of democracy and the rights of women and religious minorities. But the gray zones persisted, leading Brown, Hamzawy, and Ottaway to identify ambiguities and inconsistencies in the group's positions on the application of Islamic law, the use of violence, political pluralism, civil and political rights, the equality and rights of women, and the equality and rights of religious minorities. In 2007 the supreme guide of Egypt's Muslim Brotherhood, Mohamed Mahdi Akef, was responsible for the drafting of the brotherhood's first political platform. Among other things, it advocated banning women as well as Coptic Egyptians, who make up one-tenth of Egypt's population, from election to the presidency and raised the specter of an Iran-style religious council. Akef and his associates viewed globalization as naked U.S. ambition and regarded Western democracy as "subservient to whims of the masses, without moral absolutes." Apart from vague references to social justice, the Muslim Brotherhood does not evince interest in economic issues and has not developed a critique of Egypt's neoliberal economic strategy. According to Mona El-Ghobashy, "They still grant culture and identity issues pride of place in their platform." According to Alison Pargeter, the Muslim Brotherhood is in essence a reactionary movement unable to break from its past.[27]

The Egyptian Center for Women's Rights (ECWR) has monitored the social realities of women's lives—most notably, lobbying against the widespread problem of sexual harassment of women—while also integrating itself into the larger movement for clean elections, human rights, and democratization. In August 2010, the ECWR issued a statement criticizing the Muslim Brotherhood's Youth Forum for denying, during its mock presidential elections, a request by the forum's Muslim Sisters' Group to be included as potential nominees. The following November, the ECWR issued another press release protesting the parliament's overwhelming vote against the appointment of women judges. In March 2011, the ECWR decried the absence of women from the committee drafting Egypt's new constitution.[28]

"Gray zones" exist in the Islamic Republic of Iran as well, although there they are codified. The authorities claim that the Islamic republic is a regime of all its citizens, and yet Shia Islam is privileged above any other religious affiliation. Although religious minorities are not persecuted and in fact are entitled to representation in parliament, they cannot assume high political office and are disadvantaged in family law (if they are part of a Muslim family) and the penal code. What is more, women remain second-class citizens in the country's legal frameworks, especially in the family law provisions of its civil code. This is quite apart from the fact that neither independent organizing nor public dissent is tolerated in the Islamic Republic of Iran, and the prisons are filled with opposition figures and dissidents, most of whom simply want more political freedoms and civil rights or the right to form an independent trade union, as mentioned in chapter 3. Others have been charged with "endangering national security" through involvement with international organizations or U.S. foundations. More than thirty years after assuming power, political Islam in Iran has built a large, modern state system that functions impressively but seems incapable of transforming itself into a political system that fosters equality of citizens and welcomes feminists, socialists, democrats, and liberals.

In an early essay, Graham Fuller identifies three obstacles to the liberal evolution of political Islam. The first comes from the local political scene, where Islamists are routinely suppressed, jailed, tortured, and executed. Such circumstances encourage the emergence of secret, conspiratorial, and often armed groups rather than liberal ones. As such, his analysis is similar to that of Wiktorowicz and Hafez. The second obstacle, he writes, comes from international politics, which often pushes Islamist parties and movements, including Muslim national liberation movements, in a militant direction. The third "comes from the Islamists' own long list of grievances against the forces and policies perceived to be holding Muslims back in the contemporary world, many of them associated with liberalism's supposed avatar, the United States."[29] Fuller's second and third points may also pertain to the hardline stance of the Islamic Republic of Iran as it reacts to U.S. and European pressure.

Scholars of Middle Eastern politics continue to debate the prospects of a liberal, reformist, and democratic Islamist movement and its place within the political process. Jillian Schwedler examined shifting discourses and practices of Islamist parties in Jordan and Yemen as evidence of real moderation. Vickie Langohr has pointed out that what is on offer to Islamist movements in most countries is participation in electoral contests for political office in state systems that remain highly authoritarian.[30] Even so, with a collective action repertoire of marches, rallies, banners, and petitions, Islamist parties have made headway in a number of Muslim-majority countries, including Turkey, Morocco, Kuwait, Jordan, Palestine, Yemen, Indonesia, and Malaysia. With the political revolutions in Egypt and Tunisia and the rise of Islamic parties there, will we see a replication of the model of Turkey's AKP? Or will the Islamist parties follow the monopolistic model of the Islamic Republic of Iran?

What of moderate, reformist intellectual voices such as that of Tariq Ramadan? In a penetrating review of Ramadan's 2009 book *Radical Reform, Islamic Ethics and Liberation,* Mona Siddiqui, a professor of Islamic studies and public understanding at the University of Glasgow, writes that the real challenge is "how reformers can liberate themselves from the shackles of the law when their goals . . . are still conceptualized within medieval legal frameworks." She concludes that Ramadan's "is a pertinent voice, but in the end, it is just not bold enough."[31] Boldness certainly is needed to help change certain hardline religious attitudes in the Muslim world. A 2010 Pew Research Center survey of attitudes toward sharia-derived punishments in Egypt, Pakistan, Jordan, Nigeria, Indonesia, Lebanon, and Turkey found that an astonishing 82 percent of Jordanians and Egyptians, 78 percent of Pakistanis, and 50 percent of Nigerians favored the death penalty for people who leave Islam. More than 80 percent of Egyptians and Pakistanis, 70 percent of Jordanians, 58 percent of Nigerians, and 40 percent of Indonesians favored stoning for adultery. Almost 80 percent of Egyptians and Pakistanis and 60 to 62 percent of Jordanians and Nigerians endorsed whippings and cutting off of hands for theft. Conversely, very few Muslims in Lebanon and even fewer in Turkey favored any of these punishments. The survey suggests the extent to which radical Islamist frames could resonate in Egypt, Pakistan, Jordan, and Nigeria.[32]

MOBILIZING STRUCTURES AND CULTURAL FRAMES

Social movement theorizing has identified the importance of informal ties and social networks to recruitment and movement formation and has focused much attention on the role and formation of organizations, networks, informal groups, and other mobilizing structures. With respect to Islamist movements, recruitment occurs through kinship connection as well as through informal organizations or networks. Wiktorowicz writes that potential recruits are usually contacted by activists in preexisting social environments—family, peer groups, mosques, workplaces—or at public demonstrations. During the initial contacts, he writes, the recruiters try "to shake certitude in previously held beliefs and generate a sense of crisis and urgency."[33] The principal vehicles for recruiting adherents and attracting supporters are mosques, madrassas (religious schools), *nadwas* (Quranic study groups), and charities. In some cases, the bazaar or souk has also played a role, mainly through partnership with a mosque. In turn, these institutions constitute an "organizational infrastructure" for Islamist movements both local and transnational. In some countries, Islamists also recruit university graduates and have influence in professional associations. For example, Carrie Wickham found that the Muslim Brotherhood recruited from student unions and professional syndicates; bin Laden's coterie included engineers and physicians, and the nineteen hijackers of September 11, 2001, were almost all university educated.

In much the same way that churches have played a role in mobilizing people and framing protest in the United States, Eastern Europe, South Africa, and elsewhere, mosques have been both places of worship and sites of religio-political mobilization in the Muslim world. The mosque was a key institution for the mobilization of protest in the years that led up to the 1979 Iranian revolution and also was used by the Islamist state for the distribution of ration coupons during the war with Iraq in the 1980s. Across the Muslim world, the mosque and its attendant institutions, such as the madrassa, the *nadwa*, and charitable foundations, connect communities of believers but also provide a base from which to organize and mobilize, whether peacefully or for violent purposes, as in the Red Mosque affair in Pakistan.[34]

Other religious institutions provide assistance, build community, and foster collective identity. Judith Harik describes how Lebanon's Hezbollah, which is both a political party and a militant Islamist organization, built a network of charities and how that investment in welfare organizations translated into electoral gains at the grassroots level, especially in the southern suburb of Beirut. Janine Clark's study of Islamist charities and social welfare organizations in Egypt, Jordan, and Yemen demonstrates their success with poor and middle-class citizens alike, though she also found that the beneficiaries of Islamic charity often receive such a pittance that they seek benefits from non-Islamic charities as well. Sarah Roy describes the active role of Hamas in Palestinian civil society, showing how the social work that Hamas does has empowered the organization and enhanced its legitimacy and popularity. Providing assistance with marriage, health care, and schooling, these and other "Islamic social institutions" have proved critical in offering marginalized and disaffected citizens both symbolic and material rewards, thus ensuring steady recruitment to the Islamist cause.[35] Charities and *nadwas* are especially successful at mobilizing women and providing them with roles to play within the Islamist movement or party, such as fund-raising for the poor during Ramadan and carrying out *da'wa*, or preaching. In some countries (Egypt is a notable example), Islamist influence has extended to professional and student associations that are able to build transnational ties of solidarity with confreres.

Elsewhere—for example, in Jordan, Turkey, Malaysia, Indonesia, Palestine, and Yemen—Islamists have mobilized support, disseminated their messages, and influenced public policy through traditional institutions as well as the political process. Thus, even before the 2011 mass movements for political change, Islamists had managed to forge large networks of faith-based social service agencies, clinics, schools, charities, youth clubs, worship centers, banks, and businesses in countries such as Egypt, Jordan, and Yemen. As a number of scholars have noted, Islamic movements have emerged as a dominant opposition in the Muslim world because they command more societal institutions and resources than other movements and because of their ability to tap religious resources.[36]

The more radical and jihadist Islamists similarly recruit members and supporters and raise funds through mosques, madrassas, religious study groups, and charities, as well as through social and family ties. In Europe, radical mosques and imams with fiery messages appealed to disaffected young men, who went on to join cells or engaged in militant activism to defend what they felt were slurs or attacks on Islam. In England, they formed groups such as Tablighi Jamaat and al-Muhajiroun.[37] Increasingly porous borders in Europe facilitated interactions between contacts, some of whom were able to engage in bombings and other violent acts. Failed or fragile states elsewhere—such as in Afghanistan, Iraq, and Sudan—enable Islamist militants to travel for purposes of recruitment, training, or militant action. After the revolt against longtime Libyan leader Muammar Ghaddafi began in early 2011, this occurred in Libya as well.

The Internet is another mobilizing vehicle as well as a framing tool. Islamists have made effective use of the new computer technologies for purposes of information exchange, dissemination of their message, and projection of desired symbols and images. Local as well as transnational Islamists control numerous websites, enabling a kind of virtual activism. Indeed, al-Qaeda had a media wing called al-Sahib. In December 2007, Ayman al-Zawahiri, Osama bin Laden's deputy, invited subscribers to jihadist websites to post questions for al-Qaeda's leadership and promised that answers would be provided by mid-January 2008. In the same message inviting postings, Zawahiri emphasized the importance of "jihadi information media," saying they were "waging an extremely critical battle against the Crusader-Zionist enemy." He noted that information "used to be the exclusive domain of the official government media and the . . . media which claim to be free and non-governmental." In early January 2008, an Islamist website posted a video featuring al-Qaeda's American-born member Adam Gadahn, who urged fighters to meet President George W. Bush with bombs when he visited the Middle East later that month.[38] The many Islamist websites function as loci of self-advertisement, recruitment, and communication; in this they are sometimes helped by some Arab media. In broadcasting Islamist messages and images, Al Jazeera and Al Arabiyya, for example, help disseminate the idea that Islam and Muslims are in danger and need to fight back. As Manfred Steger has noted, Arab satellite media are part of a "chain of global interdependencies and interconnections" that make possible the instant broadcast of messages and images, including those of militant Islamists. What is more, "bin Laden may have denounced the forces of modernity with great conviction, but the smooth operation of his entire organization was entirely dependent on advanced forms of technology developed in the last two decades of the twentieth century." Similarly, Gary Blunt has investigated English- and Arabic-language Islamic blogs and militaristic websites from across the globe that create online Muslim identities or reinforce existing ones. The Islamic blogosphere, he argues, fosters new forms of Muslim networking, as "iMuslim netizens" use blogs to impact society both locally and globally via dialogue and debate or protest, information gathering and dissemination, or propagation of Islamic beliefs and values. He also shows the operations of e-jihad, whereby the Internet is used as a logistic device for funding, information sharing, and planning. Another report shows that across the Muslim world, many privately financed religious and lifestyle channels promote Salafism and broadcast a strident, aggressive tone against Shia and Christian minorities.[39]

Thus over and above the effective use and creation of mobilizing structures, Islamists have taken advantage of the opportunities afforded by globalization—specifically, the Internet, global media, and shifting geographies—to organize, build networks, coordinate activities, disseminate their message, and otherwise engage in collective action. Indeed, the making of an Islamist transnational public sphere has been facilitated by globalization. And this discursive space has been taken up by themes such as attacks on Islam; the occupations of Iraq, Afghanistan, and Palestine; corrupt and dictatorial regimes; and the need to proselytize Islam and spread the faith across the globe. The Internet has thus broadened the range of contemporary global Muslim discourses, even those that are locally grounded, creating transnational Islamic identities.

Millions of Muslims worldwide practice Islam in peace and with quiet dignity. Those who turn to violent contention, however, can justify their actions by selective recourse to Islamic scriptures regarding the imperative to defend Islam against its enemies. As sociologist Farhad Khosrokhavar has explained, Islamic martyrdom differs from Christian martyrdom in that it is an offensive tactic (rather than a passive response) to ward off challenges to the religion and thereby protect what is cherished and valued.[40] Concerns about cultural invasion, or the Israeli occupation of Palestinian land, or the presence of "infidel" soldiers and "crusaders" in Saudi Arabia, Afghanistan, and Iraq, or even relatively minor events such as satirical cartoons about the Prophet Muhammad in a Danish newspaper or the awarding of a British Medal of Honor to the writer Salman Rushdie—all these can trigger intense emotions and strong beliefs about insults to Islam, a war against Islam, and the religiously mandated imperative to defend the faith in a militant fashion. In this way, Muslim militants can draw on a ready-made cultural frame while also utilizing the existing organizational infrastructure.

REPERTOIRES OF CONTENTION: ISLAMIST AND LEFT-WING TERRORISTS

Can we better understand contemporary militant Islamism by way of comparison with other militant groups? Could Islamist terrorism represent not a growing worldwide movement but a futile attempt at power? Syrian political philosopher Sadik al-Azm has compared Islamist terror networks to those of the extreme Left in Europe in the 1970s. The latter's acts included the abduction and murder of the German industrialist Hans Martin Schleyer by the Baader-Meinhof Gang in the summer of 1977 and the similar abduction and assassination, a year later, of Aldo Moro, dean of Italy's senior political leaders after World War II, by the Italian Red Brigades. Carlos the Jackal, the Red Army Faction in West Germany, the Japanese Red Army, and other extreme leftist groups and individuals dominated the European scene at the time. The left-wing terrorism of the 1970s in Europe, al-Azm maintains, was a "desperate attempt to break out of the historical impasse and terminal structural crisis reached by communism, radical labor movements, Third Worldism, and revolutionary trends everywhere, by resorting to violent *action directe* of the most extraordinary and phenomenal kind." The terrorism of that period, he argues, was "(a) the then barely viable manifestation of that impasse and crisis, and (b) the prelude to the final demise of all those movements and trends including world communism itself."[41]

Similarly, "the *action directes* Islamists have also given up on contemporary Muslim society, its socio-political movements, the spontaneous religiosity of the masses, their endemic false consciousness, mainstream Islamic organizations, [and] the attention of the original and traditional Society of Muslim Brothers (from which they generally hail in the same way the original *action directes* hailed from European communism)." They have rejected all this, he writes, in favor of "their own brand of blind and spectacular activism, also heedless and contemptuous of consequences, long-term calculations of the chances of success or failure and so on." This kind of politics takes the form of "local attacks, intermittent skirmishes, guerrilla raids, random insurrections, senseless resistances, impatient outbursts, anarchistic assaults, and sudden uprisings." Al-Azm refers to "an Islamist impatient rejection of and contempt for politics in almost any form: conventional, radical, agitational and/or revolutionary in favor of the violent tactics of nihilism and despair. For them, the only other alternatives available are either cooptation or plain withdrawal or an admission of defeat." The *action directe* Islamists, like their European counterparts, "evince a sense of entrapment within an alien and alienating monolithic socio-political reality."[42] Al-Azm continues,

> With maximalist Islamism we get *action directe* terrorism on a global scale where the only kind of politics permitted is direct and immediate

armed attack against the enemy. The assumption in all this is that such apocalyptic Islamist self-assertion will (a) explode the obstacles blocking the way to the global triumph of Islam, (b) overcome the structural impasse in which the Islamist project finds itself at present, (c) develop better objective conditions for the success of that project, (d) catalyze the Muslim people's energies in its favor, and (e) create poles of attraction around which the Muslims of the world could immediately rally, for example the Al-Qaeda set of networks, organizations, training camps, etc., and the Taliban model of the supposedly first authentic Muslim society and government in modern times.[43]

While the analogy is useful in showing how repertoires of violent contention can travel from one geocultural space to another, the scale of European extremist left-wing violence was far smaller, and its time span shorter, than that of contemporary Islamism. This may be because the European extremists were more isolated, less networked, and less popular than contemporary Islamists; they also had fewer resources, including culturally resonant frames, at their disposal.

CONCLUSION

Political Islam appeared on the international stage in the late 1970s in the context of specific national and global opportunities and includes an array of locally based groups and transnationally active networks. Some groups have attempted the overthrow of local regimes; others have long been entrenched in cooperative relations with them; yet others have sought to bring about social, political, and legal reforms by "bypassing the state" and building strong grassroots institutions. Moderate Islamists take part in the electoral process and promote democracy to widen their social base and advance their interests; radicals rail against national and international injustices and call for strict adherence to Islam; extremists spread their message and assert themselves through violence. Many jihadists around the world enjoy sufficient "street credibility" to sway younger hearts and minds. The older ones won their spurs as fighters in the U.S.-backed campaign against the Soviet intervention in Afghanistan.

Since the late 1970s, Islamists of different orientations have come to power in Iran, Pakistan, Bangladesh, Sudan, Afghanistan, and Turkey, as well as in parts of Nigeria, Malaysia, and Indonesia. As Middle

Eastern and other states in the Muslim world have expanded, members of Islamist movements, in their capacity as well-educated members of their societies, have become employees of state bureaucracies. In Turkey, the Islamist movement had placed a sizable number of its members in the state bureaucracy by the mid-1990s. In Jordan, Islamic Action Front members were awarded the Ministry of Education, and in Kuwait's 1999 elections, Islamists won 40 percent of parliamentary seats. These developments have given rise to questions about the compatibility of Islamism with democracy and human rights. To date, no Islamist movement has been instrumental in the transition from authoritarianism to democracy, equality, and civil liberties, although in this connection, Tunisia's an-Nahda is being closely watched. As two scholars associated with liberal Islam note, "The challenge for Muslims is how to capture the massive dissonances of these times by retrieving the depth of faith without slipping into monasticism or zealotry. A democratizing and synthesizing Islam, reflecting influences from the bottom, is better placed to respond to globalization."[44] As we have seen, even moderate and parliamentary Islamists evince ambiguities and ambivalences in their views and practices regarding minority rights, women's rights, and various social freedoms. As such, Islamist movements would seem to be at the opposite end of the spectrum from feminist and global justice movements.

The radical Islamist focus on the West as the source of all ills—economic, political, and cultural—is of course the mirror image of Samuel Huntington's thesis of "the clash of civilizations" whereby the most profound clash is that between Islam and the West.[45] In both cases, cultural values and norms are emphasized as preeminent and seen to be at stake. In the Huntington perspective, the world of Islam is at odds with Western notions of democracy, tolerance, and pluralism. The solution is to keep a distance, close ranks, and protect Western values. In the Islamist perspective, the West is responsible—through such ills as secularism, feminism, gay liberation, and support for repressive regimes—for undermining Muslim societies and exerting control over them. The solution is to reject Western values and institutions and adhere strictly to Islamic laws, norms, and institutions. Both arguments essentialize religion and culture and cast the religio-cultural differences between Islam and the West into sharp relief. In the perspective taken in this book, rather than toward a clash of civilizations, cultures, or religions, attention should be directed at the broad macro-level processes and forms of masculinity that engender violent contention, as well as the organizational and cultural resources available to challengers.

Globalization processes have provided both grievances and opportunities for the emergence and growth of Islamist movements and institutions. Concerns over cultural invasion, political and military interventions in Muslim lands, and economic difficulties have galvanized militant Muslims, while the Internet has allowed them to disseminate their messages, coordinate activities, recruit followers, and maintain networks. If Islam is a world religion, Islamism has become a globalized ideology and movement.

CHAPTER 5

FEMINISM ON A WORLD SCALE

The world will not change without feminism; and feminists cannot change women's lives unless we change the world.

—World March of Women, 2002

The women's rights movement has been the subject of considerable scholarly analysis. Feminist theorizing has focused on national-level factors such as the growth of the population of educated women with grievances about their second-class citizenship, varieties of feminism, the evolution of women's movements and campaigns, and cross-regional similarities and differences in mobilizing structures and strategies. Research also distinguishes the terms "feminist movement" as a social movement guided by feminist ideas and "women's movement" as defined by a demographic group or constituency, with the former being a subset of the latter.[1]

Since the 1990s a growing literature has connected women's movements and organizations to global processes such as the role of international organizations or the UN Decade for Women, and it has examined the ways that women's organizations engage with the world of public policy. While not all feminists agree on the matter, many argue that the "women's movement" is a global phenomenon and that, despite cultural differences, country specificities, and organizational priorities, there are observed similarities in the ways women's rights activists frame their grievances and demands, form networks and organizations, and engage with state and intergovernmental institutions.[2] Some of these similarities include adoption of discourses of women's human rights and gender equality; references to international agreements such as the Convention on the Elimination of All Forms of Discrimination against Women (CEDAW) and the Beijing Platform for Action; campaigns for legal and policy reforms to ensure women's civil, political, and social rights; solidarity and networking across borders; and coalitions with other civil society groups. Another observation is that women's rights activists—whether in South Asia, Latin America, the Middle East, or North Africa—are opposed to "fundamentalist" discourses and agendas and espouse feminist discourses and goals, whether explicitly or implicitly. Valerie Sperling, Myra Marx Ferree, and Barbara Risman have correctly concluded that "feminist action" is an appropriate term to define "that in which the participants explicitly place value on challenging gender hierarchy and changing women's social status, whether they adopt or reject the feminist label." Similarly, Mary Hawkesworth defines "global feminist activism" as international feminist mobilizations involving women in more than one country or region "who seek to forge a collective identity among women and to improve the condition of women." I have identified such mobilizations as "transnational feminist networks" that advocate for women's participation and rights while also engaging critically with policy and legal issues and with states, international organizations, and institutions of global governance.[3]

Like the Islamist movement studied in the previous chapter and the global justice movement to be examined in the next, the women's movement is transnational and diverse, exhibiting the segmentary, polycentric, and reticulate features that Luther Gerlach identified as common to many social movements (see chapter 1). These features of the global women's movement were especially evident during the Fourth World Conference on Women, which took place in Beijing, China, in September 1995. For three weeks, women's groups from across the world met to take part in the massive nongovernmental forum that preceded but also overlapped with the official, intergovernmental conference. At the latter, those women's groups with UN accreditation were able to enter conference halls, lobby delegates, disseminate their literature, and hold rallies. This was hardly a movement with a center or a bureaucracy or hierarchy. It was a movement of movements, albeit highly networked. And although the women's groups at Beijing had something to say about an array of issues, they also had common grievances concerning war, peace, fundamentalisms, and the new economic order.[4]

This chapter examines the relationship between globalization and the global women's movement, with a focus on three types of transnational feminist networks (TFNs) that emerged in the 1980s and continue to be active to this day. Discussed in this chapter are networks that target the neoliberal economic policy agenda; those that focus on fundamentalism and insist on women's human rights, especially in the Muslim world; and women's peace groups that target conflict, war, and empire. I discuss their activities, the strategies they pursue, and their framing devices. The chapter begins with a discussion of the global context and the opportunity structure(s) within which transnational feminism emerged.

THE ROAD TO TRANSNATIONAL FEMINISM

Chapter 1 described the precursors to the contemporary women's movement, including international women's organizations and campaigns of the early twentieth century. At mid-century the women's movement began to diverge, grouping itself within national boundaries or economic zones, emphasizing different priorities, and aligning with divergent ideological currents. In particular, North-South differences became pronounced as feminists in the core countries and those in the developing world expressed radically different grievances and formed divergent strategies.

The women's movement of the second wave, which began in North America and Europe in the 1960s, consisted of feminist groups that emerged within national borders and addressed themselves to their own nation-states, governments, employers, male colleagues, and kin. As women's groups expanded across the globe, they remained largely nationally based and oriented. Feminist groups encompassed liberal, radical, Marxist, and socialist ideologies, and these political differences constituted one form of division within feminism. The Cold War cast a shadow on feminist solidarity, in the form of the East-West divide; there was, for the most part, antipathy between women's groups aligned with the communist movement and liberal feminist groups aligned with the so-called Free World. Another division took the form of North-South, or First World–Third World, differences in terms of prioritizing feminist issues; many First World feminists saw legal equality and reproductive rights as key feminist demands and goals, while many Third World feminists emphasized underdevelopment, colonialism, and imperialism as obstacles to women's advancement. Disagreements over what constituted top-priority feminist issues came to the fore at the beginning of the UN Decade for Women, especially at its First and Second World Conferences on Women, which took place in Mexico City in 1975 and in Copenhagen in 1980. The disagreements at the Mexico City and Copenhagen conferences pitted women activists from the North and South against each other and revolved around prioritizing issues of legal equality and personal choice versus those pertaining to global economic and political hierarchies.[5]

A shift in the nature and orientation of international feminism began to take place in the mid-1980s, during preparations for the UN's Third World Conference on Women, held in Nairobi, Kenya, in 1985. The shift took the form of bridge and consensus building across regional and ideological divides and the emergence of a women's organization of a new type. Three critical economic and political developments within states and regions and at the level of the world-system enabled the shift: (1) the transition from Keynesian to neoliberal economics, along with a new international division of labor that relied heavily on (cheap) female labor; (2) the decline of the welfare state in the core countries and the developmental state in the Third World; and (3) the emergence of various forms of fundamentalist movements. These changes led to new thinking, ways of organizing, frame alignments, and collective action repertoires on the part of activist women in developing and developed countries. Let us examine these issues in more detail.

FEMINIZATION OF LABOR

Beginning in the late 1970s, cross-national research, including studies by those working in the field of women-in-development or women-and-development (WID/WAD), showed that an ever-growing proportion of the world's women was being incorporated as cheap labor into what was variously called the capitalist world-economy, the new international division of labor, or the global assembly line. Maquiladoras along the U.S.-Mexico border and export-processing zones in the Caribbean and Southeast Asia relied heavily on female labor, while garment factories geared to the world market employed women in North Africa and Bangladesh. Studies showed that women were gaining an increasing share of many kinds of jobs, but this was occurring in a context of growing unemployment, a decline in the social power of labor, and an increase in temporary, part-time, casual, and home-based work—that is, in the context of the shift in the capitalist world-system from Keynesian to neoliberal economic policy. Disproportionately involved in irregular forms of employment increasingly used to maximize profits, women also remained responsible for reproductive work and domestic labor. In addition, women remained disadvantaged in the new labor markets in terms of wages, training, and occupational segregation. In the late 1980s, International Labour Organization (ILO) economist Guy Standing termed this phenomenon the "feminization of labor." He argued that the increasing globalization of production and the pursuit of flexible forms of labor to retain or increase competitiveness, as well as changing job structures in industrial enterprises, favored the "feminization of employment" in the dual sense of an increase in the numbers of women in the labor force and a deterioration of work conditions (labor standards, income, and employment status).[6] By the 1990s, women comprised nearly half of the world labor force, though most working women experienced poor working conditions, low wages, and minimal benefits.

WELFARE AND DEVELOPMENT CUTS

The new labor markets meant that employers could offer more jobs with part-time or temporary contracts. Privatization and denationalization meant the contraction of the public sector, which historically entailed good benefits and stable employment, if not the highest wages, and tended to be the preferred employer for women in many countries. At the urging of the World Bank, the old social contracts guaranteed by the "developmental state" in the Global South were replaced by the introduction of "user fees" for purposes of "cost recovery" in the sectors of health and education, while the generous social policies were whittled away. Cutbacks in social services as part of structural adjustment policies or the new neoliberal policy package meant that women's growing labor-market participation was not accompanied by a redistribution of domestic, household, and child-care responsibilities. Rather, the changing nature of the state vis-à-vis the public sector meant the withdrawal, deterioration, or privatization of many public services used by working- and middle-class women and their families. Contraction of the public-sector wage bill meant fewer good job opportunities for women.

As global restructuring expanded to encompass the former communist bloc, studies showed that women in Eastern Europe and the former Soviet Union were adversely affected by unemployment and the loss of income and benefits that accompanied privatization. A body of research also emerged to address another new global phenomenon: the "feminization of poverty," or the growing female share of the population living under the poverty line. Much of this research was carried out by scholar-activists with links to the women's movement, and this academic involvement helped to shape feminist strategies across the globe, including in the North.[7]

FUNDAMENTALISMS

Another important development that led to the narrowing of the political and ideological divide between First and Third World feminists was the rise of Islamic fundamentalism in Muslim countries and Hindu communalism in India. These movements sought to recuperate traditional norms and codes, including patriarchal laws and family roles for women; they put pressure on states to enforce public morality, increase religious observance, and tighten controls over women—ostensibly to protect the nation or culture from alien influences and conspiracies. In many cases there was collusion between states and the religio-political movements, usually to the detriment of women's rights. Such movements alarmed feminists in the peripheral and semiperipheral countries where the movements emerged. At the same time, feminists in the United States began to take notice of the increasing influence of the Christian Right.[8]

Divergences, therefore, began to narrow in the mid-1980s as a result of the changing environments in both the North and the South, notably with the rise of neoliberalism and the growth of fundamentalist movements. The new economic and political realities gradually led to a convergence of feminist perspectives across the globe: for many First World feminists, economic issues and development policy became increasingly important, and many Third World feminists directed greater attention toward women's legal status, autonomy, and rights. Regionally, too, changes came about. In Latin America, divisions among participants of the *encuentros feministas*, or feminist gatherings—which first took place in Bogotá, Colombia, in 1981 and in Lima, Peru, in 1983, and where women identified themselves as either "feminists" or "politicos/militants"—were eventually eclipsed by common concerns and frames.[9] New framings—women's empowerment, human rights, gender equality—were accompanied by new mobilizing structures, notably the formation of a number of transnational feminist networks that brought together women from developed and developing countries alike to respond to economic pressures and patriarchal movements. The new mobilizing structures included Development Alternatives with Women for a New Era (DAWN), Network Women in Development Europe (WIDE), the Women's Environment and Development Organization (WEDO), Women Living under Muslim Laws (WLUML), and the Sisterhood Is Global Institute (SIGI). Others formed in the 1990s. They engaged in policy-oriented research, advocacy, and lobbying around issues pertaining to women and development and women's human rights. Many of the women who formed or joined the TFNs were scholar-activists who had been involved in the WID/gender-and-development (GAD) research community. With the formation of these networks and other women's activist groups, a global social movement of women was in the making (see table 5.1).

During this period, however, international feminism paid surprisingly little attention to one important issue: the conflict in Afghanistan and the implications for women of Western support for the Islamic-tribal alliance of the mujahideen (holy warriors). The Afghan revolution and change in regime had taken place in April 1978, one year before the Iranian revolution and the victory of the Sandinistas in

Table 5.1. Types of Transnational Feminist Networks

	Website	Location/HQ
Critique of Economic Policy		
Development Alternatives with Women for a New Era (DAWN)	http://www.dawnnet.org	Philippines
Marche Mondiale des Femmes	http://www.marchemondiale.org	Quebec etc.
Network Women in Development Europe (WIDE)[a]	http://www.wide-network.org	Brussels etc.
Women's Environment and Development Organization (WEDO)	http://www.wedo.org	New York
Advocacy for Women's Human Rights		
Arab Women's Solidarity Association (AWSA)	http://www.awsa.be	Egypt, United States
Association for Women's Rights in Development (AWID)	http://www.awid.org	Canada
Equality Now	http://www.equalitynow.org	United States & Kenya
International Women's Tribune Center (IWTC)	http://www.iwtc.org	United States
MADRE	http://www.madre.org	United States
Women's Caucus for Gender Justice	http://www.iccwomen.org	Netherlands
Women's Human Rights Network (WHRNet)	http://www.whrnet.org	N/A
Women's Learning Partnership (WLP)	http://www.learningpartnership.org	United States
Women Living under Muslim Laws (WLUML)	http://www.wluml.org	United Kingdom, Nigeria, Pakistan
Women for Women International	http://www.womenforwomen.org	United States

Peace, Antimilitarism, Conflict Resolution

Association of Women of the Mediterranean Region (AVMR)[b]	http://digilander.libero.it/awmr/int http://www.mediterraneas.org/article.php3?id_article=17	United States and Cyprus
Code Pink	http://www.codepink4peace.org	United States
Grandmothers for Peace International	http://grandmothersforpeace.org	United States
MADRE	http://www.madre.org	United States
Marche Mondiale des Femmes	http://www.marchemondiale.org	Quebec etc.
Medica Mondiale	http://www.medicamondiale.org	Germany
Women in Black	http://www.womeninblack.org	17 countries
Women's International League for Peace and Freedom (WILPF)	http://www.wilpfinternational.org	Switzerland and United States
Women for Women International (WWI)	http://www.womenforwomen.org	United States
Women's Initiatives for Gender Justice	http://www.iccwomen.org	Netherlands (and Cairo and Kampala)

[a] Since 2005 includes the Women's International Coalition for Economic Justice.
[b] Inactive.

Nicaragua. The new Democratic Republic of Afghanistan set about leg-islating land reform, equality for the diverse ethnic groups, and rights for women and girls in the family and society. Almost immediately, the United States, Saudi Arabia, Pakistan, Egypt, and other countries formed a coalition in opposition to the pro-Soviet Afghan government. When the Islamist rebellion, backed by the CIA since the summer of 1978, came to threaten the viability of the new republic, the Soviet Union reluctantly agreed to the Afghan government's request for troops to help stabilize the situation. Shortly thereafter, the United States beefed up its covert operation to support the mujahideen (the coalition of Islamist rebels) and end communism in both Afghanistan and the Soviet Union. That women and girls would forfeit schooling, the right to work, and rights in the family under an Islamist regime was of no consequence to U.S. policy makers.[10] Surprisingly, it was of no appar-ent consequence to international women's groups either. Feminists in the United States and Europe were silent; they extended no support to Afghan women and did not express any concerns about the implica-tions of American support for Islamists. The silence and confusion of the 1980s may have been due to the anticommunism of liberal feminist groups, to an idealization of "Islamic guerrillas," to a misplaced cultural relativism, or to ignorance about Afghanistan. In any event, the left-wing government was defeated in late April 1992, and the mujahideen came to power—only to turn on each other and introduce a reign of lawlessness and warlordism. It was not until the mid-1990s, after the Taliban had removed the mujahideen from power and instituted a dra-conian gender regime, that feminists around the world began to take notice and respond to appeals from Afghan and Pakistani feminists for solidarity and support. By this time, transnational feminist networks were more vocal and visible. Thus began the highly effective interna-tional feminist campaign against diplomatic recognition of the Taliban. In the United States, the Feminist Majority led the campaign against "gender apartheid" in Afghanistan.

UN CONFERENCES AND THE INFORMATION AND COMMUNICATION TECHNOLOGIES REVOLUTION

As TFNs proliferated in the 1990s, they helped bridge the North-South divide among women activists and transcended the earlier political and ideological differences through the adoption of a broader feminist agenda that included a critique of neoliberalism and structural adjustment policies as well as an insistence on women's full citizenship, reproductive rights, bodily integrity, and autonomy, no matter what the cultural context. Eventually, that common agenda took the form of the 1995 Beijing Declaration and Platform for Action. Along the way to Beijing, though, there were other venues where the world's women agreed on issues pertaining to gender justice, notably the UN world conferences of the 1990s: the United Nations Conference on Environment and Development (UNCED) in Rio de Janeiro in 1992, the Human Rights Conference in Vienna in 1993, the International Conference on Population and Development (ICPD) in Cairo in 1994, and the World Summit for Social Development (the Social Summit) in Copenhagen in 1995. At these conferences, women declared that environmental issues were women's issues, that women's rights were human rights, that governments were expected to guarantee women's reproductive health and rights, and that women's access to productive employment and social protection needed to be expanded. Slowly, new frames emerged that resonated globally and have come to be adopted by women's groups throughout the world: women's human rights, gender justice, gender equality, ending the feminization of poverty, and ending violence against women.

TFNs worked with various UN agencies, notably the United Nations Development Fund for Women (UNIFEM) and United Nations Population Fund (UNFPA), but they were also consulted by various multilateral organizations. As a result, TFN activities as well as partnerships with other advocacy networks resulted in some successes at the UN conferences of the 1990s and afterward. TFN lobbying led to the insertion of important items in the final Vienna Declaration of the 1993 Conference on Human Rights, such as the assertion that violence against women was an abuse of human rights and the demand for attention to the harmful effects of certain traditional or customary practices, cultural prejudices, and religious extremisms. The declaration also stated that human rights abuses of women in situations of armed conflict—including systematic rape, sexual slavery, and forced pregnancy—are violations of the fundamental principles of international human rights and humanitarian law. TFNs were influential in lobbying delegates for a favorable outcome document at the 1994 ICPD, which included references to women's rights to reproductive health and services. They were active at the March 1995 Social Summit, where they drew attention to structural adjustment's adverse effects on women and the poor, and, as noted, they were especially prominent at the September 1995 Beijing conference. TFNs endorsed and helped secure support for the establishment of "national machinery for women"—or women's policy agencies—as well as gender budgets in a number of countries. As such, TFNs influenced institution building, policy dialogues, and norm diffusion in connection with women's participation and rights.

These and other activities were boosted by the computer revolution. The new ICTs helped women connect and share information, plan and coordinate activities more rapidly, and mobilize more extensively. Two feminist networks focusing on communications came to serve as conduits for activist materials. These were the International Women's Tribune Center, based in New York, and ISIS International Women's Information and Communication Service, with one center in Quezon City, Philippines, and another in Santiago, Chile. ISIS International produced *Women in Action*, *Women's World*, and other communications. A 2002 issue of *Women in Action* included articles on media (mis) representations of the Afghan crisis and the Israeli-Palestinian conflict, while a 2002 issue of *Women's World* contained updates on women in Sierra Leone, the Democratic Republic of Congo, Sudan, Burundi, Afghanistan, Pakistan, Albania, India, Kosovo, and Colombia, as well as about Sudanese refugees in Kenya.

Some scholars have distinguished between professionalized women's lobbying groups (NGOs or international NGOs) and "grassroots" women's groups. The former are said to be elitist while the latter are more movement oriented. This may be an arbitrary distinction, however, because many of the professionalized TFNs are led and staffed by feminist activists with strong commitments to gender equality, women's empowerment, and social transformation. Moreover, the women's movement is diffuse and diverse, with different types of mobilizing structures, discourses, and action repertoires. The overarching frame is that of achieving gender equality and human rights for women and girls. Across the different types of feminist organizations, strategies vary and include research and analysis, lobbying efforts, coalition building, feminist humanitarianism, and public protests (see table 5.2). All of these means, therefore, are movement oriented.

Table 5.2. Strategies Deployed by Transnational Feminist Networks

	Code Pink	DAWN	MADRE	Marche Mondiale	Women for Women International	WIDE	WLF	WLUML
Grassroots organizing	X			X		X		
Research and analysis	X	X	X	X	X	X	X	X
Lobbying		X			X	X		
Public advocacy and education	X		X	X	X	X	X	X
Coalition building	X	X	X	X		X	X	X
Humanitarian action	X		X		X			
International solidarity	X	X	X	X	X	X	X	X
Public protests	X			X				

NEOLIBERALISM AND THE WOMAN QUESTION

"The woman question" was the phrase used by socialist, communist, and nationalist movements in the nineteenth and early twentieth centuries to describe both the oppression that women faced in most societies and the alternative vision that the movements offered. I use it here to refer to more recent feminist contentious politics concerning the impacts of neoliberal economic policies on women and the prescribed alternatives.

The latter part of the 1990s saw feminists addressing issues of globalization and the new global trade agenda. As noted, feminist scholar-activists had been critical of structural adjustments—with their conditionalities of privatization and liberalization—and were now alarmed by the global reach of neoliberalism. A wave of workshops was organized and publications produced to increase knowledge about the technical details of trade liberalization and its gender dynamics. Of concern was that neoliberal policies—with the attendant features of flexible labor markets, privatization of public goods, commercialization of all manner of services, and "free trade"—threatened the economic security of workers, small producers, and local industries; placed a heavy burden on women to compensate for social cutbacks and deteriorating household incomes; and led to increased vulnerability and poverty. TFNs and other advocacy networks argued that the new rules of global free trade undermined existing national laws that protected workers, the environment, and animals and that World Trade Organization (WTO) intellectual property provisions allowed large corporations to appropriate (through patents) the knowledge and products of Third World countries and their local communities. Additionally, transnational feminists argued that the employment losses and dislocations brought about by the new international trade agreements would be disproportionately borne by women.[11]

TFNs such as DAWN, WIDE, and WEDO prepared documents analyzing the policies and activities of multinational corporations, the World Bank, the International Monetary Fund (IMF), and the WTO, as well as the policy stances of the U.S. government. They criticized the World Bank and IMF for their corporate bias and for policies that undermined the well-being of workers and the poor, while the WTO was charged with conducting its deliberations in secret and not subjecting them to rules of transparency and accountability. TFNs joined broad coalitions such as Jubilee 2000 for Third World debt cancellation, which involved challenges to corporate capitalism and global inequalities by labor, religious, environmental, and human rights groups. As such, transnational feminist groups were allied with, and indeed became part of, the global justice movement as it took shape in the late 1990s and into the new millennium. It is important to note, however, that the global feminist agenda on neoliberalism preceded that of the global justice movement by about a decade.[12]

An example of transnational mobilizing around neoliberalism is the World March of Women 2000. The initiative, launched two years earlier in Montreal, Canada, by the Fédération des Femmes du Québec, culminated in a series of coordinated marches and other actions held around the world to protest poverty and violence against women. Nearly six thousand organizations from 159 countries and territories were represented in the rallies and marches held. It is noteworthy that women activists from Middle Eastern and especially North African countries, not usually visible in transnational feminist organizing and mobilizing around economic justice, were involved in the planning and execution of the march, in part because of the shared knowledge of French. Women trade unionists were also involved; for example, in April 2000, some three thousand trade unionists, including many women workers, marched in Durban, South Africa, in an event organized jointly by the International Confederation of Free Trade Unions (ICFTU) and its South African affiliates. The demands included affordable and accessible housing and transportation, protection against all forms of violence, equal rights for women in the workplace and throughout society, an end to structural adjustment programs and cutbacks in social budgets and public services, cancellation of the debt of all Third World countries, making gender issues central to labor policies and programs, and treatment and protection for people with HIV/AIDS.[13]

The initiative's *Advocacy Guide to Women's World Demands* described the world as governed by two forces, neoliberal capitalism and patriarchy, which were singled out as the structural causes of poverty and forms of violence against women:

> We live in a world whose dominant economic system, neo-liberal capitalism, is fundamentally inhuman. It is a system governed by unbridled

competition that strives for privatization, liberalization, and deregulation. It is a system entirely driven by the dictates of the market and where full employment of basic human rights ranks below the laws of the marketplace. The result: the crushing social exclusion of large segments of the population, threatening world peace and the future of the planet. . . .

Neoliberalism and patriarchy feed off each other and reinforce each other in order to maintain the vast majority of women in a situation of cultural inferiority, social devaluation, economic marginalization, "invisibility" of their existence and labor, and the marketing and commercialization of their bodies. All these situations closely resemble apartheid.

The World March of Women proposed concrete measures to combat poverty and incidents of violence against women: an end to structural adjustment policies and to cutbacks in social budgets and public services, implementation of the Tobin tax on speculative transactions and for financial justice, changes to global governance such as the democratization of the United Nations (including the Security Council), and the establishment of a World Council for Economic and Financial Security. These demands were presented to the president of the World Bank on October 15, 2000.[14]

Continuing its activities to this day, the World March of Women remains an important actor within the global justice movement and the World Social Forum. It participated actively in the World Social Forum in Porto Alegre, Brazil, in 2001; was involved in the People's Summit in Quebec in April 2001; and was present during the anti-G8 demonstrations in Genoa, Italy, in July 2001 and again in 2002 in Porto Alegre, where it organized a seminar on feminism and globalization. In 2005 the network launched another global mobilization, its first since 2000, centered on the Women's Global Charter for Humanity. As described by Pascale Dufour and Isabelle Giraud, the run-up to the mobilization entailed compromises on the network's agenda (for example, on language pertaining to abortion and homosexuality) but had the effect of including many more women's groups, especially African and Indian ones. While painful to some members, the decision was important to the goal of building a global social movement with a collective identity.[15]

The WIDE network was formed in 1990 and quickly became one of the principal transnational feminist networks focused on economic development and social rights. Its argument has been that recent global economic processes trade and investment liberalization; financialization of the economy; structural adjustment policies and austerity measures, including deep cuts in social policy budgets—are undermining gender equality and women's human rights. Identifying neoliberalism as the root cause of these adverse global processes and their social/gender effects, WIDE has called for "changes in currently unjust economic policies and shifts in social mindsets in Europe and globally" in order to contribute to "gender equality and social, economic, and ecological justice globally; and women's empowerment and women's power to claim their human rights, for building participative democracy and shaping a just economy." To this end, WIDE has engaged in coalition building with other feminist groups and progressive groups, helped to strengthen women's organizations, and extended international solidarity. Throughout the years, it has undertaken research, produced reports on gender and economic processes, and lobbied EU agencies.[16] WIDE's economic justice frame allows for bridge building with other progressive organizations, including those associated with the World Social Forum, while its feminist frames enables coalitions with an array of women's rights groups. Despite the fact that it is a professional organization with paid positions, WIDE plays a key role in the global feminist movement.

FUNDAMENTALISM AND THE WOMAN QUESTION

Chapter 4 described the rise of Islamism and the collusion of states, including the United States, in its emergence and growth. Part of the collective action repertoire and framing strategy of Islamist movements was to demand the reinforcement and strengthening of existing Islamic laws and norms or their introduction and strict application. In addition to the prohibition against alcohol and usury and the insistence that women veil in public, Islamists demanded an orthodox interpretation and implementation of Muslim family laws, which regulate marriage, divorce, child custody, inheritance, and other aspects of family relations. In particular, Muslim family laws—which date from the Middle

Ages, reflect one or another of the four Sunni schools or the Shia school of jurisprudence, and were codified in the modern period of state building—place females under the authority of male kin and wives under the control of husbands. Although notions of Islamic "complementarity" of sex roles may once have been considered equitable and natural, the rise of second-wave feminism and subsequently of "global feminism" put feminism and fundamentalism on a collision course.

This is the global context in which the international solidarity network Women Living under Muslim Laws was formed. Other networks of antifundamentalist feminists were formed by expatriate Iranian women in Europe and the United States and by South Asian feminists in Britain. The Sisterhood Is Global Institute, a network created by veteran American feminist Robin Morgan, was directed by an expatriate Iranian feminist, Mahnaz Afkhami, during most of the 1990s; under her leadership, SIGI emerged as an active network dedicated to Muslim women's human rights through practical means such as training workshops, conferences, policy dialogues, manuals, and publications.

In July 1984, nine women—from Algeria, Sudan, Morocco, Pakistan, Bangladesh, Iran, Mauritius, and Tanzania—set up a WLUML action committee in response to "the application of Muslim laws in India, Algeria, and Abu Dhabi that resulted in the violation of women's human rights."[17] By early 1985, the committee had evolved into an international network of information, solidarity, and support, with such key figures as Marieme Hélie-Lucas of Algeria and France, Salma Sobhan of Bangladesh, Ayesha Imam of Nigeria, and Khawar Mumtaz and Farida Shaheed of Pakistan. These and other feminists associated with the network were concerned about changes in family laws in their countries, the rise of fundamentalism and aggressive Islamist movements, and threats to the legal status and social positions of women in Muslim-majority societies. Tasks for the network were established at the first planning meeting in April 1986, involving ten women from Algeria, Morocco, Tunisia, Egypt, Sudan, Nigeria, India, Pakistan, and Sri Lanka. The tasks were to create international links between women in Muslim countries and communities; to share information on their situations, struggles, and strategies; and to strengthen and reinforce women's initiatives through publications, exchanges, and an action alert system. Since then, WLUML has become a network of women who are active in their local and national movements but meet periodically to reach a strategic consensus. In 1997, some thirty-five activists from eighteen countries gathered in Dhaka, Bangladesh, to agree on a plan of action. A new plan was adopted in Dakar, Senegal, in January 2006.

As a fluid group rather than a membership-based organization, WLUML gave priority to creating strong networks and ties of solidarity among women across countries rather than seeking to influence national or global policy through interaction with governments or intergovernmental bodies.[18] Nonetheless, it was present at the United Nations World Conference on Human Rights, held in Vienna in 1993, and sponsored the participation of Khalida Messaoudi, an Algerian feminist leader. WLUML also attended the 1994 UN Conference on Population and Development, where it joined other feminist networks in criticizing efforts by the Vatican, conservative states, and Christian and Muslim fundamentalists to remove references to women's reproductive rights in the conference declaration. These conferences helped WLUML to expand its collaborations and alliances with transnational feminist networks such as WIDE and DAWN—in addition to its ongoing links with the Center for Women's Global Leadership at Rutgers University; Shirkat Gah in Lahore, Pakistan; and Baobab in Lagos, Nigeria.[19]

From the outset, WLUML's collective action repertoire has included gathering and disseminating information on formal and customary laws in the Muslim world, as well as on women's struggles and strategies. Common projects are identified by women in the network and reflect their diverse concerns. A ten-year project on reinterpreting the Quran culminated in a book and increased awareness of the religious women involved in the misapplication of Islamic law in the Muslim world; in this connection, the Malaysian women's group Sisters in Islam played a major role. The central activity of the network may be identified as its solidarity and support work. WLUML receives appeals and responds to, as well as initiates, campaigns pertaining to violations of human rights, including women's human rights.[20] In keeping with its focus on monitoring the human rights of women in Muslim countries, extending solidarity, and raising international awareness, WLUML has issued numerous action alerts. These have been disseminated by the international coordination office in Europe, the Asia office in Pakistan, and the Africa and Middle East office in Nigeria (now in Dakar). Another activity is documenting and disseminating information in the form of dossiers, or occasional journals, which describe the situation of Muslim women and legal codes in various countries and report on the activities of women's organizations. One key resource was the news sheet produced and disseminated by the Asia coordination office and specifically the women's resource center Shirkat Gah. In the late 1990s, many articles were devoted to describing the plight of women in Algeria and Afghanistan. Indeed, after the Taliban took control of Afghanistan in September 1996 and instituted a harsh gender regime, WLUML helped disseminate appeals from expatriate Afghan women in Pakistan for international solidarity and support. Throughout the world, feminists brought pressure to bear on their governments not to recognize the Taliban; as a result, only three governments—those of Pakistan, Saudi Arabia, and the United Arab Emirates—came to recognize the Taliban regime. Among such feminist groups, WLUML has been consistently antifundamentalist as well as a strong advocate of gender justice. As early as 1990, WLUML began to issue warnings about an "Islamist international"—with the organizational, human, financial, and military means to threaten secularists, feminists, and democrats—and some of its prominent members were critical of European governments granting political asylum to radical Islamists. In the new century, WLUML pointed to the Front Islamique du Salut's and Armed Islamic Group's record of terrorism, including harassment, kidnapping, rape, and murder of Algerian women, to oppose any legalization of these groups without prosecution of those responsible for crimes.[21]

At the same time, WLUML was critical of the U.S. bombing raids in Afghanistan, which were conducted to bring down the perpetrators of September 11, identified as Osama bin Laden, his al-Qaeda network, and their Taliban hosts. WLUML was concerned that the raids brought devastation to ordinary Afghans. And the network accused Western countries of having turned a blind eye to Islamists—and in the case of the United States, having actively supported them. An article in a WLUML newsletter declared,

> Western governments are the prime responsible ones for the creation of these big and small monsters that they are now attempting to fight against. The West never cared when the Taliban attacked Afghan women's rights, when they assaulted them, when they killed them. It

has looked in the other direction while in Algeria the radical Islamic groups have kidnapped, raped, killed and ripped to pieces scores of women—the latest aggression taking place barely two months ago—while in Bangladesh many women have to live with their faces scarred by the acid thrown in their faces by fundamentalists.

And now. Is an end to western hypocrisy going to come with the resounding measures being taken against the terrorism of the radical Islamic networks? Will they be compatible with measures of justice? It does not seem just to carpet-bomb a people, the Afghan people, who in the last years have been the prime victim of a regime which has been indirectly tolerated and harbored. There must be another way of achieving justice.[22]

Exemplifying the fluid and flexible nature of contemporary transnational social movements and their organizations, WLUML's work is maintained through the activities of "networkers" who communicate largely via the Internet but meet occasionally to agree on plans. The January 2006 action plan meeting in Dakar was attended by fifty networkers from twenty-two countries, but input was received by affiliates via e-mail. This double strategy of real and virtual communication enabled the network to agree on four priority issues: "peace-building and resisting the impact of militarization; preserving multiple identities and exposing fundamentalisms; widening debate about women's bodily autonomy; and promoting and protecting women's equality under laws."[23] Long engaged in virtual activism, WLUML wages numerous e-campaigns for women's human rights. The network has issued countless appeals on behalf of Iraqi women; it was the prime vehicle through which information was distributed worldwide in 2005 concerning the planned establishment of a sharia court in Ontario, Canada; and it has initiated or disseminated numerous petitions to protest violations of women's rights. WLUML has worked with other feminist networks and web-based projects—such as the Women's Human Rights Net, a project of the Canada-based Association for Women's Rights in Development—to highlight women's human rights violations as well as examples of feminist collective action. In 2008 its website listed seventy-five linked networks, many of them in Middle Eastern or Muslim countries. In all these ways, WLUML links dispersed communities, creating a new cyberculture and reinforcing a collective identity. Mobilization to protest gender injustices occurs rapidly and often effectively.

The Women's Learning Partnership for Rights, Development, and Peace (WLP) was formed in 2000 by veteran women's rights activist Mahnaz Afkhami. Dedicated to women's leadership and empowerment, WLP defines itself as "a builder of networks, working with eighteen autonomous and independent partner organizations in the Global South, particularly in Muslim-majority societies, to empower women to transform their families, communities, and societies." The goals are to "improve the effectiveness of feminist movements in Muslim-majority societies and globally" and to help women secure human rights, contribute to the development of their communities, and "ultimately create a more peaceful world."[24] WLP puts emphasis on women's leadership in an explicit and systematic manner, principally through the production and circulation of curricular and training manuals. The promotion of women's human rights and the creation of egalitarian democratic societies through women's leadership are central objectives achieved in part through the use of *Leading to Choices* and other manuals and through the training of trainers in a long-term, bottom-up, participatory process. The materials have been developed in a protracted and deliberative process, with consultation and testing across the partnership. In this way, WLP evinces the kind of democratic practices and internal democratic culture emphasized by many feminist organizations.

Virtual activism and communication are other key features. For WLP, the goals of building capacity (strengthening women's organizations) and building democracy (strengthening civil society and the public sphere) are carried out in both virtual and physical spaces. Through its own website and links to partner websites, WLP creates a virtual community for women's human rights and a transnational and collective identity via websites, blogs, and e-communications. WLP is an exceptionally tech-savvy TFN, with such Internet-related features as Facebook, Twitter, Flickr, and YouTube accounts; the Our Vision & Our Voices blog; and an information technology manual titled *Making IT Our Own*. Of course, face-to-face meetings are needed to enhance such community, identity, and solidarity; WLP makes this happen at annual meetings, trainings, and regional institutes. But WLP has harnessed the opportunities afforded by the new information and communication technologies for rapid communication and mobilization regarding Muslim women's human rights. In 2007–2008, for example, WLP was active in mobilizing international support for Iranian feminists who were subjected to harassment, imprisonment, or prosecution by the authorities of the Islamic Republic of Iran.

Through their virtual activism, therefore, both WLP and WLUML exemplify at least two key characteristics of social movement networks in an era of globalization: creating or actively participating in the transnational public sphere and creating and maintaining a collective identity as networkers for women's human rights.

CONFLICT, WAR, AND EMPIRE: FEMINIST RESPONSES

Chapter 1 mentioned one of the oldest transnational feminist networks and, indeed, one of the world's oldest peace organizations. The Women's International League for Peace and Freedom (WILPF) was founded in 1915 by thirteen hundred women activists from Europe and North America opposed to what became known as World War I. Feminists and women's groups have long been involved in peace work, with analyses of the causes and consequences of conflict, methods of conflict resolution and peace building, and conditions necessary for human security. The activities of antimilitarist and human rights groups such as WILPF, Women Strike for Peace (United States), the Women of Greenham Common (United Kingdom), and the Mothers and Grandmothers of the Plaza de Mayo (Argentina) are well known, and their legacy lies in ongoing efforts to "feminize" or "engender" peace, nuclear disarmament, and human rights. Women's peace activism has been long associated with world affairs.[25]

At the UN's Third World Conference on Women, which took place in Nairobi in 1985, the themes of equality, development, and peace were addressed by attendees in various ways. The Nairobi conference took place in the midst of the crisis of Third World indebtedness and the implementation of austerity policies recommended by the World Bank and the IMF. Feminists were quick to see the links among economic distress, political instability, and violence against women. As the Jamaican scholar-activist Lucille Mathurin Mair noted after Nairobi,

> This [economic] distress exists in a climate of mounting violence and militarism. . . . Violence follows an ideological continuum, starting from the domestic sphere where it is tolerated, if not positively ac-

cepted. It then moves to the public political arena where it is glamorized and even celebrated. . . . Women and children are the prime victims of this cult of aggression.[26]

The era of globalization and a new wave of conflicts brought even more urgency to the matter, spurring the formation of a number of new women-led peace and human rights organizations as well as greater professionalization of networks. It also led to a new international agreement concerning women, peace, and security. The 1990s saw conflicts in Afghanistan, Algeria, Bosnia, and Central Africa (principally Rwanda and Burundi), all of which were marked by serious violations of women's human rights. Women's groups responded by underscoring the specific vulnerability of women and girls during wartime, the pervasive nature of sexual abuse, and the need to include women's groups in peace negotiations. Newly formed feminist peace, human rights, and humanitarian organizations and networks included Women in Black, Medica Mondiale, Women Waging Peace, and Women for Women International. Advocacy networks and scholar-activists produced research to show that women's groups had been effective in peace building in Northern Ireland as well as in Bosnia, Burundi, and Liberia.

In response to such research, lobbying, and advocacy initiatives, the UN Security Council issued a resolution that was embraced by women's groups, if not necessarily by all governments. In March 2000 the Security Council, in its Proclamation on International Women's Day, recognized that gender equality is an integral component of peace. In October the council convened a special session to consider the situation of women in armed conflict. On October 31 it passed Resolution 1325, calling on governments—and the Security Council itself—to include women in negotiations and settlements with respect to conflict resolution and peace building.[27] Key points of the resolution are as follows:

- Increasing the representation of women at all decision-making levels
- Integrating a gender perspective into peacekeeping missions
- Appointing more women as special representatives and envoys of the secretary-general
- Supporting women's grassroots organizations in their peace initiatives

- Involving women as participants in peace negotiations and agreements
- Ensuring protection of and respect for the human rights of women and girls
- Protecting women and girls from gender-based violence
- Integrating a gender perspective into disarmament, demobilization, and reintegration of former combatants

While Security Council Resolution 1325 was widely hailed as a historic achievement in a domain usually considered off-limits to women and the preserve of men, its impact was unfortunately muted not long afterward, when new conflicts erupted that would sideline the resolution in the name of the "global war on terror."

The aftermath of September 11, 2001, and the invasion of Iraq in 2003 galvanized many women, who rallied to existing peace organizations or built new ones. In India, women's groups joined a coalition called Jang Roko Abhiyan (Antiwar Campaign), which condemned the massacre of American civilians on September 11 but called on the United States to accept responsibility for the fallout from past foreign policies and to refrain from military retaliation in Afghanistan that would very likely cause considerable civilian death and suffering.[28] In Pakistan, women's groups held a protest rally on September 25, 2001, against terrorism, religious fundamentalism, and war. The U.S.-based Feminist Majority issued a very measured statement on September 11 that pointed out the U.S. role in the 1980s in supplying "billions of dollars to fund, train, and arm the mujahideen, which gave rise to the Taliban." The statement continued, "Just as we must not condemn the Afghan people for the acts of terrorists, we also should not condemn Arabs and Muslims, the vast majority of whom do not support this so-called religious fanaticism. This extremism, which has now taken the lives of so many American citizens, Afghans, and others, is not about Islam, but is about the use of violence to achieve a political end."[29] A statement from the Medica Mondiale Kosovo women's center was especially pertinent:

> We have lived through war. We know what it is like to be attacked, to grieve, and to feel anger. We understand the urge for revenge is strong. And we know that it must not be given in to. We know that a violent

response can only bring more violence not justice. Instead, it kills more innocent victims and gives birth to new holy avengers. It begins a new cycle and perpetuates more hate, more insecurity, more fear and ultimately more death amongst civilians. We therefore urge the U.S. and its allies to temper their anger and to refrain from the folly of sweeping military solutions. Terrorists are not nations. And nations must not act like terrorists.[30]

The invasion of Iraq was preceded by massive antiwar protests across the globe. In the United States, progressive women's groups and feminist activists refused to side with the George W. Bush administration and took part in street and media protests. The radical feminist magazine *Off Our Backs* carried an article by veteran activist Starhawk, who wrote, "Oppression of women is real, in Muslim societies and non-Muslim societies around the globe. But women cannot be liberated by the tanks and bombs of those who are continuing centuries-old policies of exploitation, commandeering resources for themselves, and fomenting prejudice against the culture and heritage which is also a deep part of a woman's being."[31] A press release issued on March 28, 2003, by the U.S.-based feminist humanitarian group MADRE described a meeting of women's organizations worldwide (including itself) that gathered at the United Nations and urged the General Assembly to "unite for peace." It added, "This action follows a recent call in New Delhi made by women's organizations from over thirty-five countries condemning the Bush administration's war against Iraq and urging the General Assembly to challenge U.S. aggression."[32] The spring 2003 issue of *Ms. Magazine* carried a special action alert titled "No Time for Despair: Women Take Action Worldwide," signed by American feminists Robin Morgan, Ellie Smeal, and Gloria Steinem. Its authors referred to "an elective war launched against Iraq, where 50 percent of the population is under age fifteen. Yes, they are oppressed by a brutal dictatorship, but it's also clear—from polls showing that some 70 percent of Americans oppose Bush's unilateral action against Iraq—that a majority of us don't trust the judgment of our leader." At the bottom of the statement was a listing of women's organizations and progressive groups that *Ms. Magazine* readers could contact. Also included was a "National Council of Women's Organizations Statement on War with Iraq," stating in part that "U.S. foreign policy should be driven by human rights, justice, and equality—values that will decrease the threat of terrorism—and not by corporate interests or the desire to secure natural resources for U.S. consumption." The issue of Ms. Magazine also carried a statement by author and poet Grace Paley titled "Why Peace Is (More Than Ever) a Feminist Issue."[33]

The invasion of Iraq produced another women-led peace and antiwar organization—Code Pink—which grew in numbers and notoriety (among the Right) and fame (among the Left) throughout the decade. Code Pink was formed in 2002 by a group of women who had worked with each other as well as in other networks. Medea Benjamin cofounded Global Exchange in 1988 with Kevin Danaher; Jodie Evans had worked for former California governor Jerry Brown; and Gael Murphy was a longtime public health advisor in Africa and the Caribbean. The group's name is a play on the national security color codes established by the Bush administration in the aftermath of September 11, and Code Pink activists have shown their creativity and innovative style of protest in various ways. Wearing pink costumes and engaging in daring acts of public protest, they have become known for infiltrating congressional meetings, unfurling antiwar banners, shouting antiwar slogans, and badgering members of Congress about their stand on the war, military spending, health care for veterans, and support for Iraqi civilians. One of their innovations is the issuance of "pink slips" to political culprits. In one daring act, a Code Pink activist, her hands painted red, approached Secretary of State Condoleezza Rice on Capitol Hill and accused her of having the blood of the Iraqi people on her hands.[34]

In addition, Code Pink's repertoire includes feminist humanitarianism and international solidarity, as evidenced by visits to Baghdad to demonstrate opposition to war and solidarity with the Iraqi people. Medea Benjamin, Jodie Evans, and Sand Brim travelled to Iraq in February and December 2003. In December 2004, Code Pink coordinated the historic Families for Peace delegation to Amman, Jordan, involving the three Code Pink founders and a member of the antiwar group United for Peace and Justice (UFPJ), along with several relatives of fallen American soldiers and families of September 11 victims. According to one report, "In an inspiring act of humanity and generosity, they brought with them $650,000 in medical supplies and other aid for the Fallujah refugees who were forced from their homes when the

Americans destroyed their city. Although the American press failed to cover this unprecedented visit, the mission garnered enormous attention from Al-Jazeera, Al-Arabiyya, and Dubai and Iranian television, who witnessed firsthand the depths of American compassion."[35] Code Pink's recent literature presents its activities and goals as "bringing our war dollars home; holding our leaders accountable for war crimes; responding to Obama's promises; boycotting war profiteers; defending the truth tellers and changing the game; demilitarizing our society; countering corporate corruption; building bridges, not bombs; cultivating vibrant communities and a healthy planet; and declaring (loudly and proudly) that war is insane."

Code Pink has been involved in coalitions with other feminist and social justice networks, including the National Organization for Women and United for Peace and Justice, and takes part in the World Social Forum. It may be the most colorful as well as audacious of women's peace groups, but it is not alone. MADRE, Women in Black, Women for Women International, and Code Pink carry out operational activities, information exchange, and solidarity work. Networks such as the Women's Initiatives for Gender Justice, Women in Conflict Zones Network, and Women Waging Peace engage in research, advocacy, and networking to ensure that war criminals are brought to justice and that local women's peace groups are recognized. They also advocate for the International Criminal Court (established in 1999 as the first international war crimes court) and for Security Council Resolution 1325. Six women Nobel Peace Prize winners formed the Nobel Women's Initiative in 2007, and its first international conference focused on women, conflict, peace, and security in the Middle East.[36] Of the peace-oriented transnational feminist networks, Code Pink is politically closest to MADRE. But while Code Pink is known for its direct action, MADRE has built a reputation for its operational work, or what I call feminist humanitarianism.

While almost all transnational feminist networks may be regarded as internationalist and solidaristic—inasmuch as they are concerned about the plight of "sisters" across borders and boundaries of nationality, religion, and class—not all engage in feminist humanitarianism. I define feminist humanitarianism as operational work, carried out by women's groups to alleviate suffering or to meet basic needs while being informed by the strategic goal of achieving women's human rights and gender equality. This understanding is very different from the "humanitarian intervention" that was conceptualized in the 1990s to justify bombing Serbia and later invading Iraq.

MADRE began its work during the U.S.- sponsored Contra war in Nicaragua in 1983 and initially devoted itself to that issue. MADRE's work in Iraq dates back to the 1991 Gulf War, when it began collecting an assortment of needed supplies for Iraqi families, including milk and medicine. It continued this work throughout the 1990s and frequently decried the detrimental effects on women and children of the sanctions regime. After the 2003 invasion and occupation of Iraq, MADRE partnered with UNICEF-Iraq and provided twenty-five thousand citizens with supplies and emergency aid, including essential drugs and medical supplies for those in need. At the same time, it has worked in Cuba, Nicaragua, El Salvador, Palestine, and Haiti. In all countries MADRE partners with sister organizations.[37]

KOFAVIV (Komisyon Fanm Viktim pou Viktim; Commission of Women Victims for Victims) is one of MADRE's programs based in Haiti. First formed in late 2004, the group is run by women from Port-au-Prince who were raped in their poor neighborhoods during the attacks of the 1991–1994 military dictatorship. According to the MADRE website, "The women of KOFAVIV attempted to prepare a landmark legal case against the perpetrators, including the military's top dictators and paramilitary leaders, for the use of rape as a political weapon." In February 29, 2004, the attempt was interrupted due to the violence associated with the removal of President Jean-Bertrand Aristide from office.[38] MADRE also made efforts toward developmental issues and human rights policies in Sudan. Working with Zenab for Women in Development to provide emergency aid to displaced women and families in Darfur, MADRE in 2005 sent $500,000 worth of clothing and bedding to small refugee camps for use during harsh weather and in combating illnesses such as malaria and meningitis.[39]

In another example of its feminist humanitarian work, MADRE has partnered with UNICEF to provide supplies in Iraq; it has also worked with the Organization of Women's Freedom in Iraq (OWFI) to support the creation of women's shelters for victims of domestic and community violence in Iraqi cities such as Baghdad, Kirkuk, Erbil, and Nasariyeh. The OWFI-MADRE campaign against "honor killings" gave rise to a web of shelters and an escape route for Iraqi women, which came to be known as the Underground Railroad for Iraqi Women.[40]

In addition to the collective efforts spearheaded by transnational feminist networks, scholar-activists have penned numerous op-ed pieces, journal articles, and books on wars in Afghanistan and Iraq, tying these to capitalism, militarism, and empire. Zillah Eisenstein's *Against Empire*, for example, is a powerful indictment of neoliberal globalization, imperial arrogance, and racism and a clarion call for a polyversal feminism and humanism. Cynthia Enloe's *Globalization and Militarism* offers a trenchant critique of masculinist international relations, especially in the context of the war against Iraq, while also noting the contributions of women peace builders across the globe.[41] Global peace action is a key strategy of transnational feminist activism.

GLOBAL FEMINISM AND GLOBAL JUSTICE

The global women's movement and the global justice movement are internetworked social movements. Many transnational feminist networks are active in the global justice movement and participate regularly in the World Social Forum (WSF). In the first forum (2001), women made up 54 percent of participants but less than 15 percent of the most important panelists in the official forum program. By the third forum (2003), two major feminist groups—the World March of Women and Latin America's Mercosur Feminist Articulation—were responsible for two of the five thematic areas. At the Fourth WSF in Mumbai, feminists were placed in charge of the development of several of the self-organized panels, and in 2005 over six thousand women's groups participated in the WSF. The Feminist Dialogues that took place at the Fifth World Social Forum focused on three key problems: neoliberal globalization, militarism and war, and fundamentalisms.[42] For several years, many activists felt that feminist issues were not present outside the Feminist Dialogues and sessions. For example, in a report on the Third European Social Forum (held in London, October 14–17, 2004), Amandine Bach of WIDE noted that the main demands were "stop the war; no to racism; end privatization; for a Europe of peace and social justice" and that gender justice seemed outside the forum's scope.[43] At the Africa Social Forum later that year (held in Lusaka, Zambia, December 10–14, 2004), women were in the minority because, in the words of the authors of a report on the forum, "the leadership of organizations and movements (i.e., those likely to represent organizations at international forums) are men." Amanda Alexander and Mandisa Mbali, the authors of the report, continued, "Essentially, we know that patriarchy and other forms of dominance are being re-inscribed within our movements for resistance." They cited Shallo Skaba, an Ethiopian coffee worker who had appeared at the African Court of Women to complain that "no one is looking for women's problems. No one considers all that women are doing."[44]

Feminist presence at the World Social Forum has improved. According to Jane Conway, "The 2004 WSF in Mumbai and the Americas Social Forum in Quito merit special attention as historical high points in making the forum feminist." She highlights the role of the World March of Women on the WSF International Council and notes that its slogan, "The world will not change without feminism, and feminists cannot change women's lives unless we change the world," met with roars of approval at the closing ceremonies at the 2002 WSF. What was distinct about the Mumbai WSF, she writes, was that its political vocabulary was expanded to include struggles against patriarchy, militarism and war, racism, casteism, and religious communalism alongside neoliberalism. The Feminist Dialogues that take place during the WSF frame feminism as "an ideology [that] attempts to understand the oppression and agency of women within a patriarchal structure and in the present neoliberal economic, social and political systems[; . . .] that is against fundamentalism, global capitalism, and imperialism[; . . .] which allies itself with the marginalized, dalit and indigenous peoples [; and . . .] which unfolds its practice everyday in our lives and continues the quest for collective and democratic functioning."[45]

In its April 2011 newsletter, WIDE reported that the WSF in Dakar showed that "another world is possible with women's rights and gender justice at its core." WIDE was pleased to see that representatives of the World March of Women (WMW), the Feminist Dialoguers, and La Via Campesina led many of the women's assemblies and that the WMW international coordinator, Miriam Nobre, served as co-coordinator in the Assembly of Social Movements (the plenary bringing together about three thousand people). This was an important acknowledgment, the WIDE report continued, of women's struggles as common social struggles.[46]

Global feminism shares with the global justice movement a common opposition to neoliberalism and militarism but also emphasizes an antifundamentalist action frame. In particular, WLUML has been alarmed by what it perceives to be a sympathetic stance toward Islamists on the part of some antiglobalization activists, on the basis of a common opposition to empire and to military occupations in Afghanistan, Iraq, and Palestine. In an appeal issued in February 2005 that was prepared for the World Social Forum in Porto Alegre and discussed at the Feminist Dialogues that immediately preceded the forum, WLUML decried what it saw as the beginning of an "unholy alliance between a growing number of anti-globalization activists, human rights activists and progressive people in the West in general with Muslim fundamentalists, and the gradual abandonment of progressive democratic forces from within Muslim countries and communities."

The statement continued,

> Disturbed by the discrimination and exclusion that affect people of migrant descent in Europe and North America, progressive forces in the West are keen to denounce racism—and rightly so. But subsequently, they often choose to sacrifice both women and our own internal indigenous democratic progressive opposition forces to fundamentalist theocratic dictatorship, on the altar of anti-racism. Or they censor their expressions of solidarity with us for fear of being accused of racism.
>
> Derailed by neocolonial invasions and wars, progressive forces are prepared to support any opposition to the superpowers. We have already witnessed prominent Left intellectuals and activists publicly share the view that they could not care less if fundamentalist theocratic regimes come to power in Palestine or Iraq, provided that the USA and Israel get booted out. We have witnessed representatives of fundamentalist organizations and their ideologists invited and cheered in Social Fora. We have witnessed prominent feminists defend the "right to veil"—and this sadly reminds us of the defense of the "cultural right" to female genital mutilation, some decades ago.
>
> We call on the democratic movement at large, on the antiglobalization movement gathered in Porto Alegre, and more specifically on the women's movement, to give international visibility and recognition to progressive democratic forces and to the women's movement within it, that oppose the fundamentalist theocratic project. We urge them all to stop supporting fundamentalists as though it were a legitimate response to situations of oppression.[47]

This outcry was prompted by two particular complaints: first, at several antiwar rallies in London, speakers from Muslim groups invited to share the platform began and ended their talks with chants of "Allah-u-Akbar," and second, an invitation to speak at the World Social Forum had been extended to the European Muslim intellectual Tariq Ramadan, who had earlier made statements defending the veil as integral to Islamic identity.[48] Similarly, WLUML considered French feminist Christine Delphy's defense of Muslim women's "right to veil" incoherent in the absence of an analysis of the complex context in which (re)veiling occurs. Pointing out that Islamists have no quarrel with capitalism, WLUML appealed to progressives not to sacrifice women's human rights in the name of a broad antiwar and anti-imperialist front.

Another outcry occurred in 2010 when antifundamentalist feminists took issue with human rights organizations' defense of several radical Islamists. Gita Sahgal, who led the gender department of Amnesty International, resigned in protest when the organization described Moazzam Begg as a "human rights defender." In the United States, the American Civil Liberties Union and the Center for Constitutional Rights (CCR) sued the U.S. government for the right to represent Anwar al-Awlaki, a U.S. citizen linked to al-Qaeda. As Meredith Tax rhetorically asked in one posting, "What does it mean for a human rights organization to take al-Qaeda as a client? . . . Can the same organization defend Islamic fundamentalists and their victims? . . . Who will defend the people on al-Awlaki's hit list from being assassinated by his followers?" She continued, "If the CCR becomes identified as defenders of al-Awlaki, will women who are victims of salafi/jihadists feel they can trust you with their own cases?" She referred to an analysis by Algerian American law professor and activist Karima Bennoune, who pointed out that civilians are caught between torture and terror, between the national security state, which is willing to torture, kidnap, assassinate, and use remote control bombers to eliminate its enemies, and Islamists who are willing to kidnap, assassinate, and blow themselves and others up to achieve their ends. To get beyond the dichotomy, Bennoune writes, "the human rights community, as a matter of basic principles of human rights, must hear (and respond to) the voices of victims of terrorism, their survivors, and all those who live in fear of such violence. . . . A human rights analysis of terrorism centers the discussion on victims and human dignity, instead of only on national security."[49]

STRATEGIES, COLLECTIVE IDENTITIES, AND CULTURAL FRAMES

Earlier in this chapter we referred to some of the tactics and strategies that transnational feminist networks deploy to achieve their goals: research, outreach, and advocacy; lobbying and engaging with domestic and global policy makers; organizing and coalition building; public protests and direct action. Here we revisit Chadwick Alger's framework (see chapter 2) to examine more closely the strategies pursued. First, like other transnational social movement groups, they create, activate, or join global networks to mobilize pressure outside states. TFNs build or take part in coalitions, such as Jubilee 2000, the Coalition to End the Third World Debt, the Women's International Coalition for Economic Justice, the Women and Trade Network, 50 Years Is Enough, Women's Eyes on the Bank, and United for Peace and Justice. After the Battle of Seattle in November 1999, feminist groups became active players in the global justice movement, helping to form the World Social Forum and the regional forums. And while women's groups have long been identified with peace movements, the new conflicts associated with globalization and American militarism have led to the creation of new transnational feminist peace networks. Working alone or in coalitions, transnational feminist networks mobilize pressure outside states via e-petitions, action alerts, and appeals; acts of civil disobedience; other forms of public protest; and sometimes direct action.

Second, TFNs participate in multilateral and intergovernmental political arenas. They observe and address UN departments such as the Economic and Social Council (ECOSOC) and bodies such as the Commission on the Status of Women (CSW), and they consult for UN agencies and regional commissions. As mentioned, they partner with the more sympathetic UN agencies, such as UNIFEM, UNFPA, and the new UN Women, but also lobby or bring pressure to bear on other multilateral organizations for policy changes. WIDE directs much of its attention to the international development policies of the European Union, preparing its own or joint statements for high-level EU meetings. Transnational feminist networks such as WLP or WIDE may provide technical assistance to partner organizations in the preparation of policy or legal briefs. By taking part in and submitting documents to intergovernmental organization (IGO) meetings, and by preparing background papers, briefing papers, and reports, they help to set agendas and increase expertise on issues. By lobbying delegates, they raise awareness and cultivate supporters. The purpose of such interaction with IGOs is to raise new issues—such as gender and trade, women's human rights, and violence against women in war zones—with a view toward influencing policy.

Third, TFNs act and agitate within states to enhance public awareness and participation. They work with labor and progressive religious groups, the media, and human rights groups on social policy and humanitarian, development, and militarization issues. They link with and support local partners, take part in local coalitions, and provoke or take part in public protests. In the context of the Arab Spring, TFNs extended solidarity to Arab women while also disseminating the concerns raised by Arab feminist organizations about the place of women's participation and rights in the new polities. Fourth, TFNs network with each other, in a sustained process of inter-networking and Internet-working. Many take part in the biannual meetings of the Association for Women's Rights in Development (AWID); they assist in each other's campaigns; and individuals might be active in more than one TFN. A coalition of women's groups—including WIDE, AWID, the Center for Women's Global Leadership, and the Feminist Alliance for International Action—issued a joint statement in March 2011 asking that UN Women "design its policy and program on women's economic empowerment from an economic, cultural, and social rights framework."

In all these ways, feminist activism spans local, national, regional, and global terrains. The ultimate goal of the strategies deployed by TFNs is not just to set agenda for policy reform but to contribute to normative cultural change and broader societal transformation. As such, transnational feminist networks reflect the possibilities inherent within global civil society. Transnational feminist activism also reflects the reach of, and mobilization opportunities afforded by, the new information and communication technologies.

The Internet has allowed transnational feminist networks (and other advocacy and activist networks) to retain flexibility, adaptability, and nonhierarchical features while also ensuring more efficiency in their operations. That is, TFNs are now able to perform optimally without having to become formal or bureaucratic organizations. Avoiding bureaucratization is particularly important to feminists, who prioritize process, inclusion, and participation. The network form of feminist organizing suggests a mode of cooperation that may be more conducive to the era of globalization, as well as more consistent with feminist goals of democratic, inclusive, participatory, decentralized, and nonhierarchical structures and processes. And the "gift" of the Internet has allowed them to transcend borders, boundaries, and barriers in their collective action against neoliberalism, militarism, and fundamentalisms.

What leads women from across the globe to common mobilizing structures and frames? Earlier in the chapter we identified three processes at the global level that had led women's rights activists to overcome North-South differences and form transnational feminist networks with such resonant frames as women's empowerment, women's human rights, gender equality, and gender justice. Here we identify material conditions at both the macro and micro levels that influence feminist activism. At a macro level, adverse economic policies, war, and patriarchal fundamentalisms—all aspects of globalization—affect and disadvantage women in distinct ways. These can have a galvanizing effect, especially when political opportunities and resources are available. A second macro-level influence is what we may call the global women's rights agenda, which includes international conventions and declarations such as CEDAW, ILO conventions on nondiscrimination and on maternal employment, the Beijing Declaration and Platform for Action, Security Council Resolution 1325, and Millennium Development Goal 3. Promoted by the United Nations and advocated by TFNs, the global women's rights agenda is especially resonant cross-culturally with working women across the globe and can inspire, motivate, and mobilize women. The repertoire of conventions and declarations constitutes an important set of tools that can legitimate women's rights activism in difficult cultural or political circumstances.

At a micro level, women's lived experiences within the family and society, including experiences of marginalization in the labor market and the polity, the continuing significance of the sexual division of labor, the largely unacknowledged importance of women's reproductive labor, and violence against women, can set the stage for receptivity to mobilizing processes. Such common material conditions and experiences can help create collective identities that are then fostered through sustained activism, whether in the virtual public sphere, on the streets, or at conferences. Similarly, framing strategies across movements or networks can create or reinforce collective identities.

However, we have seen that transnational feminism remains divided on some issues, notably abortion (as distinct from contraception) and sexual identity, which may have distinct resonances in specific cultural contexts. Peruvian feminist and WSF veteran Virginia Vargas makes a point of referring to "the diverse and plural feminisms that exist."[50] She notes that although all feminists are opposed to fundamentalism, they differ on reproductive and sexual rights. An example is what she calls "the dialogue of differences" between activists from India and Latin America. Latin American feminists view the right to contraception and abortion as central to female autonomy and bodily integrity, and they fight for their legalization and availability. In India, reproductive rights are recognized in Indian law, but this has not provided women with power or autonomy. Instead, abortion rights have been abused to favor female feticide and the birth of sons. For this reason, abortion is not viewed as a priority issue for many Indian feminists. Similarly, at the 2007 World Social Forum in Nairobi, heated arguments took place between representatives of progressive church groups and those supporting abortion and sexual rights.

Will these differences be resolved? Or will they persist, in the interest of maintaining and respecting diversity within global feminism? An advantage of the Internet is that sensitive issues can be discussed in less emotive ways than is sometimes the case with face-to-face encounters. On the other hand, the virtual public sphere can bypass direct observation, experience, and knowledge of others, which can assist in overcoming biases and creating new bonds of solidarity. For these reasons, activism will continue to proceed on both fronts—in the real and the virtual spheres alike. Differences and diversity, meanwhile, will be recognized and celebrated, or they will be accommodated and absorbed within the segmentary, polycentric, and reticulate nature of the global women's movement. After all, transnationalization is both a function of globalization's opportunity structure and a deliberate strategy to broaden the scope, reach, and representation of a social movement.

CONCLUSION

This chapter has discussed the women's rights movement as a global social movement—albeit one with segmentary, reticulate, and polycentric characteristics—and identified key social movement organizations and transnational feminist networks focused on issues of neoliberalism, antifundamentalism, women's human rights, and peace. The chapter has drawn attention to varieties of global feminist activism: research, advocacy, and lobbying; conferences, seminars, and meetings; solidarity and international networking; progressive humanitarian work; and protest and direct action. Transnational feminist frames such as women's human rights, empowerment, gender equality, and gender justice derive from analyses and critiques of the sexual division of labor and hypermasculinity and of institutions of global governance, U.S. militarism, and specific actions by states and nonstate actors; solidarity with women across the globe; and recommendations for a women-friendly democratic polity and set of social and economic policies. These have been presented at such global venues as UN conferences, meetings of multilateral organizations, and the World Social Forum. While feminists are cognizant of the strategic importance of securing allies in the world of multilateralism, they celebrate the WSF as an autonomous space for the convergence of social movement and civil society organizations, including feminist ones, and a critical venue for deliberative democracy. As such, they play an important role in helping to shape the agenda of the WSF and advancing feminist concerns and objectives. Clearly, transnational feminist politics is goal directed rather than identity based.

We have seen, too, that global feminists have had to tackle differences within their own movement as well as with other movements. Their capacity to acknowledge differences within an overall common frame of feminist opposition to patriarchy and neoliberalism attests to the strength of their democratic practices. Whether they are taking on neoliberal economic policy, violations of women's human rights, or war, there are striking similarities in the way that transnational feminists organize and mobilize—a combination of real and virtual activism arising from the contradictions of globalization and the persistence of gender inequality.

CHAPTER 6

THE GLOBAL
JUSTICE MOVEMENT

We don't want violence. . . . Our fight is to recover a right which is the right to education.

—Camila Vallejo, student protest leader, Chile*

The global justice movement (GJM) has been in formation since at least the late 1990s and has become the subject of many new studies. It is being analyzed as a reaction to neoliberal globalization, an expression of "globalization-from-below," a key element of global civil society, and an exemplar of the transnationalization of collective action. Comprised of NGOs, social movement and civil society organizations, transnational advocacy networks, unions, religious groups, and individual activists opposed to neoliberalism and war, the global justice movement exists, to varying degrees of coordination and activism, across regions (see table 6.1). It is arguably most active in Europe.[1] It convenes at the

Table 6.1. The Global Justice Movement: Issues and Types of Movements and Networks

Type of Movement or Network	Name	Activities and Frames
Environmental	Greenpeace; Earth First!; Friends of the Earth International	Environmental protection and sustainable development
Indigenous rights	Congreso Nacional Indígena de México; Confederación de Nacionalidades Indígenas del Ecuador; Zapatistas	Cultural and land rights
Feminist	Development Alternatives with Women for a New Era; Marche Mondiale des Femmes; Women Living under Muslim Laws; Network Women in Development Europe; Feminist Articulation Mercosur	Feminist dialogues; gender justice; women's human rights
Human rights	Amnesty International; Fédération International de Droits Humains; United Students against Sweatshops; Global Exchange	Civil, political, and socioeconomic rights of citizens and immigrants
Labor	Australian Council of Trade Unions; Canadian Labour Congress; Congress of South African Trade Unions; Korean Confederation of Trade Unions	Worker and trade union rights; combatting job loss and outsourcing; worker solidarity
Antipoverty	Oxfam; Jubilee South; Make Poverty History	Sustainable development; ending Third World debt; combatting neoliberalism
Peace	Peace Boat; Code Pink; Women's International League for Peace and Freedom; Stop the War Coalition; United for Peace and Justice	Combatting militarism and war; creating sustainable peace
Religious	Christian Aid; World Council of Churches; Catholic Agency for Overseas Development	Support for the poor; abolishing the debt; critiquing neoliberalism
Third Worldist	Focus on the Global South; Third World Network; Third World Forum	Combatting neoliberalism and imperialism; deglobalization and local/regional solutions
Anticorporate governance	50 Years Is Enough; Association for the Taxation of Financial Transactions and for Citizens' Action; Public Citizen; Occupy Wall Street	Democratizing global governance; taxing financial markets; "We are the 99%!"

Note: Some of the organizations and networks above are or have been on the International Council of the World Social Forum. Also, some are involved in two or more movements.

annual World Social Forum, regional forums, and on the web; it plans and coordinates activities; and it takes part in various forms of public engagement and protest activity to spread its ideas and recruit new supporters. Its campaigns include debt relief or cancellation as well as ending poverty in developing countries; taxing of financial speculations and movements; fair trade and labor rights; environmental protection; and reform or transformation of institutions of global governance.

The existence of the global justice movement, known as the "movement of movements," confirms that issues of class, inequality, and redistribution do not belong to a bygone era. Some theorists have counterposed the so-called old social movements of class-based mobilizations and economic demands with the more recent "new social movements," which focus on identity and lifestyle. In fact, the global justice movement is the inevitable result of the capitalistic features of the contemporary world-system and its attendant globalization processes. And while advocacy and public policy engagement certainly are part of the collective action repertoire of the movement, many activists are also likely to engage in direct action against what they see as the symbols of neoliberal capitalism. Examples are the encampments and acts of civil disobedience by participants in the Occupy Wall Street (OWS) movement in the United States and the street protests against austerity measures and cuts in social spending in Athens, Madrid, London, Santiago, and elsewhere.

This chapter describes the participants of the GJM and their organizations, leading figures, grievances and critiques, actions and strategies, and proposed alternatives. But first it examines the origins and antecedents of this movement. Although the Battle of Seattle in late 1999 is usually cited as the movement's takeoff and much of the literature notes the cycle of protests against neoliberalism that ensued throughout Europe and, to a lesser degree, North America, the movement's origins lie in an earlier cycle of protests that took place in the Third World against structural adjustment policies (SAPs). The literature on globalization and its discontents sometimes overlooks the structural adjustment episode and anti–International Monetary Fund (IMF) riots, but it should be noted that the SAPs of the 1980s and the trade agenda of the 1990s were part and parcel of the same global trend of neoliberal capitalism. Indeed, many of the older participants in today's global justice movement were involved in various protests against structural adjustments in the 1980s. Many also were active in solidarity movements for Central America, South Africa, and Palestine. Thus, in recognizing the links between structural adjustments and neoliberal financialization and trade, we also should note the two cycles of collective action, one of which took place largely in the Global South. In the present century's first decade, media reports tended to focus on dramatic protests in Europe and North America, but we should recognize the genuinely global nature of the movement for economic justice and its strong roots in the developing world, especially Brazil, where the World Social Forum (WSF), a key institution of the global justice movement, was born.

FROM STRUCTURAL ADJUSTMENTS AND ANTI-IMF RIOTS TO THE GLOBAL TRADE AGENDA AND PROTESTS AGAINST THE WORLD TRADE ORGANIZATION

Structural adjustment policies were first implemented in some African and Latin American countries as a result of the debt crisis in the 1970s and early 1980s. The policy changes were conditions for receiving new loans from the IMF or World Bank or for acquiring lower interest rates on existing loans. The conditions were implemented to ensure that the money lent would be spent in agreement with the general goals of the loan. The policies aimed to balance budgets and increase competitiveness through trade and price liberalization. Some of the conditions for structural adjustment included cutting social expenditures (also known as austerity), devaluation of currencies, trade liberalization, balancing budgets and not overspending, removing price controls and state subsidies, and improving governance and fighting corruption. By the late 1980s, some seventy countries of the Global South had submitted to the World Bank and IMF programs. Economist Lance Taylor and his associates, among others, documented the difficulties of economic reform.[2]

SAPs came to be criticized by activists for halting development, exacerbating poverty, and creating new categories of the poor. Debt servicing and balanced budgets required austerity measures that led governments to halt development planning, cut back on social spending, or seek "cost recovery" through the implementation of "user fees" in sectors such as health and education, as well as through the elimination of subsidies for utilities and basic foodstuffs. Other measures, such as foreign exchange restructuring and contraction of the public-sector wage bill, resulted in a reduction of real wages, rising unemployment, and deteriorating living standards, as studies commissioned by UN agencies such as the United Nations Children's Fund (UNICEF) and the International Labour Organization found. As one activist noted, "Ghana is supposed to be one of the Bank's success stories, but in the 1990s, the Bank itself calculated that it would take the average Ghanaian forty years to regain the standard of living she had had in the 1970s." Walden Bello of the Philippines interpreted structural adjustment as a way of not only instituting market discipline but also disciplining the Third World and imposing a single economic model, that of global neoliberal capitalism. Among the milestones he identifies in the process of institutionalizing neoliberalism are "the IMF's new role as the watchdog of the Third World countries' external economic relations in the 1970s; the universalization of structural adjustment in the 1980s; and the unilateralist trade campaign waged against the Asian 'tiger economies' by Washington beginning in the early 1980s."[3]

When highly indebted Third World countries followed the policy advice of traveling World Bank and IMF economists without consulting trade unions or civil society organizations, and when households began to feel the financial pinch, popular protest was inevitable. A cycle of protests—at the time called food riots or anti-IMF riots—enveloped the Third World from the latter part of the 1970s, when the first structural adjustment policies were introduced, to the early 1990s. This pattern of public grievances is illustrated in table 6.2.

David Seddon and John Walton's analysis of structural adjustments and their listing of the anti-IMF riots show that Mexico experienced two such riots in 1986. Some years later, Mexico entered into discussions with the United States and Canada to form a regional free trade agreement that would ostensibly improve economic relations through the freer flow of capital and goods. Thus was born the North American Free Trade Agreement (NAFTA). Very quickly it came to be seen as a joint corporate-state strategy that had eschewed consultation with unions and civil society groups. Activists viewed it as a plan that would best serve the interests of American corporations rather than workers, and therefore protests arose from those on the left in all three countries.

Table 6.2. Number of Protests against Structural Adjustment by Country and Date

Country	Date of First Protest	Number
Peru	July 1976	14
Egypt	January 1977	1
Ghana	September 1978	1
Jamaica	January 1979	3
Liberia	April 1979	1
Philippines	February 1980	4
Zaire	May 1980	4
Turkey	July 1980	1
Morocco	June 1981	3
Sierra Leone	August 1981	2
Sudan	January 1982	3
Argentina	March 1982	11
Ecuador	October 1982	5
Chile	October 1982	7
Bolivia	March 1983	13
Brazil	April 1983	11
Panama	October 1983	2
Tunisia	January 1984	1
Dominican Republic	April 1984	3
Haiti	May 1985	6
El Salvador	May 1985	4
Costa Rica	May 1985	2
Guatemala	September 1985	1
Mexico	February 1986	2
Yugoslavia	November 1986	7
Zambia	December 1986	2
Poland	March 1987	6
Algeria	November 1987	3
Romania	November 1987	3
Nigeria	April 1988	2
Hungary	August 1988	2
Venezuela	February 1989	7
Jordan	April 1989	1
Ivory Coast	February 1990	1
Niger	February 1990	1
Iran	August 1991	1
Albania	February 1992	1
India	February 1992	3
Nepal	April 1992	1

Source: Walton and Seddon 1994.

The critique of NAFTA coincided with the emergence of the Zapatista movement. Its dramatic appearance in early 1994—on the day that Mexico officially adopted NAFTA—captured the imagination of leftists and globalization critics everywhere. With the charismatic Subcomandante Marcos as its chief spokesperson, the Zapatista Army of National Liberation (its Spanish acronym is EZLN) arose from the long-standing indigenous movement but was also a direct response and reaction to Mexico's adoption of NAFTA. As Marcos observed in an interview, "The economic system is not on the table for discussion," meaning that the "dialogue" proposed by the government of Vicente Fox would not include a rethinking of the country's neoliberal economic policy path. The solution, therefore, was a movement strategy at once innovative (as in the notion of "constructing a table" at which to sit with the government and engage in dialogue) and traditional (including an armed force).[4]

The decade also saw powerful international campaigns to cancel the Third World debt, establish fair trade with developing countries, and oppose the spread of genetically modified food by major corporations. These initiatives were framed in the language of development, morality, ethics, and justice, and they brought to international prominence advocacy groups such as Food First, Oxfam, and Greenpeace. Indeed, Greenpeace was one of the founding members of the 50 Years Is Enough network, which launched a campaign in 1994 calling for an end to the World Bank and the IMF on the basis of their failed policies in the developing world. Other groups involved in the network were the Development Group for Alternative Policies (D-Gap), the International Rivers Network, Global Exchange, Friends of the Earth, the Maryknoll Office for Global Concerns, and the United Methodist Women's Division.[5] A number of TFNs, notably the Development Alternatives with Women for a New Era (DAWN) and Network Women in Development Europe (WIDE), also were involved in the campaigns.

In the latter part of the 1990s, the antidebt campaign collected millions of signatures and held successful mass actions involving tens of thousands of people. Called Jubilee 2000, the campaign took its name from the biblical notion of the Jubilee, or periodic forgiveness of debts, and attracted many progressive religious persons. This powerful coalition of left-wing and religious groups aimed to cultivate international concern and mobilization for the elimination of Third World debt. In

1998, when leaders of the core countries met in Birmingham, England, at the invitation of British prime minister Tony Blair, some seventy thousand activists congregated to form a human chain ("make a chain to break the chains of debt") to tell the G7 summit that it had to act on debt cancellation. The campaign proved highly influential and effective, and politicians agreed to cancel billion of dollars worth of debt for forty-two developing countries.[6]

In the United States, activists for labor rights launched campaigns to draw national and international attention to sweatshop conditions in the global commodity chains that were producing cheap goods for retail enterprises such as Nike, the Gap, and Walmart. The campaign drew students on college campuses across the United States, and protest actions in front of local Walmart stores became a staple of college towns.

In Europe, Asia, and Canada, concern began to grow over the new rules and regulations attached to the emerging world trade regime. Activists were alarmed by the creeping commercialization—through privatization and patents—of all manner of services, natural resources, and traditional knowledge. Other concerns were the future of biodiversity and the safety of genetically modified foods, which were being promoted by multinational agribusinesses and some governments.

Another major campaign in the late 1990s was the worldwide opposition to the Multilateral Agreement on Investment (MAI). From 1995, the MAI was being negotiated in secret at the Organisation for Economic Co-operation and Development in Paris and was tied to what activists later would call the "new global trade agenda" led by the World Trade Organization (WTO). The MAI would have enabled governments to hasten trade agreements and given huge advantages to transnational corporations, allowing them the right to sue governments for introducing measures that might limit their present or even future profits.[7] The U.S. administration of President Bill Clinton was in favor of such a fast-track negotiating authority, but the proposed MAI came to the attention of critics. Activists in the Global South raised the alarm, and in the United States, leading roles in the anti-MAI coalition were played by Ralph Nader, Lori Wallach, and others within the Washington-based advocacy association Public Citizen. After the details of the secret agreement became public across Europe and North America, the bad publicity came to worry politicians in France, whose ruling coalition of socialists, communists, and greens decided to withdraw from the MAI negotiations. This disruption effectively killed the MAI, which was considered a major victory for the emerging global justice movement.

In the Global South, the policies of structural adjustment were being succeeded by the full transition from the former model of state-directed economic development with large public sectors, high government spending, and protection of domestic industries to a neoliberal model of denationalization, privatization, and liberalization of prices and trade. The shift to free markets, however, was not smooth, as market volatility created regional macroeconomic and financial crises in Latin America and Southeast Asia. Mexico and Argentina were hit especially hard in the mid-1990s, but working people throughout the two regions experienced declining labor earnings, rising unemployment, and inflation.[0]

Concern over global developments and the social implications of the neoliberal economic policy turn set the stage for the now famous Battle of Seattle. In late November 1999, the WTO's Ministerial Conference was scheduled to hold a millennial round of world trade negotiations in Seattle, a coastal city in the U.S. state of Washington that was home to the Boeing Corporation and Microsoft. There, some thirty thousand militants blocked the delegates' entry to the conference. The Battle of Seattle has become a watershed event in the history of the global justice movement and is widely seen as the precipitating act. It was followed by a cycle of protests against the WTO, the World Bank, the IMF, and the G8. (The G7 became the G8 with the inclusion of Russia.) Although there was a brief lull in the protests following the attacks of September 11, 2001, the actions against neoliberal capitalism continued and expanded into work against the invasion and occupation of Iraq and U.S. plans for the privatization and sale of Iraqi economic assets and natural resources, including its oil industry. What is more, the mobilizations assumed an increasingly coordinated nature, culminating in the creation of a new global activist institution, the World Social Forum, which first convened in Porto Alegre, Brazil, a stronghold of the left-wing Workers' Party (PT), in 2001.

TRANSNATIONAL OPPORTUNITIES

The preceding narrative of movement activity and emphases—from sporadic, nationally based structural adjustment protests and "food riots" to highly coordinated trade and antiglobalization demonstrations—helps us to understand the links between global economic restructuring and collective action, or how globalization-from-above engendered globalization-from-below. Still, such a discussion raises questions about how and why global mobilizations were able to emerge when they did. To better explain the rise of the global justice movement and its new institution, the World Social Forum, we return to social movement theory and examine the political opportunities that were available to movement activists. In particular, we identify three transnational opportunities that were conducive to the emergence and expansion of the new mobilizing structures: the spread and increasing use of the Internet, the UN conferences of the 1990s, and the coming to power of the Workers' Party in Brazil. That these events should have occurred at the same time as neoconservative intellectuals were touting the "end of history" and a world future of liberal democracy and capitalism captures the ironies and paradoxes of history. Let us examine these events more closely.

The end of the Cold War coincided with the spread of new information and communications technologies, and together these developments offered opportunities for cross-border meetings, organizing, and mobilizing. Travel across borders once difficult to traverse became easier and cheaper, while the Internet made communications faster and more expansive. Personal computers were now cheaper to buy, and e-mail became an increasingly common form of communication. The Internet allowed for the formation of numerous websites that became increasingly interactive; they were important sources of information and exchange as well as highly effective mobilizing tools for planning "global days of action." Movement media such as Indymedia captured various protests on film, issuing videos that were shown on campuses and at community meetings in North America, helping to recruit more people to the emerging global justice movement. In the new century, scholars studied the implications of Internet-based mobilizations, or "cyberactivism," in terms of not only recruitment but also the creation of a "virtual civil society," a "transnational public sphere," and, indeed, "cyberdemocracy."[9]

The United Nations held a series of world conferences in the 1990s, beginning with its Conference on Environment and Development (UNCED) in 1991, and activist groups were able to network at the parallel NGO forums (see table 6.3). The UN meetings in particular offered political space for the discussion of proposals such as the Tobin tax, while the many conventions, standards, and norms associated with UN conferences provided moral legitimacy to the movement's call for the globalization of rights. We can regard the occurrence of UN meetings in the 1990s as the making of a transnational political opportunity structure conducive to the growth of all manner of nongovernmental

Table 6.3. UN Conferences of the 1990s: Transnational Opportunities for Mobilizations and Framings

UN Conference	Intergovernmental Conference Themes	NGO/Activist Frames
Conference on Environment and Development (Rio de Janeiro, June 1992)	Environmental protection; poverty and environmental degradation; sustainable development	The "plunder of nature and knowledge"; protecting biodiversity; ending privatization and commercialization of "the commons"; reducing pollution, CO_2 emissions, and waste
World Conference on Human Rights (Vienna, June 1993)	Status of human rights conventions and practice in the world	Human rights; indigenous people's rights; "women's rights are human rights"
International Conference on Population and Development (Cairo, September 1994)	Population growth; family planning	Reproductive health and rights for women
World Summit on Social Development (Copenhagen, March 1995)	Poverty alleviation; employment generation; tackling social exclusion	Promoting welfare; financing development through the Tobin tax; combatting structural adjustment and Third World debt
Fourth World Conference on Women (Beijing, September 1995)	Addressing twelve critical areas of concern regarding women and girls	Political and economic empowerment; gender equality; human rights for women and girls
Conference on Human Settlements (Habitat II; Istanbul, 1996)	Promoting socially and environmentally sustainable human settlements and adequate shelter for all	Empowering the urban poor; transforming cities into safer, healthier, greener places; reversing or preventing privatization of public utilities

organizations, activist groups, and transnational advocacy networks. At the UN conferences, activists could lobby delegates and policy makers, disseminate their publications, and interact with each other.

In the 1990s, therefore, global developments provided an impetus for concerted and collective action. Both symbolic and material resources became available to groups critical of the growing power of multinational corporations, international financial institutions, and the neoliberal economic policy agenda. Scholar-activists not only in Europe and North America but also in India, the Philippines, Malaysia, Brazil, and sub-Saharan Africa mobilized their own resources to form or join networks critical of creeping globalization. These included Focus on the Global South, Environnement et Développement du Tiers Monde (ENDA), and the Third World Network, formed by activists from the Philippines, Malaysia, Thailand, Senegal, and India. In some regions, opposition to the presence of the U.S. military was also on the agenda. Regional activism in Southeast Asia helped shut down American military bases in the Philippines in the early 1990s.[10]

A third important opportunity came in the form of the October 2002 Brazilian elections that saw the formation of a left-wing government headed by President Luiz Ignacio "Lula" da Silva of the Workers' Party. The city of Porto Alegre had become the stronghold of the PT, and movement activists were invited there to strategize and plan activities. In 2001 the city played host to the First WSF, planned explicitly as a counterconference to the World Economic Forum, held in Davos, Switzerland, and attended by world politicians, policy makers, and corporate heads. As Bello observed, "What the Brazilians were proposing was a safe space where people in the movement could come together to affirm their solidarity."[11] The election of Lula da Silva proved especially fortuitous to the global justice movement's resource mobilization and to the WSF: the PT continued to lend moral and financial support to this important transnational institution.

THE GLOBAL JUSTICE
MOVEMENT'S CYCLE OF PROTESTS

Documenting the growth of mobilizations across the globe is a key research strategy of scholars of transnational social movements. Italian scholars Mario Pianta and Raffaele Marchetti, among others, tracked the growth of global civil society events and showed a steady and rapid increase after 1998. These included protests against the U.S. war against and occupation of Iraq held on February 15, 2003, March 20, 2004, March 19, 2005, and March 18, 2006.[12] U.S. sociologist Bruce Podobnik carried out events analysis to examine the global spread and sustained nature of protests between 1998 and 2004, as well as the number of protesters at each event. He has also grouped the protests into five categories of "summit events": WTO ministerials, IMF/World Bank annual meetings, G8 summits, World Economic Forums, and World Social Forums.[13] Faculty and students of world-system theory from the University of California, Riverside, distributed surveys at the World Social Forum to capture some key characteristics of movement participants.

In short, the next major mobilizations after the Battle of Seattle took place in Bangkok in February 2000, when a thousand activists marched on a UN trade conference calling for radical changes to the global financial system, which they claimed kept a majority of the world in poverty. This event was followed by the UN Millennium Forum of NGOs in New York in May 2000, with 1,350 representatives of more than one thousand NGOs. The cycle of protests continued through most of 2000 and 2001 and included the anticapitalist protests in London on May Day 2000, the antiglobalization protests in Melbourne and Prague in September 2000 and in Montreal the following month, and protests in Zurich in January 2001. When the World Economic Forum met at Davos in February 2001, protests took place there too. The cycle of protests continued in Quebec City, Canada, in April 2001, in Goteborg, Sweden, in June during the EU summit, and the following month in Genoa, Italy, where the G8 were meeting. The demonstrators in Genoa numbered three hundred thousand. In Genoa the police turned nasty; one protester was killed, and dozens were hospitalized, while many activists were taken into custody after the police raids. The tragedy of September 11 put a temporary halt to the antiglobalization protests, especially in the United States, but they resumed in early 2002. In February 2002 the World Economic Forum met in New York, and about one thousand antiglobalization protesters appeared. That same month in Italy, fully 3 million people came out to protest a new labor law. In March, as the EU summit took place in Spain, about five hundred thousand people held an anticapitalist protest in Barcelona.[14]

The year 2002 saw increasing activism on war and peace issues, which intensified after the decision by the governments of U.S. president George W. Bush and British prime minister Tony Blair to invade Iraq. In addition to protesting neoliberal capitalism, the Barcelona activists who gathered in March denounced Israeli actions in Palestine and U.S. plans to invade Iraq. The antiglobalization movement joined forces with the growing antiwar movement, culminating in a huge demonstration in Florence, Italy, in November 2002, where over half a million people from all over Europe gathered to protest capitalism and impending war. The start of 2003 saw demonstrations across the globe against the impending invasion of Iraq. On February 15, millions of people around the world joined in huge protests against the imminent war. Antiwar demonstrations in London and Washington, DC, also took place, led in part by activists from the global justice movement. And when the leaders of the main core countries, the G8, met in Evian, France, in early June 2003, an alternative summit, along with protests, took place in nearby Geneva, Switzerland.[15] After the 2003 invasion and occupation of Iraq by U.S. and U.K. forces, global protests increasingly took on an antiwar frame. In November 2007, activists from the No Bases Initiative in the Czech Republic staged protests against the plans of the Czech government to host the radar for a U.S. antimissile system. Throughout this period, participation at the World Social Forum grew significantly after its first meeting in 2001 (see table 6.4).

As Pianta and Marchetti aptly observed, "At the turn of the millennium, a structural scale shift occurred in the nature, identities, repertoires of actions, and strategies of global social movements."[16] The Battle of Seattle symbolized a radical challenge to neoliberal globalization and precipitated a cycle of protests, but this impetus converged with other factors, such as the coming to power of the Workers' Party in Brazil, to help launch the World Social Forum. The scope and scale of transnationalization increased dramatically, with activists sharing information and coordinating actions across borders and continents. Greater transnational cooperation among labor, environmental, feminist, and human rights activists was created through participation in the international conferences organized by the United Nations, as well as through cross-border labor struggles, transnational lobbying

Table 6.4.   Global Justice Movement Protests since the Battle of Seattle

Location	When	What Was Protested
Bangkok	February 2000	UN trade conference
Washington, DC	April 2000 and 2002	IMF/World Bank meeting
New York	September 2000	UN Millennium Summit
Melbourne	September 2000	World Economic Forum
Prague	September 2000	IMF/World Bank meeting
Quebec	April 2001	FTAA meeting
Genoa	July 2001	G8 summit
Gothenburg	June 2001	EU summit
Barcelona	March 2002	EU summit
Evian, Geneva	June 2003	G8 summit
Sheffield	June 2005	G8 summit; poverty
Global	2003–2007	Iraq invasion and war
Prague	November 2007	Planned U.S. bases
London	April 2009	G20 summit
Abruzzo	July 2009	G8 summit
Greece	May 2010[a]	Greek debt bailout
Toronto	June 2010	G20 summit
Barcelona, Madrid	May 2011[a]	Financial crisis; unemployment; welfare cuts
New York	September 2011[a]	Financial crisis; income inequality
Global	October 2011	Financial crisis; income inequality

Sources: Global Policy Forum, http://www.globalpolicy.org/ngos/advocacy/protest/archive/htm (accessed October 24, 2007); "Quebec City Protests April 2001," Internet Archive, http://www.archive.org/details/quebeccityprotest2001 (accessed April 18, 2012); Pianta and Marchetti 2007; Campaign for Peace and Democracy, http://www.cpdweb.org/statements/1007/stmt.html; Waddington and King 2007; various media reports.

[a]Continued in 2012.

campaigns, and global protest events planned and coordinated via the Internet. To illustrate this point, the Global Day of Action in solidarity with Occupy Wall Street took place on October 15, 2011, in nearly every European country, some fifteen countries in Latin America and about eleven in Asia, four countries in the Middle East (Egypt, Israel, Tunisia, and Turkey), and in South Africa, Canada, Australia, and New Zealand. In total, more than nine hundred cities across the world took part in the action day. Leading figures from various movements traveled across borders to forge alliances. Chilean student leader Camila Vallejo was quoted as saying, "This is a world battle that transcends all frontiers." While targets of protesters' anger differed from place to place, they revealed a common grievance against social and economic injustices.[17]

MOBILIZING STRUCTURES

The global justice movement is understood to be a "movement of movements," but it is possible to identify mobilizing structures, key institutions, and public intellectuals. As noted, a principal institution in the new century is the World Social Forum, coordinated by an International Council. As Virginia Vargas has stated, "The WSF harbors a multiplicity of movements whose common denominator is the struggle against the catastrophic consequences of neoliberalism. That struggle is their common ground."[18] In a sense, the WSF mirrors the global justice movement itself, and a conscious effort was made to include within the International Council as many associations as possible that reflected the GJM's breadth. The GJM is highly networked, but according to one survey, the overall structure "shows a multicentric network organized around four main movements that serve as bridges that link other movements to one another: peace, global justice, human rights, and environmental."[19] Participants are activists, policy experts, students, intellectuals, journalists, and artists. Campaigns focus on ending poverty in developing countries, the taxing of capital movements, debt relief or cancellation, fair trade, global human rights, and reform of international intergovernmental organizations.

Italian sociologist Donatella della Porta has drawn attention to the crucial role played by transnational networks in the organization of the global justice movement. She defines a transnational network as "a permanent coordination among different civil society organizations (and sometimes individuals such as experts), located in several countries, based on a shared frame on at least one specific global issue, and developing joint campaigns and social mobilizations against common targets at the national or supranational levels."[20] This would be an apt definition for the GJM's sustained and coordinated activities, carried out by organizations in both the Global South and the Global North. Well-known networks in the former region include the Third World Network, Focus on the Global South, ENDA, and DAWN. In Europe and North America, one finds the Council of Canadians; Association for the Taxation of Financial Transactions and for Citizens' Action (ATTAC), with networks in France, Germany, Sweden, Norway, Italy, and other countries; Christian Aid and Globalize Resistance (United Kingdom); Movimiento de Resistancia Global (Spain); Center of Concern and Global Exchange (United States); and transnational feminist networks such as WIDE, Women's Environment and Development Organization, and the Women's International Coalition for Economic Justice. In North America, the movement also includes university-based student groups and left-wing community organizations.[21]

For reasons having to do with the more social democratic nature of its political culture as well as the availability of all manner of resources, Europe has an especially strong presence in the GJM, involving unions, progressive religious groups, the Old and New Lefts, farmers, environmentalists, and representatives of some political parties (notably greens and communists). A brief diversion on ATTAC is instructive about the strength of the global justice movement in Europe, the influence of this particular civil society movement, and its global reach via cyberactivism. ATTAC, "an action-oriented popular education movement," was founded in France in late 1998 and, as of 2012, existed in thirty-four countries. Inspired by the late Professor James Tobin's proposal, it aims to tax financial markets and transnational corporations in order to redistribute income globally. ATTAC is also against Third World debt and tax havens and demands the complete restructuring of the World Bank, IMF, and WTO in order to move toward greater global economic justice.[22] ATTAC does not regard itself as an NGO but as a movement—one of the key movements within the global justice movement. Its website offers information in four languages—including the recurrent message "The world is not for sale"—and some of its documents are translated into thirteen languages. According to one account, ATTAC's website receives around 4 million hits from 130 countries per month, about thirty-nine thousand documents are downloaded every day, and more than eighty thousand people are subscribed to ATTAC's weekly e-mail newsletter.[23] Public intellectuals associated with ATTAC—including Bernard Cassen and Susan George—have been prominent in the global justice movement as a whole, as well as in the World Social Forum.

Other public intellectuals associated with the GJM are Arundhati Roy, Vandana Shiva, Naomi Klein, Medea Benjamin, Virginia Vargas, Tariq Ali, Walden Bello, Martin Khor, Samir Amin, Immanuel Wallerstein, José Bové, Kevin Danaher, George Monbiot, and Teivo Teivainen. They also play prominent roles in the World Social Forum.

THE WORLD SOCIAL FORUM

Organized as the popular alternative to the World Economic Forum, which brings together elites to develop global economic policies, the World Social Forum was initially supported by the Brazilian Workers' Party and the Brazilian Sem Terre (landless peasant movement). Intended as a forum for grassroots movements from all over the world, the WSF has most frequently been held in Porto Alegre, Brazil, a traditional stronghold of the PT. The first meeting of the WSF in 2001 reportedly drew 5,000 registered participants from 117 countries, but by the 2005 meeting, there were 155,000 registered participants from 135 countries.[24] The first three meetings took place in Porto Alegre, and in 2004 the venue shifted to Mumbai, India. It reverted to Porto Alegre in 2005, but in 2006 a "polycentric" WSF took place at three main venues: Bamako, Mali; Caracas, Venezuela; and Karachi, Pakistan. The meetings in 2007 and 2011 took place in Nairobi, Kenya, and Dakar, Senegal, respectively, in an effort to involve more Africans. In addition to the annual WSF since 2001, hundreds of regional, thematic, and local social forums have been organized, mostly within Latin America and Western Europe. Local forums have been slower to develop within the United States, but they have been held in Boston, Milwaukee, Austin, and Raleigh. In June 2007, the first U.S. social forum took place in Atlanta, Georgia, and the second convened in Detroit, Michigan, in June 2010.

The size and scale of networks within the GJM/WSF is considerable. As Tom Mertes explains, the Brazilian Sem Terre itself counts in its ranks over a third of a million landless families—"and this is not a passive, card-carrying membership but one defined by taking action: risking the wrath of *latifundários* and the state by occupying land. Within this layer there are, again, around twenty thousand activists."[25] Mertes goes on to compare the massive size of the landless peasant movement to the far smaller scale of individual North Atlantic networks. On the other hand, there are numerous, and very active, North Atlantic networks, including unions, progressive religious groups, feminist groups, and an array of left-wing and social justice activists. They have the human, organizational, and financial resources to attend meetings, conferences, and protest events in their own countries and elsewhere.

While the World Social Forum may be described as an institution—with a mission and vision and a structure that includes a coordinating group (the International Council)—it is regarded by its adherents as an "open space" where activists from around the world can meet, exchange ideas, participate in cultural events, and coordinate actions. The events and the opportunity for democratic deliberation are open to all those opposed to neoliberal globalization and militarism but "exclude groups advocating armed resistance."[26] Research conducted by scholar-activists such as Donatella della Porta, Christopher Chase-Dunn, Boaventura de Sousa Santos, Jackie Smith, Marina Karides, and others shows that participants are connected with different movements and types of organizations, including local or national groups. Some participants are longtime veterans of transnational organizations and the Left. What connects them all, in addition to a shared antipathy for neoliberal globalization, is attachment and commitment to an expanded and inclusive form of democracy that encompasses civil, political, and social rights, enables active participation, and encourages civil dialogue and discussion.

In addition to democratic practices, on display at the social forums are alternative values, diverse cultures, and an emphasis on supporting local products. Fair trade, organic farming, environmental protection, and diversity (bio- and cultural) are promoted, along with concepts of equality, justice, and human rights. The products of neoliberalism are opposed: genetically modified foods, sweatshop labor, commercialization, and global capitalist structures. Opposition is mounted through publications, meetings, boycotts, marches, and (at times) direct action. Protest marches are often accompanied by a carnivalesque atmosphere and evidence of individual and collective creativity, including massive puppets, whistles, drums, and costumes. The global justice movement may be angry at neoliberal globalization, but it demonstrates creativity, parody, playfulness, and joy.

Who participates in the WSF? Led by Christopher Chase-Dunn, a team from the University of California, Riverside, launched a research project on the characteristics, political views, and political activity of WSF participants by surveying individuals attending these meetings. Research has found that most participants tend to come from the country or region in which the WSF is located. Thus, from 2001 to 2005, most participants were from Brazil and the larger Latin American region, followed distantly by participants from Europe and North America. Another survey similarly reported a preponderance of participants from Brazil and elsewhere in Latin America: Santos found that at the 2003 WSF, fully 86 percent of participants were Brazilians, but this proportion decreased to 80 percent at the 2005 WSF. At the 2005 WSF, the next largest group came from Argentina (13 percent), followed by the United States (9.5 percent). A significant proportion of participants are youth (fifteen to twenty-four years of age)—42 percent in 2005, most of whom declared themselves to be students. Most WSF participants are highly educated, with at least some years of university education. Still, 22 percent had between zero and twelve years of schooling only. This is suggestive of the cross-class as well as cross-cultural nature of WSF participants. At the 2005 WSF in Porto Alegre, the Riverside research team found that over one-fifth of their respondents were affiliated with a union. While many were members of professional or artists' unions, this outcome does suggest an affinity with the labor movement and the possibility for more coordinated action between sectors represented within the GJM.[27]

The study by Peter Smith and Elizabeth Smythe shows that WSF attendance increased dramatically after 2001, when twenty thousand persons attended the First WSF. In 2003, the number was 100,000, and in 2009 it was 115,000. Attendance also increased at regional and subregional forums, including in Algeria, Morocco, and Tunisia. In each region, social forum organizations have grown, although the authors found that the largest number of such organizations is found in Europe, notably in France and Italy.[28]

As noted, the International Council of the WSF has sought to be as representative as possible. As of 2006, out of 136 members, 33 percent were from Europe; 28 percent, from Latin America and the Caribbean; 12.5 percent, from North America; 9.6 percent, from Africa; 6.6 percent, from Asia; and 2.9 percent, from the Middle East (that is, four members). The council includes representation by a large number of major trade unions, regional associations, feminist groups, progressive religious groups, progressive media, and an array of civil society organizations. Feminist groups with members on the International Council have included Mercosur Feminist Articulation, DAWN, Forum des Femmes Africaines pour un Monde de l'Économie Solidaire, Fédération Démocratique Internationale des Femmes, International Gender and Trade Network, National Network of Autonomous Women's Groups, Rede Mulher e Habitat (Women and Shelter Network), Women's

Global Network for Reproductive Rights, and Marche Mondiale des Femmes/World March of Women.[29] In November 2011, most of these feminist organizations were still on the council. What is more, at least five Arab organizations were on the council. By reaching out to even small civil society organizations and including them in decision making and leadership, the International Council may be seen as a transmitter of the democracy frame and practice.

WOMEN, FEMINISM, AND THE WSF

Not all women's organizations are feminist in their discourses or goals; women-led organizations or campaigns may prioritize human rights, bread-and-butter issues, or environmental concerns over gender hierarchy. One such group, which is also very active within the World Social Forum is the Mothers and Grandmothers of the Plaza de Mayo. Initiated as a human rights group led by Argentinian women who had lost children to the military junta's "dirty war" of the 1970s, it aimed to gain information on the whereabouts of grandchildren born during their parents' incarceration and to achieve an end to dictatorship and the military's impunity. Famous throughout the world, it became one of the most studied women's movements in Latin America. Elizabeth Borland describes how the group's discourses and activism have in recent years encompassed issues related to neoliberalism, such as external debt, hunger, unemployment, and corruption.[30] This kind of frame alignment reflects the capacity of social movement organizations to resonate with diverse audiences, and it shows their recognition that new political realities require new repertoires of collective action.

As demonstrated in the previous chapter, global feminism and global justice share a common frame of challenging neoliberalism and militarism and calling for democratic decision making at all levels. At the 2002 World Social Forum, the International Gender and Trade Network (IGTN) produced a statement pointing out that "in the current trading system, women have been turned into producers and consumers of traded commodities and are even traded themselves." The document continued,

> In solidarity with our sisters across the globe, we acknowledge that another world will be possible when systems of inequitable power among

governments, among institutions, among peoples, and between women and men have been changed to represent the needs of the majority of people and not the market. . . .

IGTN representatives from Africa, Asia, Latin America, the Caribbean and North America here in Porto Alegre are calling for a halt to WTO, FTAA, the Cotonou Agreement and other regional negotiations that are inherently flawed and demand an alternative multilateral trading system that will include the incorporation of a democratic process, corporate accountability, gender and social impact assessments and a commitment to put human rights and social development at the core of all negotiations. Women have much to lose! Today, we women celebrate our power, our partnership and our vision for peace and social justice, and we will continue in the struggle because—ANOTHER WORLD IS POSSIBLE![31]

Initially the WSF saw feminist criticisms of underrepresentation and of the selection process for invited guests. Santos cites critiques from the Mothers and Grandmothers of the Plaza de Mayo, Flora Tristan Feminist Centre of Peru, and the Mercosur Feminist Articulation, but criticisms also were aired by DAWN and WIDE. At the Third WSF (2003), Santos notes, just 26 percent of speakers were women (ten women and twenty-eight men).[32] This marked an improvement in women's representation, but sadly there were cases of violence against women in the Youth Camp, where thirty-five thousand young people stayed. As a result, a security force was organized, the Brigadas Lilas, and this too became an issue.[33] Hegemonic masculinity seemed to be operating at two levels: that of representation of women and feminist issues and that of the security of young women. The potential crisis was resolved through dialogue and mechanisms to improve both safety and representation. At the Fourth and Fifth WSFs, feminist groups were put in charge of a number of key sessions. Women's attendance at the WSF has grown: about half of all participants are women, and many prominent spokespersons are women, including Arundhati Roy, Vandana Shiva, Virginia Vargas, Naomi Klein, Susan George, and Medea Benjamin. In addition, scholar-activists have noted women's growing presence and influence within La Via Campesina, a transnational peasant movement that has an active presence in the WSF. The influence of feminist and women's groups at the WSF has been steady, leading to an integration of women's rights issues into WSF declarations and objectives. For example, the Declaration of the Social Movements Assembly at both the 2011 WSF in Dakar and the 2012 WSF in Porto Alegre included the following frames:

Fight against transnational corporations
Fight for climate justice and food sovereignty
Fight against violence against women
Fight for peace and against war, colonialism, occupations and militarization of our territories[34]

DEMOCRATIC DELIBERATION AT THE WSF

Boaventura de Sousa Santos is a Portuguese scholar who is also on the Secretariat of the WSF. In a book he authored on the WSF, he describes the institution as "a set of forums—world, thematic, regional, subregional, national, municipal and local—that are organized according to the Charter of Principles." The fourteen-point Charter of Principles, drawn up and adopted in 2001, emphasizes the free flow of ideas and exchanges. It begins with the following statement:

The World Social Forum is an open meeting place for reflective thinking, democratic debate of ideas, formulation of proposals, free exchange of experiences and interlinking for effective action, by groups and movements of civil society that are opposed to neoliberalism and to domination of the world by capital and any form of imperialism, and are committed to building a planetary society directed towards fruitful relationships among Humankind and between it and the Earth.[35]

Apart from agreeing with the Charter of Principles, what do participants understand about globalization and its alternatives? A survey at the 2003 WSF found that for participants, globalization meant the following: a concentration of wealth that makes the rich richer and the poor poorer (81 percent); dominion of the world by capital, commanded by the big corporations (75 percent); and a new name for imperialism (68 percent). On the question of "the possibility of societies connecting on the planetary scale," responses were polarized: 47 percent totally or partially agreed, 34 percent totally or partially disagreed, and 20 percent were indifferent. Fully 78 percent disagreed with the statement that globalization meant "more opportunities for all, rich and poor." Participants had strong feelings about the means by which "another possible world" could be achieved: through the strengthening of civil society (94 percent), democratization of governments (78 percent), or democratization of multilateral organizations (63 percent). As for whether direct action with use of force could help achieve another world, fully 84 percent of respondents totally or partially disagreed.[36]

Many participants see the WSF as an important instrument for achieving cohesiveness and more effective strategizing within the global justice movement. It is argued that movements are more likely to be cohesive when participants share political goals and beliefs, use similar strategies, and are culturally or socially alike. One result of the diversity within the WSF has been the emergence of a number of polarizing debates. A difference of opinion divides those who would like to see the WSF remain broad, inclusive, and fluid, primarily a site for democratic dialogue, and those who would like to see more deliberate action and a more unified movement. Other sites of disagreement include the issue of socialism or social emancipation (sometimes also framed as reform or revolution); whether to regard the state as enemy or potential ally; whether to focus on local, national, or global struggles; whether to engage in direct action, institutional action, or civil disobedience; and whether to place greater emphasis on the principle of equality or on the principle of respect for difference.[37] Those in favor of more deliberate action issued the Manifesto of Porto Alegre, which is discussed below.

Ellen Reese, Chase-Dunn, and their team identify five general debates:

> Whether to reform existing social structures and global governance institutions or to fundamentally transform them;
>
> Whether to create more economic growth in order to meet workers' demands for employment and goods or to reduce growth in order to protect the environment;
>
> Whether upholding international social and labor standards will protect human rights or simply protect Northern workers' interests at the expense of Southern workers' interests;
>
> Whether to uphold Western values as universal goals, to respect cultural diversity, or to reconstruct universal values in order to acknowledge the experiences of the marginalized;
>
> Whether to prioritize democratic initiatives at the local, national, or global levels.[38]

This diversity of perspectives is perhaps inevitable, given that WSF participants encompass indigenous groups, trade unionists, leftists, feminists, and social justice Catholics. This diversity parallels the different strands of the GJM identified by Pianta and Marchetti: (1) reformists with the aim of humanizing or civilizing globalization, (2) radical critics with a different project for global issues, (3) alternatives who self-organize activities outside the mainstream of the state and market spheres, and (4) resisters of neoliberal globalization who strive for a return to local and national spheres of action. These categories—which may be extended to describe those who participated in the Occupy Wall Street encampments and their numerous outside supporters—may be seen as dividing lines or as reflections of healthy debate around the common theme of opposition to neoliberal capitalism, imperialism, and war. For Kevin Danaher of Global Exchange, "Inside, outside, we're all on the same side."[39] In other words, there is a shared antipathy toward neoliberal economic policy and the inequalities that it has engendered.

FRAMING THE PROBLEM
AND PROPOSING SOLUTIONS

The global justice movement may have a diversity of grievances and critiques, but opposition to neoliberalism is its master frame and the basis for its collective action. We have seen how the critique of neoliberalism evolved from the earlier critique of structural adjustments and from the global shift away from Keynesian economics. Neoliberalism was behind the onerous Third World debt, deteriorating standards of living, and competition, conflict, and war. It was imposed by "globalizers" such as the World Bank, the IMF, multinational corporations, the WTO, and an emerging transnational capitalist class. But whereas Margaret Thatcher declared, "There is no alternative" to neoliberal globalization, the OWS frame of "We are the 99%!" draws attention to the gross inequality and unsustainability of neoliberalism's preference for the top 1 percent, while participants of the social forums confidently proclaim, "Another world is possible." What are the key elements of this "other world," or of the "other globalization" (*altermondialisation*)? First and perhaps foremost is the concept of international solidarity and identity construction of global citizenship. While many participants retain national attachments and remain rooted in local and national struggles, they are also highly vested in broader planetary and human rights concerns. Thus they have expressed strong opposition to the war in Iraq, sympathy with Palestinians and Lebanese victims of Israeli bombings, and concerns about environmental degradation and global climate change. "Another world" would be one without invasions, occupations, or wars; without hunger, poverty, exploitation, or pollution. A second feature is the GJM's focus on the world's policy environment, which has been captured by political and economic elites, or what some refer to as an oligarchy (the 1 percent identified by the OWS movement). "Another world" would be one in which the resources captured and monopolized by the 1 percent would be redistributed far more broadly. Grievances, critiques, and proposed alternatives may be summarized as follows:

- Against neoliberal globalization and "market fundamentalism" implemented by large corporations, the World Bank, the IMF, the WTO, the transnational capitalist class, and the United States
- Against the persistent North-South divide
- Against capital's domination over labor and the environment
- Against war and imperialism
- For economic justice, environmental justice, and gender justice
- For economic, social, and cultural rights, including rights of indigenous peoples and the landless
- For people-oriented sustainable development
- For local and global democracy
- For global solidarities
- For multilateralism and reform of institutions of global governance
- For a new worldwide program of taxation and redistribution[40]

Is another world, then, possible? Susan George of ATTAC is certain that it is, and she offers a set of ten guidelines for how to achieve it. First, activists need to know "what we're talking about." Globalization is not a harmless process of integrating states and markets, she observes, but rather the latest stage of world capitalism and the political framework that it helps to thrive, replete with inequalities. Second, the planet needs to be salvaged. The new world trade order permits corporations to produce, buy, sell, invest, and even patent life-forms across national borders, but it does not require companies to reduce waste, pollution, and environmental destruction. Third, the actors need to be identified. The World Bank and IMF (which George calls "the Terrible Twins") are responsible for imposing neoliberal restructuring on indebted Third World countries, while the WTO seeks to commercialize not only goods but also all services. Meanwhile, corporations are constantly seeking to lower labor costs, and the system's shift to the primacy of financial markets portends instability and crisis. Fourth, it is important to target the right adversaries. In this respect, George identifies various public and private actors on national, regional, international, and planetary (environmental) levels, such as states and their specific policies, employers' associations, regional bodies aligned with the neoliberal agenda, agribusinesses, the "Terrible Twins," the WTO, and various corporations. Fifth, Europe should "win the war within the West." George is clearly among those who view the EU and the European social model as an alternative to the American model of neoliberal capitalism and war making. But she adds that efforts by the European Commission and other regional bodies to take the neoliberal route must continue to be resisted. Sixth, the movement must include everyone and forge alliances. In her book, she goes on to discuss, in nuts-and-bolts terms, how to attract, recruit, and retain activists and how to forge alliances with progressive faith-based groups, peace groups, and political parties. Seventh, activists must combine knowledge and politics. She cites the example of the anti-MAI campaign, noting that the highly technical aspects of the secretive agreement had to be understood by activists and disseminated in ways that could resonate with a broader public. Eighth, educators must educate. Here she notes the important role of scholar-activists, or the many academics and "professional knowledge workers" involved in the GJM, and the ways that academics can advance "critical globalization studies." Ninth, George argues for the abandonment of cherished illusions. Here she warns NGOs against accepting corporate-initiated "dialogues" without setting clear objectives and conditions, and she notes the limits of individual lifestyle and consumption changes when compared with larger, sustained collective action such as boycotts. Finally, she insists that the movement continue to practice nonviolence. Nonviolence, she maintains, distinguishes the GJM from "the violence of the strong, the powerful, and the state." She also notes that activist recourse to violence is counterproductive, as the media tend to exaggerate it, causing it to eclipse other aspects of the movement or campaign.[41]

Other sets of proposals for overcoming neoliberal globalization and creating an alternative world have been issued from within the GJM. The Manifesto of Porto Alegre, produced and signed by a number of prominent scholar-activists at the 2005 WSF, proposed twelve ways to make another world possible. The first set of proposals pertained to economic measures, such as cancelling all debts in the Global South, establishing a tax on financial transactions, removing tax and bank account havens, ensuring that all citizens enjoy social security and pensions, promoting fair trade, ensuring food security and sovereignty, and prohibiting every form of patenting knowledge. Another group of recommendations had to do with promoting "cooperative life" in peace and justice, including combating all forms of discrimination and xenophobia, ending the destruction of the environment, and closing down military bases in foreign countries. The last set of proposals, on local and global democracy, called for the free flow of communication and information and for reforming and democratizing international organizations.[42]

Some activists and prominent figures within the GJM prefer "deglobalization" and a focus on local communities. In 2001, the International Forum on Globalization issued a statement titled "Alternatives to Economic Globalization" and proposed eight principles, summarized here: (1) a new democracy and popular sovereignty; (2) subsidiarity, or favoring the local; (3) ecological sustainability; (4) human rights; (5) jobs, livelihood, and employment; (6) food security and food safety; (7) equity; and (8) cultural, biological, economic, and social diversity.[43] Two of the signatories, Walden Bello of the Philippines and Vandana Shiva of India, have written extensively about globalization, the new global trade agenda, and alternative arrangements. Bello is a prominent advocate of deglobalization, by which he means the removal of all the new rules and regulations of trade, along with the attendant institutions of global governance. The new structures, he argues, constitute an "iron cage" that can only encourage "oligarchic decision-making" and an entrenchment of existing inequalities. The solution, he asserts, lies in "a fluid international system, where there are multiple zones of ambiguity that the less powerful can exploit in order to protect their interests." Vandana Shiva, a member of the International Forum on Globalization, has argued,

We want a new millennium based on economic democracy, not economic totalitarianism. The future is possible for humans and other species only if the principles of competition, organized greed, commodification of all life, monocultures and monopolies, and centralized global corporate control of our daily lives enshrined in the WTO are replaced by the principles of protection of people and nature, the obligation of giving and sharing diversity, and the decentralization and self-organization enshrined in our diverse cultures and national constitutions.[44]

And what is occurring "on the ground," in terms of alternatives to neoliberalism? Earlier in the century, Naomi Klein documented the Latin American "pink tide," noting that after Argentina's financial and political chaos in 2001, elections brought to power progressive, anti-neoliberal governments in Argentina, Bolivia, Brazil, Chile, Ecuador, Nicaragua, and Venezuela. New policies included nationalization of key sectors of the economy, land reform, and major investments in education, literacy, and health care. The governments of Venezuela, Costa Rica, Argentina, Uruguay, and Bolivia announced that they would no longer send students to the School of the Americas (now called the Western Hemisphere Institute for Security Cooperation), the police and military training center in Fort Benning, Georgia, that became infamous for graduating future torturers. In Brazil, the farmers of the Landless Workers' Movement (MST) formed hundreds of cooperatives to reclaim unused land. In Argentina, the movement of "recovered companies" was led by workers who resuscitated two hundred bankrupt businesses and turned them into democratically run cooperatives. Venezuelan president Hugo Chávez made the cooperatives in his own country a top political priority, giving them first refusal on government contracts and offering them economic incentives to trade with one another. Klein also describes the Bolivian Alternative for the Americas (ALBA), "the continent's retort to the Free Trade Area of the Americas, the now-buried corporatist dream of a free-trade zone stretching from Alaska to Tierra del Fuego." In this fair trade plan, Bolivia would provide gas at stable, discounted prices; Venezuela would offer heavily subsidized oil to poorer countries and share expertise in developing reserves; and Cuba would send thousands of doctors to deliver free health care all over the continent, while training students from other countries at its medical schools. Last but not least, a Bank of the South, planned as a regional alternative to current international financial institutions, would make loans to member countries and promote economic integration among them. Do these initiatives represent "another world" in practice? It may be too soon to tell, but Klein suggests that, at the very least, they augur a crisis of credibility for the World Bank, IMF, and WTO.[45] The crisis of credibility she identifies deepened in the wake of the economic and financial collapse of 2008 and is reflected in the emergence of anti-austerity protests in Europe and Chile, the spread of the Occupy Wall Street movement, and even those protests in Egypt and Tunisia that demanded less inequality and more attention to the social rights of citizens.

Another developing alternative to the hegemony of neoliberalism and the capitalist crisis is the solidarity economy, also known as the social economy. It refers to collective practices of sustainable development that are meant to contribute to building a more just and egalitarian world. Such forms of social enterprises—characterized by cooperatives or collectives under worker control or partnerships between groups of private citizens and (progressive) government geared toward the common good and citizen empowerment—are found in Quebec, Brazil, Spain, Bolivia, and Ecuador, among other countries. Workshops on the solidarity economy were plentiful at the United States Social Forum (USSF) in Detroit in June 2010, drawing interested crowds, especially from among young Americans who knew less about this alternative form of economic production and distribution. The U.S. Solidarity Economy Network (SEN), founded at the Atlanta social forum in 2007, organized many of the workshops, and representatives took part in the International Forum on Social and Solidarity Economy, which convened in Montreal in October 2011. As an alternative to corporate capitalism and state capitalism alike, the solidarity economy may be the pathway to the kind of economic citizenship that has eluded citizens throughout the world.[46]

CONCLUSION

In a sense, if contemporary globalization's origins lie in the changes to the world-economy that began in the 1970s and took off in the 1980s, then opposition to neoliberal globalization can be regarded as almost continuous. Nevertheless, it has been useful to distinguish two cycles of collective action as well as to establish their connections and their relationship to globalization. Santos correctly notes that the WSF was born in the Global South—at least in the Latin American South—and represents "an epistemology of the South." This is an important point confirming our argument that the semiperiphery of the world-system is the locus of much social movement activism and that a connection exists between the activities, institutions, and intellectuals of the contemporary global justice movement and those involved in earlier cycles of mobilizations and protest in the Third World. Such observations and affirmations, moreover, help to globalize social movement theory.

We have seen how the "movement of movements" has created a dynamic transnational public sphere replete with discussions, debates, research, and collaborative action. The GJM meets in physical space—notably at the World Social Forum and at various other regional forums, as well as on the streets of New York, London, Paris, Athens, and Santiago—but it has also created a virtual community through the Internet. What is more, the global justice movement is—like the women's rights movement—an integral part of global civil society, a democratic sphere beyond the spheres of the state and the market.

The study of the GJM calls into question previous hypotheses and claims regarding the evolution of social movements. In the 1980s and 1990s, some scholars were too quick to argue that the "new social movements" privileged identity, lifestyle, and values (in contradistinction to the "old social movement" issues of class, inequality, and power); that single-issue campaigns were more effective than broad politics; and that lobbying was now the preferred strategy. These hypotheses were premature even in the 1980s, when transnational feminist networks emerged and addressed major global issues.[47] The Battle of Seattle, the World Social Forum, the Arab Spring, and Occupy Wall Street have shown that a broad-based politics against economic injustice, inequality, and exploitation could feature as prominently in the twenty-first century as it did in centuries past.

CHAPTER 7

CONCLUSIONS AND PROGNOSTICATION

The philosophers have only interpreted the world, in various ways; the point, however, is to change it.

—Karl Marx, *Theses on Feuerbach*

This book has examined three transnational social movements, their relationship to globalization processes, and the similarities and differences among them. Drawing on a number of theoretical frameworks—primarily social movements, feminism, the world-system, and the world polity—we have looked at how social movements respond to political opportunities on a global scale, frame grievances and alternatives, and create new mobilizing structures. In the course of our study, we have drawn attention to the opportunities and resources available for movement building, the use of violence in social movements and transnational networks, the relationship of war to the global capitalist order, the salience of masculinities in global processes, and the contribution of social movements to democratization. This book began by posing a number of questions: What is the connection between globalization and social movements? How have people collectively responded to globalization? Have social movements changed to better confront globalization's economic, political, and cultural manifestations and challenges? And how are contemporary social movements and networks affecting the progression of globalization?

The economic, political, and cultural dimensions of globalization, I have argued, create opportunities and engender grievances that have resulted in a range of forms of collective action responses on a transnational scale, including those that are nonviolent and progressive and others that are violent and extremist. This book has considered the democratic potential of various types of social movements, specifically assessing the capacity of global feminism, global Islamism, and the global justice movement to build or deepen democracy. Questions were raised about the democratic potential of Islamist movements. The Arab Spring and the coming to power of Islamist parties in Egypt, Morocco, and Tunisia will be a good test of two opposing propositions: that moderate Islamist parties may indeed adopt democratic practices and work in coalitions with non-Islamist parties to build institutions enabling their citizens to enjoy civil, political, and social rights; and that moderate Islamist parties will remain fixated on cultural and identity issues, unwilling to share power and unable to build stable, democratic, and prosperous societies. Thus far, even moderate Islamist parties appear wanting in a commitment to human rights, women's equality, and a deliberative and participatory democracy that would also prioritize the social and economic rights of citizens.

We have seen how social movements utilize technology to their advantage; the Internet, in particular, has become a key mobilizing resource, a framing device, and a means by which collective identities are created and maintained. Although the Internet has not replaced physical sites of recruitment and action, it has enabled the creation of virtual activism and facilitated the emergence of transnational public spheres. Cybernetworking has helped movement mobilizations to proceed rapidly and effectively, challenging the hegemony of global capital, institutions of global governance, and repressive states.

All three movements considered in this book are counterhegemonic, even though they are starkly different in some ways. A key difference between the Islamist movement, on the one hand, and the feminist and global Justice movements, on the other, lies in their framings as well as their collective action repertoires. Islamists are not preoccupied with neoliberal capitalist globalization; rather, the problem is framed as Western imperialism or cultural invasion or Islam in danger. Global social democracy, or even local democratic practice, is not presented as a solution; rather, "Islam is the solution." In contrast, transnational feminism and global justice have a shared antipathy toward the current model of capitalist globalization and a common commitment to deliberative democratic processes, whether within their own organizations, in intergroup and coalition politics, or in the world-system at large. What is more, while conferences, activist research, lobbying efforts, cyberactivism, protest rallies, and civil disobedience constitute the collective action repertoire of feminist and global justice movements, many Islamists deploy militant and violent tactics not only against state repression but also in response to what they perceive as insults to their religion and culture. Moderate Islamists will engage with elections, the media, professional associations, and other societal institutions to extend their influence, but they have not satisfied skeptics who raise questions about Islamist commitment to democratic processes, civil liberties, and inclusive citizenship. Their unwillingness to engage with the feminist critique of patriarchy is also a cause for concern.

Despite their differences, the three transnational movements originate in the same structural sources: neoliberal inequalities, the global diffusion of world culture, and (to a lesser degree) Internet-based activism. Neoliberal globalization has exacerbated inequalities across and within countries, leading to the emergence of the various types of contenders and challengers that we have examined in this book: jihadists and moderate Islamists, transnational feminists, and global justice activists. The global spread of Western cultural products, discourses, values, and norms has been rejected tout court by militant Islamists and selectively by feminists and global justice activists. That is, while transnational feminists and global justice activists embrace the discourses and values of human rights, women's rights, and environmental protection, they reject the dominant values of consumerism, commercialization, and privatization.

If social movements and activism have a place in civil society, then transnational social movements and global civil society are similarly connected. Civil society is the sphere of associational life that provides citizens with an alternative site of engagement and resources outside (and presumably beyond the clutches of) the state and the market. Civil society includes informal networks, social clubs, voluntary associations, nonstate religious organizations, professional and civic associations, trade unions, and social movement organizations. Global civil society is made up of those actors that consciously communicate, cooperate, and organize across national boundaries. Clearly, a well-developed infrastructure exists for the practice of an alternative to the status quo, "business as usual," and, specifically, the logic of neoliberal capitalist globalization. What is required, however, is more deliberate strategizing across movements—labor, feminist, progressive religious, environmental, antiwar, global justice—toward a common vision and plan of action.

In this book we have encountered two approaches to the study and understanding of civil society, one normative and subjective and the other empirical and objective. Is civil society exclusively a domain of democratic interaction and progressive transformation? Rupert Taylor and his colleagues have argued that it is, but others have noted that nonstate actors, including social movements and networks themselves, are diverse and not necessarily emancipatory. According to John Guidry, Michael Kennedy, and Mayer Zald, "This is not to suggest that social movement theory should abandon the normative impulses that have drawn so many to engagement with movements. Rather, we suggest that it could be driven to engage the resonant and dissonant motifs in the civilizational concerns of movements across the world."[1] In this book, we have done precisely that, by engaging with the dissonant motifs and civilizational concerns of Islamist movements and suggesting that social movements create multiple transnational public spheres that in some cases overlap and in others diverge absolutely.

Paradoxically, then, globalization processes have given rise to both nonviolent democratic movements and violent antidemocratic ones. As noted by Benjamin Barber, it was "McWorld" that engendered jihad. But globalization has also been confronted by democratic movements such as feminism and global justice. Scholars have established links between not only economic globalization and terrorist activity but also economic globalization and world culture, on the one hand,

and the spread of democratic counterhegemonic social movements, on the other. If on a conceptual level this duality appears unsatisfying or logically inconsistent, it should be recalled that globalization is a widespread and multidimensional process of worldwide restructuring. As such, its entailments and outcomes are not uniform or linear but, rather, contentious and seemingly "messy."

Similarly, social movement theorizing that places a premium on cost-benefit analysis, cool calculations, and strategic thinking in resource mobilizations needs to consider the role of emotions, grievances, moral outrage, and humiliation, as well as joy, commitment, trust, solidarity, and altruism. Social movement activism is neither a matter of individual rational choice nor an example of collective irrationality. It involves people coming together around common grievances, goals, and identities and creating meaning, forging alliances, building coalitions, and maintaining institutions. Such work is not easy. Constituting, sustaining, or participating in global social movements is a difficult enterprise. Barriers to be overcome are linguistic, monetary, and political—and sometimes cultural. Even beyond the complementarity of agendas and goals, the question of language and communication is central to the ability to participate meaningfully. Within the world of international diplomacy, simultaneous interpretation and rapid translation of documents are common, but the global justice movement, for example, lacks the financial resources for such services. Therefore, much of the work of communicating across language groups other than English, French, and Spanish—for example, at the various meetings of the World Social Forum—is done voluntarily by bilingual or multilingual activists. Multilingual websites are certainly helpful—and these are maintained by the World Social Forum as well as by transnational feminist networks such as Women Living under Muslim Laws (WLUML) and Network Women in Development Europe (WIDE)—but they do not exhaust the languages of large parts of the global community that remain excluded from the deliberative processes of democratic transnational activism.

ON THE MOBILIZING ROLE OF THE INTERNET

Social movement research has shown that recruitment into networks often occurs because of involvement in other networks. Activist networks not only ensure that a person is a member of a larger community but also frame issues and offer particular understandings. There is a large body of research on recruitment through formal networks, such as professional associations or organizations, what Mark Granovetter famously called "the strength of weak ties," or through informal networks, also known as the friend-of-a-friend phenomenon. Our analysis has shown that information and communication technologies have expanded the scope and rapidity of recruitment and mobilization, whether through formal or informal ties, and that the Internet helps create and maintain new networks. Sociologist Lauren Langman has argued this point succinctly and well. The Internet provides a variety of "virtual public spheres" where people can find information and "undistorted communication" that highlights adversity and offers frames for understanding that adversity. Virtual public spheres help to foster the embrace of what Manuel Castells has called "project identities."[2] Such identities enable mobilizations that would change that adversity and articulate a vision of what a better policy or law—or, indeed, another, better world—might look like. Transnational movements, therefore, can be regarded as Internet/networked movements. That is, much of their activist work takes place on the Internet, and they are networked with each other both virtually and physically.

Global interconnectedness through "world society" or "network society" suggests a world full of movement and a complex mix of virtual and physical interactions. What is more, the "global" stimulates the creation of a transnational identity in a new "virtual" space that transcends borders. This new transnational social space is also a subject-supporting field in that it can provide solidarity and resources for individuals and groups at the local level. In this way, the "virtual" is a tool of empowerment. Virtuality does not replace normal communication; nor does it replace existing identities. It does, however, add new identities (e.g., world citizen, transnational feminist activist, international partner). Virtual networks extend social capital through the Internet, allowing participants to build a sense of belonging that was previously difficult because of distance.

If the transnational public sphere is defined as a place where forms of organization and tactics for collective action can be transmitted across the globe, the Internet is a key medium through which this transnational public sphere takes shape. Our study of transnational

Islamism, global feminism, and the global justice movement suggests that social movement theorizing needs to consider the mobilizing role of the Internet. The Internet has become a principal site for the formation of political and cultural communities and for the meeting and linking of movement networks. Enabling virtual and transnational public spheres and rapid communication of frames, the Internet allows many movements to connect, thus facilitating the mobilization of "internetworked" social movements. Solidarities and collective action across borders are of long-standing existence, but the virtual public sphere allows for more rapid dissemination of political expressions and coordination of protest actions—including alerts, appeals, information exchange, petitions, and announcements of public rallies. The Internet enables members of some networks to learn about and join other networks. That it fosters the creation and maintenance of collective identities was evident in 2010–2012 with the *indignados* in Spain, the Arab Spring in Egypt, Tunisia, and Morocco, the anti-austerity protests in Greece, and Occupy Wall Street (OWS).

Transnational collective action does not take place exclusively in the virtual sphere, of course. The preceding chapters have shown the importance of recruitment in madrassas, charities, and mosques (Islamist movements) and of mobilization processes at international conferences (feminist and global justice movements). Nonetheless, the Internet has become a prime vehicle for the transmission of information about movement strategies, the mobilization of resources, and the exchange of ideas across borders, boundaries, and barriers. The solidarity work of WLUML, for example, is maintained through the activities of "networkers." Much of its mobilizing work is done via the Internet, in the form of e-campaigns for women's human rights. The WIDE network does hold an annual conference, and members are found at the World Social Forum and regional forums, but a major part of its work is conducted over the Internet, in the form of newsletters regularly disseminated to the organization's membership list and an extensive website with postings of research results, advocacy efforts, reports, news, and alerts. Among transnational feminist networks, the Women's Learning Partnership (WLP) is especially tech savvy, with a dynamic and interactive website that hosts webinars and blogs. The Internet has enabled transnational feminist networks to come quickly to the assistance of their sisters in need, especially those in repressive environments. In 2007 and 2008, for instance, transnational feminist networks such as WLUML, WLP, Development Alternatives with Women for a New Era, and Equality Now—along with individual Iranian feminist expatriates—disseminated information, transmitted petitions, and mobilized media interest around the One Million Signatures Campaign inside Iran (for law reform and women's rights), cases of imminent stonings of women charged with adultery, and the closure of a prominent Iranian women's magazine, *Zanan*. These examples make clear that the communications revolution associated with globalization enables actors to participate in collective action, in transnational advocacy networks, and in global social movements via cyberspace, while also helping to build a kind of cyberdemocracy. The local and the global are now linked in virtual public spheres, allowing activists to communicate, coordinate, exchange information, learn from each other, and build their collective identities and action repertoires across borders and indeed continents. In an era of globalization, mobilization processes have not replaced the traditional sites of family, neighborhood, religious groups, trade unions, and political networks, but they now extend to the virtual public sphere. As such, the Internet not only augments mobilization processes but sometimes also allows activists to circumvent obstacles and barriers created by repressive states. And in democratic polities where movement activity might be ignored by commercialized media, the Internet can provide alternative sources of information about movement strategies and achievements.

FOUR PROPOSITIONS

Chapter 1 summarized this book's main arguments, assumptions, and concepts in ten propositions, largely informed by the effects of globalization on social movements. Here I offer an additional four propositions to serve as food for thought and suggestions for future research on social movements, whether nationally based or transnational. These points pertain to the relationship between states and social movements in the era of globalization, social movements and political change, violence and social movements, and gender and social movements.

1. *States and social movements in a globalizing era:* Social movements or networks of contenders adopt a transnational form when (a)

global opportunities for legitimation or growth present themselves (here I am referring to the salience of world culture or world society integration), or (b) when collective action within domestic/national boundaries is foreclosed or repressed. We will continue to see social movements emerging throughout the world, and their tactics, scope, and prospects will depend on the combination of political opportunities, both domestic and global, as well as on the strength of their mobilizing and framing efforts. Movements are sometimes constrained from transnational activism and sometimes make strategic choices to remain domestically oriented. Globalization, of course, presents new opportunities for social movements to expand transnationally, but doing so will depend on world-system location, the strategic choice of the movement involved, and the domestic structure of political opportunity.

2. *Social movements and political change:* The Arab Spring consisted of large, peaceful protest movements that produced political revolutions in Tunisia and Egypt and constitutional reforms in Morocco. Given the inequalities and injustices of the contemporary world order, the semiperiphery of the world system will continue to be the site of social movements for political change and possibly revolutionary movements that aim to deepen or broaden a democracy oriented toward people rather than markets.

3. *Violence and social movements:* Social movements or networks of contenders assume violent methods to achieve their goals when (a) state repression forecloses open forms of peaceful collective action or protest, (b) movements or networks interpret repression as weakness, betrayal, or an opportunity to gain adherents to the cause, or (c) an extant cultural frame can be drawn upon to justify such actions. Violence as a tactic of contentious politics has been largely associated with revolutions or armed rebellions and less so with social movements, but some radical wings of social movements have been known to turn to violent means. State repression can leave a movement with little choice but to take up arms, and in some cultural contexts, violence can be justified in religious terms. However, movements have been known to make a strategic choice not to engage in violence, even when states

have taken repressive measures against them. Women's movements, for example, are invariably nonviolent. Labor movements and trade unions, too, have largely eschewed violence.

4. *Feminism, masculinities, and social movements:* The more masculine the composition and the more violent the discourse, the less likely it is that women will be involved as participants or leaders. Although some women will continue to identify with or support a masculinized movement, and the group may use some women in an instrumental fashion, such movements are unlikely to attract a critical mass of women or to incorporate them into leadership roles. With transnational networks in particular, which require a high degree of mobility, membership in movements and networks that deploy violence as the chief means of contention will continue to be overwhelmingly male.

IS ANOTHER WORLD POSSIBLE?

All three transnational movements examined in this book express dissatisfaction with the state of the contemporary world and existing power relations. Members of all three believe that another world is possible, even though the Islamist vision may differ markedly from that of feminists and global justice activists. What, indeed, are the prospects for global change, and what are the prospects for our social movements?

In examining the rise of Islamist movements, I have emphasized macro processes such as authoritarianism, economic crisis, and neoliberalism; normative disruptions caused by structural strains; the conservative tendencies of the lower middle class and the petite bourgeoisie; and the militarist implications of hegemonic masculinities. What of the future? Since at least the mid-1990s, a debate has ensued among scholars concerning the future of political Islam, especially the future of global jihadism. Some argue that militant Islam has exhausted its possibilities and is on the decline. Due to their incompetence and repression, the regimes in Afghanistan, the Islamic Republic of Iran, and Sudan do not constitute a model of governance or state-society relations. The extreme violence of jihadist groups has repelled Muslims across the globe, and many militant groups have been defeated by harsh state repression or the "global war on terror." (The U.S.-U.K. invasion of Iraq had the opposite effect of stimulating Islamist revival and reaction in that country.) At the same time, religious politics appear strong and likely to dominate elections, lawmaking, and civil society activism for the foreseeable future. All Muslim countries have populations of liberal, left wing, or secular citizens, and all have feminist groups. However, many parts of the Muslim world still exhibit the master frames of nationalism and Islam, with the result that we are likely to see the persistence of politics conducted in a religious idiom. Depending on local circumstances, the religious frame will be stronger or weaker in different Muslim-majority countries, including those in the Middle East and North Africa. Can we expect Islamism to take the form of movements and political parties that reconcile faith and heritage with "world society" links to global institutions and ideals? This has already occurred in Turkey with the ruling Justice and Development Party, or AKP, but will it occur in Egypt and Tunisia? In the meantime, transnational feminist networks and the global justice movement would do well to support and encourage democratic and progressive forces within Muslim-majority countries while continuing to oppose hegemonic politics, war, and empire.

The women's movement has been among the most successful social movements of the modern era, and feminists around the world continue to associate modernity with women's equality and rights. This is especially the case with feminist activism in countries of the Middle East and North Africa. For example, in her discussion of competing gender frames in contentious Algeria in the 1990s, Doria Cherifati-Merabtine distinguished the "Islamic female ideal" from the "modernist model."[3] Historically, women's movements have been allied with nationalist movements and with liberalism, socialism, and social democracy, and they continue to engage in coalitions with other social forces, movements, and organizations. Yet such groups—feminist movements and organizations in particular—are inclined to maintain their autonomy, and they engage in coalitions only when women's strategic interests are served rather than sidelined. This is evidence of the continuing maturity of women's social movements, especially feminist ones, which have clear goals about gender hierarchy, democratic transformations, and women's rights. For these reasons, feminist groups express strong criticism of Islamist movements and other forms of religio-politics or fundamentalism. They have a more natural affinity with the global justice movement, even though some tensions have been discerned.

With transnational feminism, the global justice movement shares a critique of neoliberalism, hegemonic governance, war, and all forms of oppression. Like global feminism, which comprises many nationally based and transnational feminist groups with their own frames and strategies, the global justice movement is a broad global "movement of movements" with no centralized leadership. (In this respect it is also similar to transnational Islamism.) Some scholar-activists have argued that for the global justice movement to more effectively challenge the hegemony of neoliberal capitalism, it needs more focus, better coordination, stronger leadership, and a more coherent strategy for action and change. As we have seen, however, others prefer that the global justice movement, and the World Social Forum itself, be as inclusive as possible and remain primarily a site for dialogue and diversity, including many different forms of action. During 2011 and 2012, with the rise and growth of Occupy Wall Street, it was evident yet again that a broad and inclusive democratic movement was preferred to a more centralized or strategically oriented political coalition. OWS—along with the anti-austerity social protest movements in Europe and Chile—certainly seemed to breathe new life into the global justice movement. But will the movement be able to present itself as an alternative form of political organizing and—along with progressive governments in Latin America and elsewhere—force changes in the institutions of global governance? Or will the global justice movement become an alternative cultural site, devoid of political power and unable to exert authority and influence over the workings of the global economy, its institutions, and its agents?

And what of the prospects for globalization itself? If globalization is a "project" with distinct institutions and agents (the "globalizers"), then a strong global justice movement could conceivably force some changes. If, however, globalization is part of a secular historic trend with deep structural roots ("the latest stage of capitalism"), it may need more time to work its way through its own dynamics and contradictions, and it might even exhaust itself as a result of a series of accumulation or legitimation crises, such as those that emerged with the 2008 global financial crisis.

Globalization has reduced the power of states, though in different ways across the world-system's economic zones. In many cases, the capacity of governments to compensate the losers and manage social tensions is curtailed, while global economic and political integration reduces the scope of democratic decision making. This was evident during the period of structural adjustments and austerities in the developing countries and in Greece in 2011–2012. And yet, the role of the state is crucial in making democracy sustainable. The era of globalization and its neoliberal ideology favors corporations, banks, and other private interests. The challenge, then, is to organize state institutions so that they will engage in activities that are socially beneficial rather than catering to the corporate sector.[4] Addressing this challenge—to help deepen democracy in the core countries, consolidate democracy in the "fourth-wave" countries, and move toward a global democracy—requires strategic engagement with policy, legal, and institutional frameworks and the building of transnational partnerships and coalitions.

How will globalization and pro-democracy movements play out in the Middle East and North Africa? In a reflection of the paradoxes of historical capitalism, the current form of globalization could have a positive impact in that region. Earlier chapters in this book described the diffusion of democracy and women's rights frames. The most globalized parts of the region, notably the Gulf sheikhdoms (though not yet Saudi Arabia), have slowly turned their backs on previously exclusionary politics in favor of the adoption of "world values." In the United Arab Emirates, which has enjoyed huge investments in international banks, properties, and retail, women won a 23 percent share of parliamentary seats in 2007, and there were some public dialogues about the rights of migrant workers and other previously excluded groups. As the Middle East becomes more integrated into world society, could we see a concerted movement toward less contentious politics? Toward democratic transition and consolidation?

Let us propose two directions that globalization could possibly take in the Middle East and in the wake of the Arab Spring. In one scenario, pro-democracy movements bring about strong civil societies, transform the relations between state and society, and establish institutions to sustain citizen rights and a democratic polity. A diversity of international links reinforces democratic institutions and norms. This route could end the kind of vulnerability that allows the hegemonic power and core countries to exert control (as with the invasions of Iraq and Libya), and it could end the anger, frustration, and humiliation that have driven Islamist movements. In the other scenario, Islamist movements sideline erstwhile coalition partners, including feminists, democrats, minorities, and those Muslims for whom "Islam is the solution" is not a resonant frame. Transnational ties, control over economic resources, and capital flows could strengthen Islamic institutions and networks, including militant ones, with the effect of expanding their global reach. In the first scenario, "world values" are expanded in a way that suggests cultural and political convergence, and hegemonic control is attenuated. In the second and more negative scenario, Islamists in power create their own version of the "state of exception," deny rights and equality to many categories of citizens, and insist on cultural and religious identity, differences, and boundaries. They may take issue with the hegemon and the core on matters of cultural practices and norms, but not on technological, military, and capital flows. Of course, time will tell which of these scenarios will be realized.

In the years ahead, we can look back on the mass social protests of 2010–2012 and assess the outcomes. After the democracy movements of Egypt, Morocco, and Tunisia; the pro-union activism in Wisconsin and Ohio in the United States; the rallies in Israel against unemployment and inequality; the many protests in Europe against neoliberalism; the student protests in Chile; and the spread of the Occupy Wall Street movement, we can ask, Did we embark on the age of global justice? Or did the era of neoliberal globalization reassert itself?

Notes

CHAPTER 1: INTRODUCTION AND OVERVIEW

1. Marx 1978: ch. 31. For studies on the world-system, see Chase-Dunn 1998; Wallerstein 1991; on the internationalization of capital, see Frobel, Heinrichs, and Kreye 1980.

2. On "new social movements," see Melucci 1989; Eyerman and Jamison 1991; Rucht 1991. See McAdam, McCarthy, and Zald 1996 on theorization of political opportunities, mobilizing structures, and cultural frames.

3. On global restructuring, see Cox 1992; Moghadam 1995a; Hopkins and Wallerstein 1996; Boswell and Chase-Dunn 2000. On "globalism" and consumer capitalism as ideology, see Sklair 2001, 2002; Steger 2002, 2009; Steger and Roy 2010. See Fukuyama 1992 for a celebration of what he sees as the triumph of liberal democracy and capitalism at the end of the Cold War.

4. On "world culture," see Meyer et al. 1997; Boli and Thomas 1997; Boli 2005; Moghadam and Elveren 2008. On norm diffusion and advocacy/solidarity across borders, see Smith, Chatfield, and Pagnucco 1997; Keck and Sikkink 1998. See also Garrett 2006 on protest in an information age.

5. Arjomand 1986: 107; Wuthnow 1986; Klatch 1994; Blee and Creasap 2010: 273.

6. On the connection with global restructuring, see Moghadam 1995a; on gender and fundamentalism, see Kandiyoti 1991 and Moghadam 1994. On Islamist movements, see Zubaida 1993; Hafez 2003; Wiktorowicz 2004b; see also Beckford 1986 for comparative perspectives and Marty and Appleby's four volumes on comparative fundamentalisms (1991, 1992, 1993, 1994).

7. Keck and Sikkink 1998: 3. See also Smith, Chatfield, and Pagnucco 1997.

8. Scholte 2000: 46; Pieterse 1998. See also Held 2000.

9. The definition is from Guidry, Kennedy, and Zald 2000a. See also Smith and Johnston 2002; Podobnik and Reifer 2004; Appelbaum and Robinson 2005; Moghadam 2005; Chase-Dunn and Babones 2006; Della Porta 2007.

10. On transnational feminism see Eschle and Maiguashca 2010; Marchand and Runyan 2000; Meyer and Prugl 1999; Moghadam 2005; Stienstra 2000. On Middle East/North African feminism, see Berkovitch and Moghadam 1999; Moghadam 2003; Moghadam and Sadiqi 2006; Moghadam and Gheytanchi 2010.

11. Supportive of the NATO "humanitarian intervention" were Middle East specialists such as Gilbert Achkar, Rami Khoury, and, most vociferously, Juan R. I. Cole, along with left-wing sociologists such as Lauren Langman and Michael Schwartz. Supporters cited the Arab League's endorsement of the Security Council resolution to allow a no-fly zone over Libya, but only nine of the twenty-two members actually voted in favor; two voted against, and the others abstained or were absent. Along with Samir Amin, Edward Herman, Gary Younge, Medea Benjamin, Alexander Cockburn, and others, I was adamantly opposed to both the NATO intervention and the violence of the rebels, leading to many impassioned e-mail exchanges and conversations. Veteran left-wing Egyptian economist Samir Amin criticized the intervention and the killing of Ghaddafi as imperialistic. In an online editorial, the editors of the left-leaning *Middle East Report* expressed the concern that Libya could turn out to "look nothing like the democratic state of liberal interventionist dreams, and quite a bit like post-Saddam Iraq." Code Pink pointed out that "democracy doesn't come on the back of a Tomahawk missile," adding that "in 2009 alone, European governments—including Britain and France—sold Libya more than $470 million worth of weapons, including fighter jets, guns and bombs. And before it started calling for regime change, the Obama administration was working to provide the Libyan dictator another $77 million in weapons, on top of the $17 million it provided in 2009 and the $46 million the Bush administration provided in 2008. . . . The U.S. government need not drop a single bomb in the Middle East to help liberate oppressed people. All it need do is stop selling bombs to their oppressors." See Medea Benjamin and Charles Davis, "FOX News video: CODEPINK's Medea Benjamin Speaks Out on Libya," Pink Tank, http://codepink.org/blog/2011/03/fox-news -video-codepinks-medea-benjamin-speaks-out-on-libya/# (accessed March 22, 2011). It is also worth noting that the governments of Argentina and Brazil, led by presidents Cristina Fernandez de Kirchner and Dilma Roussef, respectively, opposed the NATO intervention in Libya.

12. See "About MoveOn.org," MoveOn.org, http://www.moveon.org/about.html; "About Azaaz.org," Azaaz.org, http://www.avaaz.org/en/about.php.

13. On Iran's protests and the Internet, see Kamalipour 2010. On the use of mobile phones in protests, see Castells, Fernàndez-Ardèvol, and Sey 2006.

14. Walgrave et al. 2011; the quotes appear on pp. 326 and 329. See also Langman 2005.

15. Stephen Moss, "Impresario of a New Journalism," *Guardian Weekly*, July 30, 2010, 28–29; BBC World Service, October 24, 2011; see wikileaks.org (accessed October 27, 2011). A Facebook posting by Catherine Savage (November 2011) featured a photo of Julian Assange with the comment, "I give private information on corporations to you for free and I'm the villain," juxtaposed with the image of Mark Zuckerberg and the comment, "I give your private information to corporations for money, and I'm the Man of the Year."

16. The term refers to the ability of individuals to take part in protest activity due to the absence of potential obstacles, which may be family responsibilities, a high-pressure job, the fear of being sacked, or physical incapacity. Young people's availability for activism is generally deemed to be high. On "biographical availability," see McAdam 1986; Goldstone and McAdam 2001.

17. Heckscher 2002; Tarrow 1994: 48, cited in Keck and Sikkink 1998: 37.

18. Polanyi [1944] 2001; Arrighi, Hopkins, and Wallerstein 1989; Boswell and Chase-Dunn 2000; Chase-Dunn and Babones 2006; Chase-Dunn et al. 2009. Karl Polanyi's highly influential text was originally published in 1944. The 2001 edition includes contributions by economist Joseph Stiglitz and political sociologist Fred Block.

19. Smith 2008.

20. Keck and Sikkink 1998: 38.

21. Moaddel 2005: 1; Roberts 2003; Voll 1991, cited in Marty and Appleby 1991; Esposito 2002: 45–46. Salafiyists are literalists who also believe that Muslims should be ruled by an Islamic state similar to that established by the Prophet Mohammad and his successors (the Salaf). They formed partly in opposition to folkloric versions of Islam (maraboutism) practiced by rural people and the urban poor.

22. Jayawardena 1986; Berkovitch 1999; Meyer 1999; Rupp 1998; Stienstra 1994; Plastas 2011. As noted by Boxer and Quataert 1978, the socialist movement organized predominantly working-class women, such as textile workers, for revolutionary causes, while the feminist organizations were largely middle-class and reformist.

23. These arguments are associated with, respectively, Harvey 2003; Robinson 2004; and Pieterse 2004.

24. Wallerstein 2000, 2003.

25. McAdam, McCarthy, and Zald 1996; on "frames," see especially Snow 2004.

26. Gerlach 1999: 95.

27. See Goodwin, Jasper, and Polleta 2001; Flam and King 2005.

28. Bhavnani, Foran, and Talcott 2005: 330.

29. Cited in Barkawi 2006: 130. The quote is from a videotaped statement released on October 7, 2001. The mention of "eighty years" is a reference to the downfall and breakup of the Ottoman Empire and its caliphate.

30. Babones 2006; the quotes appear on pp. 13 and 26.

31. Smith and Wiest 2005; Lizardo 2006; Wiest 2007; Reid and Chen 2007; Smith et al. 2008; Allard, Davidson, and Matthaei 2008; Juris 2008. On feminism and the WSF see Conway 2007; Eschle and Maiguashca 2010.

32. In her feminist analysis of globalization, Spike Peterson (2003) has identified three gendered economic spheres: that of the production of goods and the provision of services; that of social, biological, and labor reproduction (sometimes known as the care economy); and the sphere of nonmaterial, speculative, and financial transactions (the virtual economy).

33. For examples and illustrations of anticorporate networking, see Juris 2008.

34. The phrase is from Guidry, Kennedy, and Zald 2000a: 17, but I am not suggesting that they would agree with my recommendation.

35. On critical globalization studies, see Appelbaum and Robinson 2005.

CHAPTER 2:
GLOBALIZATION AND COLLECTIVE ACTION

1. An early study was Barnet and Muller 1974. See Roberts and Hite 2007 for an elaboration of the evolution from development to globalization.

2. Harvey 2009: 39; Klein 2007b.

3. Soviet support was especially important to the South African and Palestinian liberation movements. In various parts of the world, some leftists who were appalled by U.S. support for dictators and involvement in coups d'état, or who sympathized with the Palestinian national liberation cause, formed "revolutionary cells" in Germany, Italy, Japan, and elsewhere. Extremist leftists such as the German Red Army Faction (including the Baader-Meinhof group), the Japanese Red Army, and the Italian Red Brigades wreaked havoc but did not last long. French filmmaker Olivier Assayas's three-part miniseries *Carlos*, released in 2010, provides a good visual introduction to this episode. See also chapter 4 for further discussion.

4. Some Cavtat Roundtable documents are available from the author; see also http://www.jstor.org/pss/29765806. On the NIEO, see "Declaration on the Establishment of a New International Economic Order," reprinted in Broad 2002: 99–102.

5. Loans also were taken out by dictators, which helped to entrench their rule and benefited the lending institutions to the detriment of citizens. Such loans later came to be called "odious" by advocates of debt cancellation. See chapter 6.

6. On the Drexel Lambert Burnham scandal, see Zey 1993; on the debt trap, see Payer 1975. These two books should be more widely read and cited. On structural adjustments, see Cornia, Jolly, and Stewart 1989; Bakker 1994; Sparr 1994; Moghadam 1995a, 1998a.

7. On the "deindustrialization of America," see Bluestone and Harrison 1982. On "the golden age of capitalism" and its end, see Marglin and Schor 1990. See also Rupert and Solomon 2006: 42. On the withdrawal from UNESCO, see Moghadam and Elveren 2008. In brief, the Reagan administration left UNESCO on December 31, 1984, and returned on October 1, 2003. The stated reasons for the withdrawal were the alleged bad management of the organization, the left-wing orientation of the programs, and the politicization of debates. The United States was particularly opposed to the proposal for a New World Information and Communication Order (NWICO). In 1985 the British government of Margaret Thatcher followed suit, citing similar reasons. In 1997 the government of Tony Blair decided that the United Kingdom would rejoin UNESCO after the latter abandoned the NWICO idea and undertook administrative reforms. The United States rejoined UNESCO in 2004—but then withdrew again in 2011 when the Executive Board voted to allow Palestine to join. The United States also briefly withdrew from the International Labour Organization (1977–1980).

8. See http://www.iie.com/publications/papers/williamson0904-2.pdf. See also Steger and Roy 2010: 19–20.

9. On the Millennium Development Goals, see http://www.un.org/millenniumgoals. For economists' perspectives on globalization, see Joseph Stiglitz, "Globalism's Discontents" (2002), in Roberts and Hite 2007: 295–304; Dani Rodrik, "Has Globalization Gone Too Far?" (1997), in Roberts and Hite 2007: 305–19, 314–15; Jeffrey Sachs, "The Anti-

globalization Movement" (2005), in Roberts and Hite 2007: 356–59. See also Standing 1999b; Bhagwati 2004; UNDP 1999; Oxfam 2002.

10. Harvey 2003, 2004; Peterson 2003; Robinson 2004; Wallerstein 1991; Chase-Dunn 1998.

11. Yaghmaian 2001; Sklair 2001, 2002; Steger 2002. "Globalizers" included academic economists, as seen in the 2010 documentary *Inside Job* by Charles Ferguson. See http://www.sonyclassics.com/insidejob.

12. Bello 2000; Khor 2000; Korten 1995; Mander 1996. On the Tobin tax: As early as 1978, Professor James Tobin, winner of the 1981 Nobel Prize for economics, proposed a tax on international currency transactions (for example, foreign exchange speculation) to reduce the volatility and instability of financial markets (see Tobin 1978). In 1994 he reiterated his proposal, suggesting that the proceeds of that tax be placed at the disposition of international organizations for development purposes. The idea for such a tax was endorsed by many progressive NGOs, including transnational feminist networks, and became a principal demand of ATTAC, which went on to become a key group within the global justice movement. The Tobin tax was discussed by NGOs at the 1995 UN Social Summit in Copenhagen but was turned down by most governments. James Tobin died in March 2002. (For a movement perspective on the Tobin tax, see Broad 2002.) In 2011, as part of the rescue of the Eurozone, the French government endorsed a financial tax, but this was rejected by the British government.

13. On inequalities, see the summary of Maddison's research in UNDP 1999; see also Atkinson 2001; Taylor 2000; Milanovic 2005, 2011.

14. Monbiot 2011: 19; Foroohar 2011; Newman 1999; Wilkinson and Pickett 2009; UNDP 2005.

15. On the global financial and economic crisis, see Chossudovsky and Marshall 2010; ILO 2011; IMF 2009.

16. On globalization and the state, see Mathews 1997: 50; Strange 1996: 4; Beck 2004: 144.

17. Castells 1996, cited in Zivkovic and Hogan 2007: 186.

18. Sklair 1991, 2001; Chase-Dunn 1998. Sklair (2001: 1) argues that "the transnational capitalist class has transformed capitalism into a globalizing project," while Robinson and Harris (2000: 20) state that "the transnationalization of the capital circuit implies as well the transnationalization of the agents of capital." But see Hirst and Thompson 1996 and Berger and Dore 1996 for more state-centered views.

19. Tarrow 2001; Johnston 2011.

20. Barkawi 2006: 10.

21. On the "justice cascade," see Sikkink 2011. This is an important and impressively documented book, and Sikkink does have a chapter on the United States, but the assumption that all states and officials are equally vulnerable to the new global norms and institutions of justice is flawed.

22. Morozov 2011; Dominic Rushe, "U.S. Ruling on Twitter 'a Blow to Privacy,'" *Guardian Weekly*, November 18, 2011: 12.

23. Santos 2006. See also chapter 6 in this book.

24. Barber 2001: 232, i.

25. Hardt and Negri (2000) theorized away the militarized state and coercive international relations and disputed the hegemonic role of the United States—incorrectly, in my view. For a summary discussion, see Howe 2002.

26. On the importance of the Afghanistan episode, see Cooley 1999; Rashid 2000; and Moghadam 2003: ch. 7.

27. On this latter point, see Elizabeth Drew, "The War in Washington," *New York Review of Books*, May 10, 2007, 53–55; Schumpeter, "The Civil War in Washington, DC, Is Damaging American Business," *The Economist*, August 13, 2011, 66.

28. I have discussed this at greater length in Moghadam 2012.

29. Runyan 2002: 362; Langman and Morris 2004; Connell 1998.

30. Barber 2001; Kaldor 2003; Chua 2003.

31. Moghadam 2011b; Marx 1978: ch. 31.

32. Eckstein and Wickham-Crowley 2003. See also Johnston and Almeida 2006.

33. Hadden and Tarrow 2007: 214; Tarrow 2005: 11.

34. Guidry, Kennedy, and Zald 2000a: 3; Alger in Smith, Chatfield, and Pagnucco 1997: 262, table 15.1.

35. Pianta and Marchetti 2007: 30–31.

36. Kaldor 2003: 44–45, 46; Anheier, Glasius, and Kaldor 2001: 21.

37. Taylor 2004: 4; Bauer and Hélie 2006.

CHAPTER 3: SOCIAL MOVEMENTS
AND DEMOCRATIZATION

1. On the democratic underpinnings of social movements see Guidry, Kennedy, and Zald 2000b: 14; Costain 2005; Della Porta 2005; Di Marco 2011a, 2011b; Dryzek 1990; Polletta 2002; Weldon 2011. On neoliberalism and its discontents in Latin America, see Silva 2010.

2. Johnston 2011; Meyer and Tarrow 1998.

3. On South Korea, see Cummings 2000; Im 2000; Chang 2008. On Argentina, see Di Marco 2011a.

4. On egalitarian family relations, see Okin 1989; Di Marco and Tabbush 2011; Collectif Maghreb Egalité 95 2005. See also O'Donnell and Schmitter 1986: 7, cited in Korzeniewicz and Awbrey 1992: 618.

5. Barber 1984; Schmitter and Karl 1991: 77. For more on formal and substantive democracy, politics, and citizenship rights, see Marshall 1964; Crick 2000; Lister 2003; Moghadam 2011a.

6. Fukuyama 1992; Huntington 1992.

7. On democracy and the semiperiphery, see Korzeniewicz and Awbrey 1992; Markoff 1999. On contagion, consent, control, and conditionality, see Przeworski et al. 1995: 6.

8. On democracy and structural adjustments in Africa, see Bratton and Van De Walle 1992; Ake 1993; Vieceli 1997: 90.

9. Costas Douzinas, "In Greece, Democracy Is Reborn," *Guardian Weekly*, June 24, 2011, 20. For commentaries and comparisons of Argentina's 2001 default and the Greek dilemma, see http://www.guardian.co.uk/business/2010/apr/16/argentina

-to-repay-2001-debt and http://www.nytimes.com/2011/06/24/business/global/24peso .html?pagewanted=all.

10. Kenneth Bollen cited in Korzeniewicz and Awbrey 1992: 612. See also Moore 1966; Lipset 1959; Huntington 1992; Welzel and Inglehart 2009.

11. Wejnert 2005.

12. On the ties between the 6th April Movement and Otpor, see Kirkpatrick and Sanger 2011.

13. Htun and Weldon 2011; Sikkink 2011.

14. Givan, Roberts, and Soule 2010.

15. On Latin America, see Alvarez 1990; Jaquette 2001, 2009; Waylen 1994, 2007. On the Philippines, see Roces 2010.

16. Jaquette 2001: 114.

17. Beckwith 2010; Eschle 2000; Barron 2002; Di Marco and Tabbush 2011; Moghadam 2005; Vargas 2009.

18. Keane 1996. My assertion about Tunisia's prospects comes from years of research travels, observations, and interviews in Tunisia, Egypt, Morocco, and other MENA countries, published in various books and journal articles.

19. Htun and Weldon 2011.

20. UNDP 2002: 1; Markoff 1999: 285.

21. Phillips 2003; see also UNDP 2011, which shows the extent to which U.S. inequality lowers the Human Development Index (HDI) for the United States and its ranking among countries.

22. Smith 2008; Moghadam and Elveren 2008.

23. Dunn 2005; Przeworski et al. 1995: 4; Barber 2001; Habermas 1992.

24. Chua 2003; Lukacs 2005.

25. Bennoune 1995; Cherifati-Merabtine 1995; Messaoudi and Schemla 1998; Moghadam 2001; Salhi 2011.

26. Tessler 2007: 114.

27. Diamond 2010. See also Diamond et al. (1989: xix): they justified exclusion of communist countries from their study because "there is little prospect among them of a transition to democracy, but only of liberalization of Communist rule."

28. Moghadam 2008; Bayat 2007; Beinin 2009a, 2009b; Schwedler 2006; *Arab Human Development Report*, various years, http://arab-hdr.org; ILO 2010: 23–30.

29. McAdam 1986.

30. On Mansour Osanloo, see http://united4iran.org. On the feminist movement, see Change for Equality Campaign (Iran), http://www.change4equality.com/english, and Feminist School (Iran), http://feministschool.net and http://feministschool.net/campaign.

31. Moghadam and Gheytanchi 2010; Hashemi and Postel 2011.

32. Moghadam and Gheytanchi 2010; Sater 2007, especially ch. 4.

33. Rabéa Naciri of L'Association democratique des femmes du Maroc (ADFM) was one of the initiators of the plan (Sater 2007: 133).

34. Latifa Jbabdi of l'Union d'Action Feminine, in remarks made at a seminar in Helsinki, Finland, September 9, 2004. Jbabdi's background was in the Left—she was also the daughter of leftists—and she had been a political prisoner. Jbabdi was among those with visible and vocal roles in the Truth Commission that was organized by the

Youssefi government to investigate the human rights violations of the previous era. For details, see Slyomovics 2005.

35. Skalli 2007; Sadiqi and Ennaji 2006.

36. See Collectif 2005 for the English-language translation, which was published by the Bethesda, Maryland–based Women's Learning Partnership.

37. Conversation with the author, Montecatini, Italy, March 27, 2009.

38. Larbi Sadiki, "The Arab Spring: Voting Islamism," Al Jazeera, December 7, 2011, http://www.aljazeera.com/indepth/opinion/2011/12/2011126105646767454.html.

39. Gideon Rachman, "Reflections on the Revolution in Egypt," FT.com, February 14, 2011, notes that a Pew opinion poll showed 80 percent support in Egypt for the idea that adulterers should be stoned, "the kind of figure that bolsters the fears of those who worry that Facebook Egypt will be outvoted by fundamentalist Egypt."

40. See the following 2009 sources: Anonymous, http://forums.whyweprotest .net/categories/iran.305; "Internet Brings Events in Iran to Life," BBC News, June 15, 2009, http://news.bbc.co.uk/2/hi/middle_east/8099579.stm; Angela Moscaritolo, "Iran Election Protesters Use Twitter to Recruit Hackers," *SC Magazine*, June 15, 2009, http://www.scmagazineus.com/iranian-election-protestors-use-twitter-to -recruit-hackers/article/138545 (accessed December 14, 2011).

41. Laer and Aelst 2010: 1151.

42. Florence Beaugé, "Fragile Morocco Balances Priorities," *Guardian Weekly*, October 14, 2011, 18.

43. See the following: Adbusters Occupy Wall Street, http://www.adbusters .org/blogs/adbustersblog/occupywallstreet.html; Occupy Wall Street: The Resistance Continues at Liberty Square and Worldwide, http://occupywallst.org; Kevin Voigt, "Beyond Wall Street: 'Occupy' Protests Go Global," CNN, October 7, 2011, http:// edition.cnn.com/2011/10/07/business/wall-street-protest-global; Juan Luis Sánchez, "Dreaming of a 'New Global Citizen Power,'" *Periodismo Humano*, October 15, 2011, http://takethesquare.net/2011/10/13/october-15th-dreaming-of-a-%e2%80%9cnew -global-citizen-power%e2%80%9d.

44. See http://occupywallst.org/about.

45. "About," Occupy Wall Street, http://occupywallst.org/about.

46. O'Brien et al. 2000; Smith 2008: 41–44, 46.

47. Smith 2008; the quotes appear on pp. 5, 106, 107. See also Smith and Wiest 2012.

48. Della Porta 2005, 2009. See also Smith 2008; the quotes appear on pp. 34, 214, 208.

49. On the solidarity economy, see Allard, Davidson, and Matthaei 2008. Also see McBride 2001, especially ch. 8, and UNDP 2002: 3 on the Brazilian budgeting experiment.

50. See contributions in Moghadam, Franzway, and Fonow 2011.

CHAPTER 4: ISLAMIST MOVEMENTS

1. Schwedler 2006; White 2003; Wickham 2002; Zeghal 2008; Gerges 2005; Wiktorowicz 2000, 2001, 2004a, 2004b: 15; Hafez 2003.

2. See, for example, Rahman 1982. Fazlur Rahman was a critic of political and theological dogmatism whose career included a senior civil service post in Pakistan and a professorship at the University of Chicago. Nasr Abu Zeyd, Egyptian philosophy professor, was harassed in Egypt because of his historical and hermeneutical approach to the Qur'an. When an Egyptian family court charged him with apostasy and ordered him divorced from his wife, the couple left for the Netherlands, where he held a professorship at Leiden University until his death in 2010. See Charles Kurzman's Liberal Islam project at http://www.unc.edu/~kurzman/LiberalIslamLinks.htm.

3. While they attracted many supporters in Iran and the diaspora, the religious intellectuals—Abdolkarim Soroush, Mohsen Saidzadeh, Mohsen Kadivar, Hasan Yousefi Eshkevari, and Mohammad Mojtahed Shabestari—have been harassed or forced into exile by the authorities. For more information on these proponents of a liberal Islam, see Kurzman's online sources; see also Mir-Hosseini and Tapper 2006.

4. On Tariq Ramadan, see Fourest 2004. On the Ahmadiyya—who often are persecuted as heretics—see http://www.muslimsforpeace.org. The U.S.-based ASMA society may be found at http://asmasociety.org/home/index.html.

5. Al-Azm 1993: 117. See also Marty and Appelby 1991, 1994; Kepel 2002; Juergensmeyer 2003. On Islamic activists see Wiktorowicz 2004b: 2; Hafez 2003: 5.

6. Sadik Jalal al-Azm, "What Is Islamism?" (unpublished paper given to me by the author, Damascus, Syria, December 17, 2007). Al-Azm, retired professor of modern European philosophy at the University of Damascus, is one of the most prominent critical intellectuals in the Arab world.

7. Amin 2007: 2. That Islamist movements are right-wing as well as patriarchal has long been argued by transnational feminists such as Marième Hélie-Lucas, a founder of Women Living under Muslim Laws. See chapter 5 for details.

8. Of course, Islam did not spread by the sword alone. Trade, empire, and settlement by Muslims helped the community to grow, while the decency of Muslim neighbors encouraged others to convert.

9. Regarding Iran, I have referred to two revolutions: the populist revolution against the shah in 1978–1979 and the Islamic takeover in 1979–1981 (Moghadam 1989). On the demonstration effect of Iran's Islamic revolution, see Esposito 1989.

10. On Western and Saudi support for Islamism, see Curtis 2010; Hegghammer 2010; Rubin 1997; Cooley 1999 (the quote appears on p. 1). On Indonesia, see Hefner 2000; Dhume 2009.

11. See Saad Eddin's pioneering sociological study of Islamists (Ibrahim 1980). On women, the veil, and male anxiety, see Mernissi 1987; Sabbah 1984. Other feminist studies on fundamentalism and Islamism include Kandiyoti 1991; Moghadam 1994. While some have equated Islamism with right-wing movements, at least one scholar sees similarities between contemporary Islamists and the extreme Left in Europe in the 1970s. Sadik al-Azm's views on the matter will be presented later in this chapter.

12. These propositions initially were presented in the first edition of my book *Modernizing Women: Gender and Social Change in the Middle East* (1993) and are also included in that book's second edition (Moghadam 2003, ch. 5). The propositions remain valid, and I present them here with adjustments and updates to reflect more recent developments.

13. An investigative article in Britain's *Guardian Weekly* describes "the lost boys" of Pakistan's Swat Valley, who had been pressed into the ranks of the Tehrik-i-Taliban, largely for the purpose of fighting infidels and becoming martyrs. Some of them were "lured by the swagger of the Islamic fighters"; others "were taken in the night by heavily armed figures who demanded money and recruits"; some "were sold by their parents for around $300, the going rate paid by the TTP for a healthy teenager." See Scott-Clark and Levy 2010; the quotes appear on p. 25. The authors also describe a school that tried to "deprogram teenagers brainwashed by the Taliban."

14. On "blowback," see Johnson 2001. The origin of the name "al-Qaeda" is unclear; it may refer to a "base" used by bin Laden and his associates in Afghanistan; see Halliday 2005: 196. See also Gerges 2005 on transnational Islam.

15. Wiktorowicz 2004a: 16.

16. Cesari 2004; Meer 2010. See also "Cameron Cuts Off Cash to Islamic Groups Suspected of Extremism," *Guardian Weekly*, February 11, 2011, 13. In July 2010, the French National Assembly voted 335–1 to ban the wearing of the niqab or burka (which covers the face as well as the hair and body). The law is formally called "Forbidding the Concealing of the Face in the Public Space." In Catalonia, an Islamic court run by salafists allegedly kidnapped a North African woman charged with adultery and sentenced her to death. She fled, and her captors were arrested, but not before moderate Muslim groups criticized the Catalan government for giving "a free rein to the most radical forms of Islam." See "Catalonia's 'Illegal' Islamic Court," *Guardian Weekly*, December 18, 2009, 11.

17. On the assassination of Salmaan Taseer, see "Staring into the Abyss: Pakistan's Increasing Radicalization," *The Economist*, January 8, 2011; the quote appears on p. 39. See also Declan Walsh, "Pakistan's Liberal Dream Has Died with the Assassination of Taseer," *Guardian Weekly*, January 14, 2011, 9. On the Danish cartoon controversy, see Klausen 2009; see also Olesen 2007; the quote appears on p. 42.

18. Entelis 2005; Wiktorowicz 2004a: 20; Hafez 2004; Hafez 2003; Hafez and Wiktorowicz 2004: 62.

19. The indented GIA quote appears in Hafez 2004: 52; others are found on pp. 48–49, 50. On feminist concerns and activities in Algeria, see Moghadam 2001, 2011a.

20. See Goodwin 2007.

21. Goodwin 2001.

22. Ghannouchi, cited in Fadel (2011: 4).

23. Gulalp 2001: 434.

24. Tugal 2009; Gulalp 2001.

25. Brown, Hamzawy, and Ottaway 2006: 7.

26. Abdo 2000. For a sympathetic view of the Muslim Brotherhood, see Tariq Ramadan, in *The Fundamentalisms Project*, vol. 3.

27. Pargeter 2010; El-Ghobashy 2005: 391. David Wroe, "Divisions in the Muslim Brotherhood," *The Age*, November 16, 2007, http://www.theage.com.au/news/world/divisions-in-muslim-brotherhood/2007/11/16/1194766965617.html (accessed December 12, 2007). See also Brown, Hamzawy, and Ottaway 2006.

28. Komsan 2010a, 2010b. See also http://www.ecrwonline.org.

29. Fuller 2002: 52–53.

30. Schwedler 2006; Langohr 2001.

31. Mona Siddiqui, "Call for Change, but All Too Quiet." *Times Higher Education* (London), April 2, 2009, 54.

32. "Dreaming of a Caliphate," *The Economist*, August 6, 2011, 22.

33. Wiktorowicz 2005: 85; Wickham 2002.

34. In Islamabad, Pakistan, in July 2007, thousands of militants associated with the Red Mosque and its affiliated schools barricaded themselves with arms until military units eventually attacked.

35. Clark 2004; Harik 2004; Roy 2011. Sara Roy maintains that Hamas is at heart a political organization, albeit one that has encouraged the Islamization of Gazan society. Its social work and attention to the practical needs of those in Gaza is also a political move—especially in light of competition from the Palestine Liberation Organization and from newly formed Salafist groups.

36. Wiktorowicz 2004a. See also Davis and Robertson 2009 on how certain faith-based organizations can succeed at strategies of "bypassing the state" and building grassroots organizations.

37. Al-Muhajiroun was disbanded in 2004 and its leader, Omar Bakri Mohammad, has not been allowed back into the United Kingdom since August 2005. The group's tenet was "the use of military coups to establish Islamic states wherever there are Muslims, including Britain" (Wiktorowicz 2005: 7). Considered by many UK Muslims as a "lunatic fringe," it managed to elicit considerable media attention.

38. Ian Black, "Al-Qaida Chief Launched 'Any Questions' Sessions on Web," *Guardian*, December 20, 2007, 22; Anna Johnson, "Al-Qaida Member Says Bush Should Be Greeted in Mideast with Bombs," Associated Press, January 7, 2008.

39. See "Satellites in the Arab World: Stop Their Orbit," *The Economist*, October 30, 2010, 50. See also Steger 2003: 5, 2; Blunt 2009. The dissemination of extremist messages via the media, as well as radical mosques, may help explain the string of attacks on churches in the Muslim world. For example, nine churches were attacked in Malaysia in January 2010; the perpetrators, Muslim extremists, were angered by a court ruling overturning a ban on non-Muslims using the word "Allah" for God. See *The Economist*, January 16, 2010, 8. The extremist Nigerian group Boko Haram went on a rampage in early 2012, killing Christians worshipping in church and then attacking police.

40. Khosrokhavar 2005.

41. Al-Azm 2004: 19. See also the miniseries *Carlos,* released by French filmmaker Olivier Assayas in 2010, which depicts the brief episode of Europe's experience with the extreme Left in the 1970s.

42. Al-Azm 2004: 19–20.

43. Al-Azm 2004: 20–21.

44. Pasha and Samatar 1997: 200.

45. Huntington 1996.

CHAPTER 5: FEMINISM ON A WORLD SCALE

1. See, for example, Chafetz and Dworkin 1986; Dahlerup 1987; Margolis 1993; Basu 1995; Beckwith 2007; Molyneux 2001; Ferree and Tripp 2006.

2. Stienstra 1994, 2000; Naples and Desai 2002; Moghadam 2005.

3. Sperling, Ferree, and Risman 2001: 1157; Hawkesworth 2006: 27; Moghadam 2005.

4. The Fourth World Conference on Women gathered to discuss, finalize, and adopt the draft Beijing Platform for Action, which identified twelve "critical areas of concern," including education, health, employment, poverty, the girl-child, and decision making.

5. The Palestinian question also divided participants, especially at the Copenhagen NGO Forum. See Fraser 1987.

6. Standing 1989, 1999a. Women-in-development (WID) began in the early 1970s and sought to bring attention to the problems facing women in the development process, including their marginalization from productive activities. Women-and-development (WAD) emerged as a more critical turn, and researchers raised questions about the nature of the development process that women were to be integrated into (see Beneria and Sen 1981; Elson and Pearson 1981). The gender-and-development (GAD) approach grounded itself more explicitly in feminist theorizing (see Young 1992).

7. On female poverty, see Beneria and Feldman 1992; Chant 1995; Moghadam 1998b. On restructuring in the former communist bloc, see Moghadam 1993; Rueschemeyer 1998.

8. For an elaboration of various types of fundamentalism across the globe, their gender dynamics, and their impacts on women's legal status and social positions, see contributions in Kandiyoti 1991 and Moghadam 1994, 1995b.

9. Alvarez et al. 2002.

10. Moghadam 2003, ch. 7.

11. Women in Development Europe 1998; Wichterich 1999.

12. For details on the activities of transnational feminist networks such as DAWN, WIDE, and WEDO, see Moghadam 2005: ch. 5.

13. "3,000 Trade Unionists March in Protest at Poverty and Violence against Women in Durban on April 5," International Confederation of Free Trade Unions (ICFTU), http://www.icftu.org (accessed April 15, 2002). The ICFTU is now known as the International Trade Union Confederation (ITUC), a nod to post–Cold War realities.

14. Moghadam 2005: 75–76.

15. Dufour and Giraud 2007: 310; 318–19.

16. Patricia Munoz Cabrera, "Globalising Gender Equality and Social Justice; WIDE—Women in Development Europe" (prepared for the international Women's Studies North and South conference, Bellagio, Italy, September 13–17, 2011) (conference organized by the present author).

17. Kazi 1997: 141.

18. Shaheed 1994: 7–8.

19. Personal communication from Marième Hélie-Lucas, July 3, 2003. Charlotte Bunch, founder and first director of the Center for Women's Global Leadership at Rutgers University, was instrumental not only in raising funds for women's groups and

their meetings but also in conceptualizing women's rights in the private sphere as human rights. For details on Algerian women's organizations, see Moghadam 2003, chs. 3 and 8, and Moghadam 2011a; see also Messaoudi and Schemla 1995.

20. See http://wluml.org/english/pubsfulltxt.shtml?cmd[87]=i-87-549649 (accessed January 16, 2008).

21. The cautionary message about an Islamist international was stated at a conference I organized on comparative fundamentalisms and women, which took place at UNU/WIDER in Helsinki, Finland, in October 1990. See Moghadam 1994; see also Hélie-Lucas 1993: 225. Disclosure: I provided some of the background information for a 2004 legal suit brought at the request of WLUML against an Algerian Islamist's request for political asylum in the United States.

22. Boix 2001: 6, 7.

23. See http://wluml.org/english/links.shtml (accessed January 16, 2008).

24. See http://www.learningpartnership.org. Much of the information in this section comes from my observations and interviews conducted in March 2010 at the WLP offices in Bethesda, Maryland; a transnational partners' meeting that took place in Jakarta in April 2010; and a site visit to BAOBAB in Nigeria in July 2010.

25. Enloe 2007: 14. See also Enloe 1990; Reardon 1993; Tickner 1992; Accad 2007; Flamhaft 2007; Moghadam 2007.

26. Lucille Mathurin Mair was secretary-general of the United Nations' second conference on women, which convened in Copenhagen in 1980. The passage is cited in Bunch and Carillo 1992: 71. See also Pietila and Vickers 1994.

27. See http://www.un.org/docs/scres.

28. Jang Roko Abhiyan, "Rally on the 25th [of September, 2001]," circulated via Internet by socglob@topica.com.

29. Eleanor Smeal (president of the Feminist Majority), "Special Message from the Feminist Majority on the Taliban, Osama bin Laden, and Afghan Women," Feminist Majority, September 18, 2001, http://feministmajority.org.

30. See http://www.IWTC.org.

31. Starhawk 2003: 17.

32. MADRE statement communicated to the author via e-mail in 2003.

33. The quotes appear on pp. 62, 65, and 66, respectively, of the spring 2003 issue of Ms. Magazine.

34. This occurred on October 24, 2007, and was widely reported. Rice had been on Capitol Hill to testify before the House Foreign Relations Committee.

35. Milazzo 2005: 103. See also Brim 2003: 10–12.

36. See http://www.nobelwomensinitiative.org. I was an invited participant. The six founders are Shirin Ebadi of Iran, Jody Williams of the United States, Betty Williams and Mairead Corrigan of Northern Ireland, Wangari Matthai of Kenya, and Rigoberta Menchu of Guatemala. The first international conference took place in Galway, Ireland, in May 2007, and was attended by about seventy-five women from across the globe.

37. "MADRE Programs in Iraq," MADRE, http://madre.org/programs/Iraq.html (accessed November 28, 2007).

38. "MADRE—Sister Organizations in Haiti," MADRE, November 13, 2007, http://www.madre.org/sister/Haiti.html.

39. See http://madre.org/programs/index.html.

40. "Honor Crimes," MADRE, November 28, 2007, http://www.madre.org/articles/int/honorcrimes.html. See also "Mission | Vision," MADRE, http://www.madre.org/index/meet-madre-1/who-we-are-49/mission--vision-160.html.

41. Eisenstein 2004; Enloe 2007.

42. Vargas 2005: 109–10.

43. Bach 2004.

44. Alexander and Mbali 2004.

45. Conway 2007: 50, 57, 63. In the latter quote, Conway is citing from a 2006 article by Nandita Gandhi and Nandita Shah.

46. WIDE Newsletter Special, April 2011, 1, http://www.wide-network.org.

47. Women Living under Muslim Laws 2005.

48. Tariq Ramadan is considered by many observers to be an important intellectual and a representative of a liberal or moderate Islam. But others view him with skepticism. For a critique of Tariq Ramadan's Arabic-language statements, see Fourest 2004. Caroline Fourest—who also authored a scathing critique of the French Far Right nationalist leader Le Pen—notes that in one of Ramadan's cassettes, Ramadan deliberately conflates "so-called secular Muslims" with "Muslims lacking Islam" (149). He also calls veiling a Muslim obligation and encourages young women to defend their right to veil, in part to protect themselves against the male gaze (see Fourest 2004: 212, quoting another cassette). At the First International Congress of Islamic Feminism, held in Barcelona in late October 2005 and organized by the Junta Islamica Catalan and the UNESCO office in Barcelona, Zainah Anwar of the Malaysian group Sisters in Islam told me that Tariq Ramadan had defended hijab at a meeting in Kuala Lumpur, leading to a spirited debate with the Islamic feminists who were themselves not veiled.

49. Meredith Tax, "The CCR and the Elephant in the Room," MeredithTax.org, August 22, 2010, http://www.meredithtax.org/taxonomyblog/ccr-and-elephant-room, also distributed by WLUM, September 12, 2010; Bennoune 2010.

50. Vargas 2005: 109.

CHAPTER 6: THE GLOBAL JUSTICE MOVEMENT

*This quote is from Jonathan Franklin, "Camila Takes on Chile's Elite," *Guardian Weekly*, September 2, 2011, 13. Camila Vallejo, twenty-three, a member of the Communist Party, was elected leader of the University of Chile student union and led protests against the two-tiered system of education and the underfunding of public schools and universities.

1. See, for example, Della Porta 2007.

2. Taylor 1993, 2000.

3. Bello 2000: 55. On Ghana, see Njehu 2004: 103.

4. Subcomandante Marcos 2004.

5. Njehu 2004.

6. George 2004: 194. Susan George, a veteran international activist, goes on to say that Jubilee 2000 dissolved itself in 2000, while other groups within the global justice movement continue to campaign for the abolition of all Third World debt.

7. George 2004: 196.

8. For details, see Moghadam 2005, ch. 3.

9. See, for example, Langman, Morris, and Zalewski 2002.

10. Bello 2004: 55. Bello adds that "the war on terror" resulted in a return of the U.S. military bases.

11. Bello 2004: 64.

12. Pianta and Marchetti 2007: 40–41.

13. Podobnik 2005.

14. Moghadam 2005: 31–32; Pianta and Marchetti 2007: 40–41.

15. Various news reports covered the protest events of the early 2000s—for example, Tom Hundley, "Anti-Globalization Groups Gear Up," *Chicago Tribune*, July 15, 2001; Ben White, "An Elite Cast Debates Poverty," *Washington Post*, February 3, 2002; and Leslie Crawford, "Huge Protest March Passes Off Peacefully," *Financial Times*, March 18, 2002.

16. Pianta and Marchetti 2007: 39.

17. See, for example, Esther Addley, "Local Action with Global Message," *Guardian Weekly*, October 21–27, 2011, 1.

18. Vargas 2005.

19. Reese, Gutierrez, and Chase-Dunn 2007: 4.

20. Della Porta 2007: 44.

21. For example, in West Lafayette, Indiana, where I was based from 2007 through 2011, the global justice movement was present in the form of an anti-sweatshop student group at Purdue University called POLE (Purdue Organization for Labor Equality) and a community group called the Greater Lafayette Progressive Alliance. Members of both attended the United States Social Forum (USSF) that took place in Atlanta, Georgia, in July 2007. I also participated in the second USSF in Detroit, Michigan, in June 2010 and observed many student groups and community-based activist groups in attendance.

22. See http://www.attac.org and George 2004: xi. On the Tobin tax, see chapter 2.

23. Ancelovici 2002.

24. Reese, Gutierrez, and Chase-Dunn 2007: 6.

25. Mertes 2004: 242.

26. Reese, Gutierrez, and Chase-Dunn 2007: 6. See also Smith et al. 2008.

27. Santos 2006: 95. Reese, Gutierrez, and Chase-Dunn 2007 surveyed 640 participants (out of 155,000 registered participants from 135 countries) at the 2005 WSF in Porto Alegre and found the following demographic breakdown: South Americans represented 68 percent of those surveyed (with Brazilians making up 58 percent of the total number); Western Europeans, 13 percent; North Americans, 9 percent; Asians, 8 percent; and Africans, 2 percent. Their sample included no participants from the Middle East or North Africa.

28. Smith and Smythe 2010.

29. Santos 2006: 104, 188–95 (appendix 1). See also http://www.forumsocialmundial.org.br.

30. Borland 2006.

31. International Gender and Trade Network 2002.

32. Santos 2006: 53–54. Critiques by DAWN and WIDE are found in various of their online publications.

33. Santos 2006: 60.

34. See http://www.marchemondialedesfemmes.org/alliances_mondialisation/asamblea-movimientos-sociales/declarations/poa-2012/en. On women in Via Campesina, see Desmarais 2007.

35. Santos 2006: 35. The Charter of Principles may be found at http://www.forum socialmundial.org.br/main.php?id_menu=4&cd_language=2.

36. Santos 2006: 92–93.

37. Santos 2006: 111–26.

38. Reese, Gutierrez, and Chase-Dunn 2007. Many European activists feel that a strong EU is needed as a counterweight to U.S. hegemony, but others in the global justice movement are opposed and prefer a return to local democracy.

39. Danaher cited in George 2004: 98. See also Pianta and Marchetti 2007: 48.

40. For some of these ideas, see contributions in Podobnik and Reifer 2004; George 2004; Smith et al. 2008; the WSF Charter of Principles and other documents; various publications by WIDE and Marche Mondiale des Femmes/World March of Women.

41. George 2004. Susan George was among the participants in a landmark conference, organized by left-wing sociology professors and held at the University of California, Santa Barbara, in May 2003, that sought to define and advance "critical globalization studies." Her presentation focused on the responsibility of scholar-activists. See Appelbaum and Robinson 2005.

42. Santos 2006: 205–7 (appendix 3). The Bamako Appeal of 2006 makes a similar set of proposals. See http://mrzine.monthlyreview.org/bamako.html.

43. See Broad 2002: 42–46. The statement was issued and signed, inter alia, by Maude Barlow (Council of Canadians), Walden Bellow (Focus on the Global South), Lori Wallach (Public Citizen), Vandana Shiva, and John Cavanaugh.

44. Shiva 2000: 123–24; Bello 2000: 90.

45. Klein 2007a. See also U.S. filmmaker Oliver Stone's documentary *South of the Border,* released in 2010, which provides a good visual depiction of the Latin American "pink tide."

46. On the 2011 Montreal conference, see http://www.fiess2011.org/en; on the SEN, see http://www.ussen.org; for case studies of solidarity economy, visit http://aloe.socioeco.org/page70-studies_en.html.

47. Moghadam 2005.

CHAPTER 7: CONCLUSIONS AND PROGNOSTICATION

1. Guidry, Kennedy, and Zald 2000a: 24.

2. Granovetter 1983; Langman 2005; Castells 1996; Giddens 1999.

3. Cherifati-Merabtine 1995: 42.

4. Przeworski et al. 1995, especially p. 14.

References

Abdo, Geneive. 2000. *No God but God: Egypt and the Triumph of Islam.* Oxford: Oxford University Press.

Accad, Evelyne. 2007. "Gender and Violence in Lebanese War Novels." Pp. 293–310 in *From Patriarchy to Empowerment: Women's Participation, Movements, and Rights in the Middle East, North Africa, and South Asia,* edited by V. M. Moghadam. Syracuse, NY: Syracuse University Press.

Ake, Claude. 1993. "Rethinking African Democracy." In *The Global Resurgence of Democracy,* edited by Larry Diamond and Marc Plattner. Baltimore: Johns Hopkins University Press.

Al-Azm, Sadik. 1993. "Islamic Fundamentalism Reconsidered: A Critical Outline of Problems, Ideas and Approaches." *South Asia Bulletin: Comparative Studies of South Asia, Africa, and the Middle East* 13, nos. 1–2: 93–121.

Al-Azm, Sadik. 2004. "Islam, Terrorism and the West Today." Essay written for the Praemium Esarmianum Foundation on the occasion of the award of the Erasmus Prize, Amsterdam (November). Naarden: Foundation Horizon.

Alexander, Amanda, and Mandisa Mbali. 2004. "Have the Slaves Left the Master's House?" A report on the Africa Social Forum. Alternatives . . . for a Different World (December 21). http://www.alternatives.ca/article1625.html (accessed January 16, 2008).

Allard, Jenna, Carl Davidson, and Julie Matthaei, eds. 2008. *Solidarity Economy: Building Alternatives for People and Planet, Papers and Reports from the U.S. Social Forum 2007.* Chicago: ChangeMaker Publications.

Alvarez, Sonia. 1990. *Engendering Democracy in Brazil: The Women's Movements in Transition Politics.* Princeton, NJ: Princeton University Press.

Alvarez, Sonia, et al. 2002. "Encountering Latin American and Caribbean Feminisms." *Signs: Journal of Women in Culture and Society* 28, no. 2: 537–73.

Amin, Samir. 2007. "Political Islam in the Service of Imperialism." *Monthly Review* (December): 1–18.

Ancelovici, Marcos. 2002. "Organizing against Globalization: The Case of ATTAC in France." *Politics & Society* 30, no. 3 (September): 427–63.

233

Anheier, Helmut, Marlies Glasius, and Mary Kaldor, eds. 2001. *The Global Civil Society Yearbook*. Oxford: Oxford University Press.

Applebaum, Richard, and William I. Robinson, eds. 2005. *Critical Globalization Studies*. New York: Routledge.

Arjomand, Said Amir. 1986. "Social Change and Movements of Revitalization in Contemporary Islam." Pp. 87–112 in *New Religious Movements and Rapid Social Change*, edited by James Beckford. Beverly Hills and Paris: Sage Publications and UNESCO.

Arrighi, Giovanni, Terence K. Hopkins, and Immanuel Wallerstein. 1989. *Anti-Systemic Movements*. London: Verso.

Atkinson, Anthony. 2001. "Is Rising Inequality Inevitable? A Critique of the Transatlantic Consensus." *WIDER Annual Lectures* 3 (November).

Babones, Salvatore. 2006. "Conducting Global Social Research." Pp. 8–30 in *Global Social Change: Historical and Comparative Perspectives*, edited by Christopher Chase-Dunn and Salvatore Babones. Baltimore, MD: Johns Hopkins University Press.

Bach, Amandine. 2004. "The Third European Social Forum, London, 14–17 October 2004." http://62.149.193.10/wide/download/The%203rd%20ESF.pdf?id=250 (accessed January 12, 2008).

Bakker, Isabella, ed. 1994. *The Strategic Silence: Gender and Economic Policy*. London: Zed Books with the North-South Institute.

Barber, Benjamin. 1984. *Strong Democracy: Participatory Politics for a New Age*. Berkeley, Los Angeles, and London: University of California Press.

———. 2001. *Jihad vs. McWorld*. New York: Times Books.

Barkawi, Tarak. 2006. *Globalization and War*. Lanham, MD: Rowman & Littlefield.

Barnet, Richard J., and Ronald Muller. 1974. *Global Reach: The Power of Multinational Corporations*. New York: Simon & Schuster.

Barron, Andrea. 2002. "The Palestinian Women's Movement: Agent of Democracy in a Future State?" *Middle East Critique* 11, no. 1: 71–90.

Basu, Amrita, ed. 1995. *The Challenge of Local Feminisms: Women's Movements in Global Perspective*. Boulder, CO: Westview Press.

Bauer, Jan, and Anissa Hélie. 2006. *Documenting Women's Human Rights Violations by Non-State Actors: Activist Strategies from Muslim Communities*. Québec: International Centre for Human Rights and Democratic Development and WLUML.

Bayat, Asef. 2007. *Making Islam Democratic: Social Movements and the Post-Islamist Turn*. Stanford, CA: Stanford University Press.

Beck, Ulrich. 2004. "The Cosmopolitan Turn." Pp. 143–66 in *The Future of Social Theory*, edited by Nicholas Gane. London: Continuum.

Beckford, James, ed. 1986. *New Religious Movements and Rapid Social Change*. Thousand Oaks, CA, and Paris: Sage and UNESCO.

Beckwith, Karen. 2007. "Mapping Strategic Engagements: Women's Movements and the State." *International Feminist Journal of Politics* 9, no. 3: 312–38.

———. 2010. "Introduction: Comparative Politics and the Logics of a Comparative Politics of Gender." *Perspectives on Politics* 8, no. 1 (March): 159–68.

Beinin, Joel. 2009a. "Egyptian Workers from Arab Socialism to the Neo-Liberal Economic Order." Pp. 68–86 in *Egypt: The Moment of Change*, edited by Rabab El-Mahdi and Philip Marfleet. London: Zed Press.

———. 2009b. "Workers' Protest in Egypt: Neo-Liberalism and Class Struggle in the 21st Century." *Social Movement Studies* 8, no. 4 (November): 449–54.

Bello, Walden. 2000. "Building an Iron Cage." Pp. 54–90 in *Views from the South: The Effects of Globalization and the WTO on Third World Countries*, edited by Sarah Anderson. Chicago: Food First and the International Forum on Globalization.

———. 2004. "The Global South." Pp. 49–69 in *A Movement of Movements: Is Another World Really Possible?*, edited by Tom Mertes. London: Verso.

Beneria, Lourdes, and Gita Sen. 1981. "Accumulation, Reproduction and Women's Role in Development: Boserup Revisited." *Signs* 8, no. 2 (winter).

Beneria, Lourdes, and Shelley Feldman, eds. 1992. *Unequal Burden: Economic Crises, Persistent Poverty, and Women's Work*. Boulder, CO: Westview Press.

Bennoune, Karima. 1995. "S.O.S. Algeria: Women's Human Rights under Siege." In *Faith and Freedom: Women's Human Rights*, edited by Mahnaz Afkhami. Syracuse, NY: Syracuse University Press.

———. 2010. "Remembering the Other's Others: Theorizing the Approach of International Law to Muslim Fundamentalism." *Columbia Human Rights Law Review* 41: 635–98.

Berger, Suzanne, and Ronald Dore, eds. 1996. *National Diversity and Global Capitalism*. Ithaca, NY: Cornell University Press.

Berkovitch, Nitza. 1999. *From Motherhood to Citizenship: Women's Rights and International Organizations*. Baltimore: Johns Hopkins University Press.

Berkovitch, Nitza, and Valentine M. Moghadam. 1999. "Middle East Politics: Feminist Challenges" (introduction to special issue). *Social Politics: International Studies in Gender, State, and Society* 6, no. 3 (fall).

Bhagwati, Jagdish. 2004. *In Defense of Globalization*. New York: Oxford University Press.

Bhavnani, Kum-Kum, John Foran, and Molly Talcott. 2005. "The Red, the Green, the Black, and the Purple: Reclaiming Development, Resisting Globalization." Pp. 323–32 in *Critical Globalization Studies*, edited by Richard Appelbaum and William I. Robinson. New York: Routledge.

Blee, Kathleen M., and Kimberly A. Creasap. 2010. "Conservative and Right-Wing Movements." *Annual Review of Sociology* 36: 269–86.

Bluestone, Barry, and Bennett Harrison. 1982. *The Deindustrialization of America: Plant Closings, Community Abandonment, and the Dismantling of Basic Industry*. New York: Basic Books.

Blunt, Gary. 2009. *iMuslims: Rewiring the House of Islam*. Chapel Hill: University of North Carolina Press.

Boix, Monserrat. 2001. "Women's Networks: Islamists' Violence and Terror." *WLUML Newssheet* 13, no. 4 (November–December).

Boli, John. 2005. "Contemporary Developments in World Culture." *International Journal of Contemporary Sociology* 46, no. 5–6: 383–404.

Boli, John, and George M. Thomas. 1997. "World Culture in the World Polity." *American Sociological Review* 62, no. 2 (April): 171–90.

Borland, Elizabeth. 2006. "The Mature Resistance of Argentina's Madres de Plaza de Mayo." Pp. 115–44 in *Latin American Social Movements: Globalization, Democratization, and Transnational Networks*, edited by Hank Johnston and Paul Almeida. Lanham, MD: Rowman & Littlefield.

Boswell, Terry, and Christopher Chase-Dunn. 2000. *The Spiral of Capitalism and Socialism: Toward Global Democracy*. Boulder, CO: Lynne Rienner.

Boxer, Marilyn J., and Jean H. Quataert. 1978. *Socialist Women: European Socialist Feminism in the Nineteenth and Early Twentieth Centuries.* New York: Elsevier.

Bratton, Michael, and Nicholas Van De Walle. 1992. "Towards Governance in Africa: Popular Demands and State Responses." In *Governance and Politics in Africa,* edited by Goran Hyden and Michael Bratton. Boulder, CO: Lynne Rienner Publishers.

Brim, Sand. 2003. "Report from Baghdad." *Off Our Backs* (March–April): 10–12.

Broad, Robin, ed. 2002. *Global Backlash: Citizen Initiatives for a Just World Economy.* Lanham, MD: Rowman & Littlefield.

Brown, Nathan, Amr Hamzawy, and Marina S. Ottaway. 2006. "Islamist Movements and the Democratic Process in the Arab World: Exploring Gray Zones." Washington, DC: Carnegie Endowment for International Peace, Paper No. 67 (March). http://www.carnegieendowment.org/files/cp_67_grayzones_final.pdf.

Bunch, Charlotte, and Roxanna Carillo. 1992. *Gender Violence: A Development and Human Rights Issue.* Dublin: Atlantic Press.

Castells, Manuel. 1996. *The Rise of the Network Society.* Oxford and New York: Oxford University Press.

Castells, Manuel, Mireia Fernàndez-Ardèvol, and Araba Sey. 2006. *Mobile Communication and Society: A Global Perspective.* Cambridge, MA: MIT Press.

Cesari, Jocelyne. 2004. *When Islam and Democracy Meet: Muslims in Europe and in the United States.* New York: Palgrave Macmillan.

Chafetz, Janet S., and Gary Dworkin. 1986. *Female Revolt: Women's Movements in World and Historical Perspective.* Totowa, NJ: Rowman & Allanheld.

Chang, Paul Y. 2008. "Unintended Consequences of Repression: Alliance Formation in South Korea's Democracy Movement (1970–1979)." *Social Forces* 87, no. 2: 651–77.

Chant, Sylvia. 1995. "Women's Roles in Recession and Economic Restructuring in Mexico and the Philippines." In *Poverty and Global Adjustment: The Urban Experience,* edited by Alan Gilbert. Oxford: Blackwell.

Chase-Dunn, Christopher. 1998. *Global Formation: Structures of the World Economy.* 2nd ed. Totowa, NJ: Rowman & Littlefield.

Chase-Dunn, Christopher, and Salvatore Babones, eds. 2006. *Global Social Change: Historical and Comparative Perspectives.* Baltimore: Johns Hopkins University Press.

Chase-Dunn, Christopher, et al. 2009. "The New Global Left : Movements and Regimes." IROWS Working Paper 50. http://www.irows.urc.edu/papers.

Cherifati-Merabtine, Doria. 1995. "Algerian Women at a Crossroads: National Liberation, Islamization, and Women." Pp. 40–62 in *Gender and National Identity: Women and Politics in Muslim Societies,* edited by Valentine M. Moghadam. London: Zed Books.

Chossudovsky, Michel, and Andrew Gavin Marshall, eds. 2010. *The Global Economic Crisis: The Great Depression of the XXI Century.* Montreal: Global Research Publishers, Centre for Research on Globalization.

Chua, Amy. 2003. *World on Fire: How Exporting Free Market Democracy Breeds Ethnic Hatred and Global Instability.* New York: Doubleday.

Clark, Janine. 2004. *Islam, Charity and Activism: Middle-Class Networks and Social Welfare in Egypt, Jordan, and Yemen.* Bloomington: Indiana University Press.

Collectif Maghreb Egalité 95. 2005. *Guide to Equality in the Family in the Maghreb.* Translated by Chari Voss. Bethesda, MD: Women's Learning Partnership Translation Series.

Connell, R. W. 1998. "Masculinities and Globalization." *Men and Masculinities* 1, no. 1: 1–20.

Conway, Jane. 2007. "Transnational Feminisms and the World Social Forum: Encounters and Transformations in Anti-Globalization Spaces." *Journal of International Women's Studies* 8, no. 3 (April): 49–70.

Cooley, John. 1999. *Unholy Wars: Afghanistan, America and International Terrorism.* London: Pluto Press.

Cornia, Giovanni Andrea, Richard Jolly, and Frances Stewart. 1989. *Adjustment with a Human Face: Protecting the Vulnerable and Promoting Growth.* Oxford and New York: Clarendon Press and UNICEF.

Costain, Anne. 2005. "Social Movements as Mechanisms for Political Inclusion." Pp. 108–21 in *The Politics of Democratic Inclusion*, edited by Christina Wolbrecht and Rodney Hero. Philadelphia: Temple University Press.

Cox, Robert W. 1992. "Global Perestroika." Pp. 26–43 in *Socialist Register 1992*, edited by Ralph Miliband and Leo Panitch. London: Merlin Press.

Crick, Bernard. 2000. *Essays on Citizenship.* London: Continuum.

Cummings, Bruce. 2000. "Democracy and Civil Society in Korea." Pp. 133–46 in *Pathways to Democracy: The Political Economy of Democratic Transitions*, edited by James F. Hollifield and Calvin Jillson. New York: Routledge.

Curtis, Mark. 2010. *Secret Affairs: Britain's Collusion with Radical Islam.* London: Serpent's Tail.

Dahlerup, Drude, ed. 1987. *The New Women's Movement: Feminism and Political Power in Europe and the USA.* London: Sage.

Davis, Nancy J., and Robert V. Robertson. 2009. "Overcoming Movement Obstacles by the Religiously Orthodox: The Muslim Brotherhood in Egypt, Shas in Israel, Communione e Liberazione in Italy, and the Salvation Army in the United States." *American Journal of Sociology* 114, no. 5: 1305–49.

Della Porta, Donatella. 2005. "Deliberation in Movement: Why and How to Study Deliberative Democracy and Social Movements." *Acta Politica* 40, no. 3: 336–50.

———, ed. 2007. *The Global Justice Movement: Cross-National and Transnational Perspectives.* Boulder, CO: Paradigm Publishers.

———. 2009. "Making the New Polis: The Practice of Deliberative Democracy in Social Forums." Pp. 181–208 in *Culture, Social Movements and Protest*, edited by Hank Johnston. Farnham, UK: Ashgate.

Desmarais, Annette Aurélie. 2007. *La Via Campesina: Globalization and the Power of Peasants.* Halifax, Canada, and London, UK: Fernwood Publishing and Pluto Press.

Dhume, Sadanand. 2009. *My Friend the Fanatic: Travels with a Radical Islamist.* New York: Skyhorse Publishing.

Di Marco, Graciela. 2011a. "Gendered Economic Rights and Trade Unionism: The Case of Argentina." Pp. 93–122 in *Making Globalization Work for Women: The Role of Social Rights and Trade Union Leadership*, edited by Valentine M. Moghadam, Mary Margaret Fonow, and Suzanne Franzway. Albany, NY: State University of New York Press.

———. 2011b. "Claims for Legal Abortion in Argentina and the Construction of New Political Identities." Pp. 167–89 in *Feminisms, Democratization, and Radical Democracy: Case Studies in South and Central America, Middle East, and North Africa*, edited by Graciela Di Marco and Constanza Tabbush. Buenos Aires: UNSAM Edita.

Di Marco, Graciela, and Constanza Tabbush, eds. 2011. *Feminisms, Democratization and Radical Democracy*. San Martin, Argentina: UNSAMEDITA Press.

Diamond, Larry. 2010. "Why Are There No Arab Democracies?" *Journal of Democracy* 21, no. 1: 93–104.

Diamond, Larry, Juan Linz, and Seymour Martin Lipset, eds. 1989. *Democracy in Developing Countries: Asia*. Boulder, CO: Lynne Rienner.

Dryzek, John. 1990. *Discursive Democracy: Politics, Policy, and Political Science*. Cambridge: Cambridge University Press.

Dufour, Pascale, and Isabelle Giraud. 2007. "The Continuity of Transnational Solidarities in the World March of Women, 2000 and 2005: A Collective Identity-Building Approach." *Mobilization* 12, no. 3 (November): 307–22.

Dunn, John. 2005. *Setting the People Free: The Story of Democracy*. New York: Atlantic Books.

Eckstein, Susan E., and Timothy Wickham-Crowley. 2003. "Struggles for Social Rights in Latin America: Claims in the Arenas of Subsistence, Labor, Gender, and Ethnicity." Pp. 1–56 in *Struggles for Social Rights in Latin America*, edited by Susan E. Eckstein and Timothy Wickham-Crowley. London: Routledge.

Eisenstein, Zillah. 2004. *Against Empire: Feminisms, Racism, and the West*. London: Zed Books.

El-Ghobashy, Mona. 2005. "The Metamorphosis of the Egyptian Muslim Brothers." *International Journal of Middle East Studies* 37: 373–95.

Elson, Diane, and Ruth Pearson. 1981. "Nimble Fingers Make Cheap Workers: An Analysis of Women's Employment in Third World Export Manufacturing." *Feminist Review* (spring): 87–107.

Enloe, Cynthia. 1990. *Bananas, Beaches and Bases: Making Feminist Sense of International Politics*. Berkeley: University of California Press.

———. 2007. *Globalization and Militarism: Feminists Make the Link*. Lanham, MD: Rowman & Littlefield.

Entelis, John. 2005. "Islamist Politics and the Democratic Imperative: Comparative Lessons from the Algerian Experience." In *Islam, Democracy and the State in Algeria: Lessons for the Western Mediterranean and Beyond*, edited by Michael D. Bonner, Megan Reif, and Mark Tessler. London: Routledge.

Eschle, Catherine. 2000. *Global Democracy, Social Movements, and Feminism*. Boulder, CO: Westview Press.

Eschle, Catherine, and Bice Maiguashca. 2010. *Making Feminist Sense of the Global Justice Movement*. Lanham, MD: Rowman & Littlefield.

Esposito, John, ed. 1989. *The Iranian Revolution: Its Global Impact*. Gainesville: University Press of Florida.

———. 2002. *Unholy War: Terror in the Name of Islam*. Oxford: Oxford University Press.

Eyerman, Ron, and Andrew Jamison. 1991. *Social Movements: A Cognitive Approach*. University Park: Pennsylvania University Press.

Fadel, Leila. 2011. "Islamists' Win Tests Tunisia Democracy." *Guardian Weekly*, November 4, 4–5.

Ferree, Myra Marx, and Aili Marie Tripp, eds. 2006. *Global Feminism: Transnational Women's Activism, Organizing, and Human Rights*. New York: New York University Press.

Flam, Helena, and Debra King, eds. 2005. *Emotions and Social Movements*. New York: Routledge.

Flamhaft, Ziva. 2007. "Iron Breaks, Too: Israeli and Palestinian Women Talk about War, Bereavement, and Peace." Pp. 311–26 in *From Patriarchy to Empowerment: Women's Participation, Movements, and Rights in the Middle East, North Africa, and South Asia*, edited by V. M. Moghadam. Syracuse, NY: Syracuse University Press.

Foroohar, Rana. 2011. "Whatever Happened to Upward Mobility?" *Time*, November 14, 25–34.

Fourest, Caroline. 2004. *Frère Tariq: Discours, stratégie et méthode de Tariq Ramadan*. Paris: Grasset et Fasquelle.

Fraser, Arvonne. 1987. *The U.N. Decade for Women: Documents and Dialogue*. Boulder, CO: Westview.

Frobel, Folker, Jurgen Heinrichs, and Otto Kreye. 1980. *The New International Division of Labor*. Cambridge: Cambridge University Press.

Fukuyama, Francis. 1992. *The End of History and the Last Man*. New York: The Free Press.

Fuller, Graham. 2002. "The Future of Political Islam." *Foreign Affairs* (March–April): 48–60.

Garrett, R. K. 2006. "Protest in an Information Society." *Information, Communication & Society* 9: 202–24.

George, Susan. 2004. *Another World Is Possible If . . .* London: Verso.

Gerges, Fawaz. 2005. *The Far Enemy: Why Jihad Went Global*. Cambridge: Cambridge University Press.

Gerlach, Luther. 1999. "The Structure of Social Movements: Environmental Activism and Its Opponents." Pp. 85–98 in *Waves of Protest: Social Movements since the Sixties*, edited by Jo Freeman and Victoria Johnson. Lanham, MD: Rowman & Littlefield.

Giddens, Anthony. 1999. *Runaway World: How Globalization Is Reshaping Our Lives*. London: Profile Books.

Givan, Rebecca Kolins, Kenneth Roberts, and Sarah A. Soule, eds. 2010. *The Diffusion of Social Movements: Actors, Mechanisms, and Political Effects*. New York: Cambridge University Press.

Goldstone, Jack A., and Doug McAdam. 2001. "Contention in Demographic and Life-Course Context." Pp. 195–221 in *Silence and Voice in the Study of Contentious Politics*, edited by Ronald Aminzade, Jack Goldstone, Doug McAdam, Elizabeth Perry, William Sewell, Sidney Tarrow, and Charles Tilly. Cambridge, UK: Cambridge University Press.

Goodwin, Jeff. 2001. *No Other Way Out: States and Revolutionary Movements, 1945–1991*. Cambridge: Cambridge University Press.

———. 2007. "Explaining Revolutionary Terrorism." Pp. 199–221 in *Revolution in the Making of the Modern World*, edited by John Foran, David Lane, and Andreja Zivkovic. London: Routledge.

Goodwin, Jeff, James M. Jasper, and Francesca Polleta, eds. 2001. *Passionate Politics: Emotions and Social Movements*. Chicago: University of Chicago Press.

Granovetter, Mark S. 1983. "The Strength of Weak Ties: A Network Theory Revisited." *Sociological Theory* 1: 201–33.

Guidry, John A., Michael D. Kennedy, and Mayer N. Zald. 2000a. "Globalizations and Social Movements." Pp. 1–32 in *Globalizations and Social Movements: Culture, Power and the Transnational Public Sphere*, edited by John A. Guidry, Michael D. Kennedy, and Mayer N. Zald. Ann Arbor: University of Michigan Press.

———, eds. 2000b. *Globalizations and Social Movements: Culture, Power and the Transnational Public Sphere*. Ann Arbor: University of Michigan Press.

Gulalp, Haldun. 2001. "Globalization and Political Islam: The Social Bases of Turkey's Welfare Party." *International Journal of Middle East Studies* 33: 433–48.

Habermas, Jurgen. 1992. "Further Reflections on the Public Sphere." In *Habermas and the Public Sphere*, edited by Craig Calhoun. Cambridge, MA: MIT Press.

Hadden, Hennifer, and Sidney Tarrow. 2007. "The Global Justice Movement in the United States since Seattle." Pp. 210–31 in *The Global Justice Movement: Cross-National and Transnational Perspectives*, edited by Donatella della Porta. Boulder, CO: Paradigm Publishers.

Hafez, Mohammed. 2003. *Why Muslims Rebel: Repression and Resistance in the Islamic World*. Boulder, CO: Lynne Rienner Publishers.

———. 2004. "From Marginalization to Massacres: A Political Process Explanation of GIA Violence in Algeria." Pp. 37–60 in *Islamic Activism: A Social Movement Theory Approach*, edited by Quintan Wiktorowicz. Bloomington: Indiana University Press.

Hafez, Mohammed, and Quintan Wiktorowicz. 2004. "Violence as Contention in the Egyptian Islamic Movement." Pp. 61–88 in *Islamic Activism: A Social Movement Theory Approach*, edited by Quintan Wiktorowicz. Bloomington: Indiana University Press.

Halliday, Fred. 2005. *100 Myths about the Middle East*. London: Saqi.

Hardt, Michael, and Antonio Negri. 2000. *Empire*. Cambridge, MA: Harvard University Press.

Harik, Judith. 2004. *Hezbollah: The Changing Face of Terrorism*. London: I. B. Taurus.

Harvey, David. 2003. *The New Imperialism*. Oxford: Oxford University Press.

———. 2004. "Neoliberalism and the Restoration of Class Power." *Via Portside*, August 6. http://www.scribd.com/doc/63941056/HARVEY-David-Neoliberalism-and-Class-Restore.

———. 2009. *A Brief History of Neoliberalism*. Oxford and New York: Oxford University Press.

Hawkesworth, Mary. 2006. *Globalization and Feminist Activism*. Lanham, MD: Rowman & Littlefield.

Heckscher, Zahara. 2002. "Long before Seattle: Historical Resistance to Economic Globalization." Pp. 86–91 in *Global Backlash: Citizen Initiatives for a Just World Economy*, edited by Robin Broad. Lanham, MD: Rowman & Littlefield.

Hefner, Robert. 2000. *Civil Islam: Muslims and Democratization in Indonesia*. Princeton, NJ: Princeton University Press.

Hegghammer, Thomas. 2010. *Jihad in Saudi Arabia: Violence and Pan-Islamism since 1979*. Cambridge, UK: Cambridge University Press.

Held, David, ed. 2000. *A Globalizing World? Culture, Economics, Politics*. London: Routledge.

Hélie-Lucas, Marieme. 1993. "Women Living under Muslim Laws." In *Ours by Right: Women's Rights as Human Rights*, edited by Joanna Kerr. London: Zed Books, in association with the North-South Institute.

Hirst, Paul, and Grahame Thompson. 1996. *Globalization in Question: The International Economy and the Possibilities of Governance*. Cambridge: Polity Press.

Hopkins, Terence K., and Immanuel Wallerstein. 1996. "The World System: Is There a Crisis?" Pp. 1–10 in *The Age of Transition: Trajectory of the World-System 1945–2025*, coordinated by Terence K. Hopkins et al. London: Zed Books.

Howe, Stephen. 2002. *Empire: A Very Short Introduction*. Oxford and New York: Oxford University Press.

Htun, Mala, and Laurel Weldon. 2011. "Sex Equality in Family Law: Historical Legacies, Feminist Activism, and Religious Power in 70 Countries." Background paper for the World Bank, *World Development Report 2012*, http://siteresources.worldbank.org/INTWDR2012/Resources/7778105-1299699968583/7786210-1322671773271/Htun-Weldon-family-law-paper-april-11.pdf.

Huntington, Samuel. 1992. *The Third Wave: Democratization in the Late Twentieth Century*. Norman: University of Oklahoma Press.

———. 1996. *The Clash of Civilizations and the Remaking of World Order*. New York: Simon & Schuster.

Ibrahim, Saad Eddin. 1980. "Anatomy of Egypt's Militant Islamic Groups: Methodological Notes and Preliminary Findings." *International Journal of Middle East Studies* 12, no. 4 (December): 423–53.

Im, Hyung Baeg. 2000. "South Korean Democratic Consolidation in Comparative Perspective." Pp. 21–54 in *Consolidating Democracy in South Korea*, edited by Larry Diamond and Byung-Kook Kim. Boulder, CO: Lynne Rienner Publishers.

International Gender and Trade Network (IGTN). 2002. "With Women, Another World Is Possible." IGTN statement, World Social Forum, Porto Alegre, Brazil, February. http://www.wide-network.org/index.jsp?id=198 (accessed January 16, 2008).

International Labour Organization (ILO). 2011. *The Global Economic Crisis: Causes, Responses, and Challenges*. Geneva: International Labour Office. http://www.ilo.org/wcmsp5/groups/public/---dgreports/---dcomm/---publ/documents/publication/wcms_155824.pdf.

International Monetary Fund (IMF). 2009. *World Economic Outlook, April 2009: Crisis and Recovery*. Washington, DC: IMF. http://www.imf.org/external/pubs/ft/weo/2009/01/pdf/text.pdf.

Jaquette, Jane. 2001. "Regional Differences and Contrasting Views." *Journal of Democracy* 12, no. 3 (July): 11–125.

———. 2009. "Feminist Activism and the Challenges of Democracy." Pp. 208–18 in *Feminist Agendas and Democracy in Latin America*, edited by Jane Jaquette. Durham, NC: Duke University Press.

Jayawardena, Kumari. 1986. *Feminism and Nationalism in the Third World*. London: Zed Books.

Johnson, Chalmers. 2001. "Blowback." *The Nation*, October 15. http://www.thenation.com/doc/20011015/Johnson.

Johnston, Hank. 2011. *States and Social Movements*. London: Polity Press.

Johnston, Hank, and Paul Almeida, eds. 2006. *Latin American Social Movements*. Lanham, MD: Rowman & Littlefield.

Juergensmeyer, Mark. 2003. *Terror in the Mind of God: The Global Rise of Religious Violence*. Berkeley: University of California Press.

Juris, Jeffrey. 2008. *Networking Futures: The Movements against Corporate Globalization*. Durham, NC: Duke University Press.

Kaldor, Mary. 2003. *Global Civil Society: An Answer to War*. Cambridge: Polity Press.

Kamalipour, Yahya R., ed. 2010. *Media, Power and Politics in the Digital Age: The 2009 Presidential Election Uprising in Iran*. Lanham, MD: Rowman & Littlefield.

Kandiyoti, Deniz, ed. 1991. *Women, Islam and the State*. London: Macmillan.

Kazi, Seema. 1997. "Muslim Laws and Women Living under Muslim Laws." Pp. 141–46 in *Muslim Women and the Politics of Participation*, edited by Mahnaz Afkhami and Erika Friedl. Syracuse, NY: Syracuse University Press.

Keane, John. 1996. *Reflection on Violence*. London: Verso.

Keck, Margaret E., and Kathryn Sikkink. 1998. *Activists beyond Borders: Advocacy Networks in International Politics*. Ithaca, NY: Cornell University Press.

Kepel, Gilles. 2002. *Jihad: The Trail of Political Islam*. Cambridge, MA: Harvard University.

Khor, Martin. 2000. "How the South Is Getting a Raw Deal at the WTO." Pp. 7–53 in *Views from the South: The Effects of Globalization and the WTO on Third World Countries*, edited by Sarah Anderson. Chicago: Food First Books.

Khosrokhavar, Farhad. 2005. *Suicide Bombers: Allah's New Martyrs*. Translated by David Macey. London: Pluto Press.

Kirkpatrick, David D., and David E. Sanger. 2011. "A Tunisian-Egyptian Link that Shook Arab History." *New York Times*, February 13. http://www.nytimes.com/2011/02/14/world/middleeast/14egypt-tunisia-protests.html.

Klatch, Rebecca. 1994. "Women of the New Right in the United States: Family, Feminism, and Politics." Pp. 367–89 in *Identity Politics and Women: Cultural Reassertions and Feminisms in International Perspective*, edited by V. M. Moghadam. Boulder, CO: Westview Press.

Klausen, Jyttle. 2009. *The Cartoons That Shook the World*. New Haven, CT: Yale University Press.

Klein, Naomi. 2007a. "Latin America's Shock Resistance." *The Nation*, November 26. http://www.thenation.com/doc/20071126/klein.

———. 2007b. *Shock Doctrine: The Rise of Disaster Capitalism*. New York: Henry Holt.

Komsan, Nehad Aboul. 2010a. "The Muslim Brotherhood . . . Returning Egypt to an Age without Law." Press release issued by the Egyptian Center for Women's Rights, Cairo, August 25. http://www.ecwronline.org.

———. 2010b. "Who Judges the Judges? A Black Day in the History of Justice in Egypt." Press release issued by the Egyptian Center for Women's Rights, Cairo, November 16. http://www.ecwronline.org.

Korten, David. 1995. *When Corporations Rule the World*. San Francisco: Kumarian.

Korzeniewicz, Roberto, and Kimberley Awbrey. 1992. "Democratic Transitions and the Semiperiphery of the World-Economy." *Sociological Forum* 7, no. 4: 609–40.

Laer, Jeroen Van, and Peter Van Aelst. 2010. "Internet and Social Movement Action Repertoires." *Information, Communication & Society* 13, no. 8: 1146–71.

Langman, Lauren. 2005. "From Virtual Public Spheres to Global Justice: A Critical Theory of Internetworked Social Movements." *Sociological Theory* 23, no. 1 (March): 42–74.

Langman, Lauren, and Douglas Morris. 2004. "Hegemony Lost: Understanding Contemporary Islam." In *Globalization, Hegemony and Power: Antisystemic Movements and the Global System*, edited by Thomas Reifer. Boulder, CO: Paradigm.

Langman, Lauren, Douglas Morris, and Jackie Zalewski. 2002. "Globalization, Domination and Cyberactivism." In *The 21st Century World-System: Systemic Crises and Antisystemic Resistance*, edited by Wilma A. Dunaway. Westport, CT: Greenwood Press.

Langohr, Vickie. 2001. "Of Islamists and Ballot Boxes: Rethinking the Relationship between Islamisms and Electoral Politics." *International Journal of Middle East Studies* 33: 591–610.

Lipset, Seymour Martin. 1959. "Some Social Requisites of Democracy: Economic Development and Political Legitimacy." *American Political Science Review* 53, no. 1 (March): 69–105.

Lister, Ruth. 2003. *Citizenship: Feminist Perspectives*. 2nd ed. London: Macmillan.

Lizardo, Omar. 2006. "The Effect of Economic and Cultural Globalization on Anti-U.S. Transnational Terrorism 1971–2000." *Journal of World-Systems Research* 7, no. 1: 144–86.

Lukacs, John. 2005. *Democracy and Populism: Fear and Hatred*. New Haven, CT: Yale University Press.

Mander, Jerry. 1996. "The Dark Side of Globalization: What the Media Are Missing." *The Nation* 15, no. 22: 9–29.

Marchand, Marianne, and Anne Sisson Runyan, eds. 2000. *Gender and Global Restructuring: Sightings, Sites and Resistances*. London: Routledge.

Marglin, Stephen, and Juliet Schor, eds. 1990. *The Golden Age of Capitalism*. Oxford: Clarendon Press.

Margolis, Diane. 1993. "Women's Movements around the World: Cross-Cultural Comparisons." *Gender & Society* 7, no. 3 (September): 379–99.

Markoff, John. 1999. "Globalization and the Future of Democracy." *Journal of World-Systems Research* 5, no. 2 (summer): 277–309.

Marshall, T. H. 1964. *Citizenship and Social Class*. Cambridge: Cambridge University Press.

Marty, Martin E., and R. Scott Appleby, eds. 1991. *The Fundamentalism Project*. Vol. 1: *Fundamentalisms Observed*. Chicago: University of Chicago Press.

———, eds. 1992. *The Fundamentalism Project*. Vol. 2: *Fundamentalisms and Society*. Chicago: University of Chicago Press.

———, eds. 1993. *The Fundamentalism Project*. Vol. 3: *Fundamentalisms and the State*. Chicago: University of Chicago Press.

———, eds. 1994. *The Fundamentalism Project*. Vol. 4: *Accounting for Fundamentalisms: The Dynamic Character of Movements*. Chicago: University of Chicago Press.

Marx, Karl. 1978. *Capital*. Vol. 1. Moscow: Progress Publishers.

Mathews, Jessica. 1997. "Power Shift." *Foreign Affairs* 76, no. 1 (January–February): 50–66.

McAdam, Doug. 1986. "Recruitment to High-Risk Activism: The Case of Freedom Summer." *American Journal of Sociology* 92: 64–90.

McAdam, Doug, John McCarthy, and Meyer Zald, eds. 1996. *Comparative Perspectives on Social Movements: Political Opportunities, Mobilizing Structures, and Cultural Frames*. Cambridge: Cambridge University Press.

McBride, William. 2001. *From Yugoslav Praxis to Global Pathos: Anti-Hegemonic Post-Post-Marxist Essays*. Lanham, MD: Rowman & Littlefield.

Meer, Nasar. 2010. *Citizenship, Identity and the Politics of Multiculturalism: The Rise of Muslim Consciousness*. New York: Palgrave Macmillan.

Melucci, Alberto. 1989. *Nomads of the Present*. Philadelphia: Temple University Press.

———. 1996. *Challenging Codes: Collective Action in the Information Age*. Cambridge: Cambridge University Press.

Mernissi, Fatima. 1987. *Beyond the Veil: Male-Female Dynamics in Modern Muslim Society*. 2nd ed. rev. Bloomington: Indiana University Press.

Mertes, Tom. 2004. "Grass-Roots Globalism: Reply to Michael Hardt." Pp. 237–47 in *A Movement of Movements: Is Another World Really Possible?*, edited by Tom Mertes. London: Verso.

Messaoudi, Khalida, and Elisabeth Schemla. 1998. *Unbowed: An Algerian Woman Confronts Islamic Fundamentalism.* Philadelphia: University of Pennsylvania Press.

Meyer, David S., and Sidney G. Tarrow, eds. 1998. *The Social Movement Society: Contentious Politics for a New Century.* Lanham, MD: Rowman & Littlefield.

Meyer, John, John Boli, George Thomas, and Francisco Ramirez. 1997. "World Society and the Nation-State." *American Journal of Sociology* 103, no. 1: 144–81.

Meyer, Mary K. 1999. "The Women's International League for Peace and Freedom: Organizing Women for Peace in the War System." Pp. 107–21 in *Gender Politics in Global Governance*, edited by Mary K. Meyer and Elisabeth Prugl. Lanham, MD: Rowman & Littlefield.

Meyer, Mary K., and Elisabeth Prugl, eds. 1999. *Gender Politics in Global Governance.* Lanham, MD: Rowman & Littlefield.

Milanovic, Branko. 2005. *Worlds Apart: Measuring International and Global Inequality.* Princeton, NJ: Princeton University Press.

———. 2011. *The Haves and the Have-Nots: A Brief and Idiosyncratic History of Global Inequality.* New York: Basic Books.

Milazzo, Linda. 2005. "Code Pink: The 21st Century Mothers of Invention." *Development* 48, no. 2: 100–104.

Mir-Hosseini, Ziba, and Richard Tapper. 2006. *Islam and Democracy in Iran: Eshkevari and the Quest for Reform.* London: I. B. Taurus.

Moaddel, Mansour. 2005. *Islamic Modernism, Nationalism, and Fundamentalism: Episode and Discourse.* Chicago: University of Chicago Press.

Moghadam, Valentine M. 1989. "One Revolution or Two? The Iranian Revolution and the Islamic Republic." In *Revolution Today: Aspirations and Realities. Socialist Register 1989*, edited by Ralph Miliband, Leo Panitch, and John Saville. London: Merlin.

———, ed. 1993. *Democratic Reform and the Position of Women in Transitional Economies.* Oxford: Clarendon Press.

———, ed. 1994. *Identity Politics and Women: Cultural Reassertions and Feminisms in International Perspective.* Boulder, CO: Westview Press.

———. 1995a. "Gender Dynamics of Restructuring in the Semiperiphery." Pp. 17–38 in *EnGendering Wealth and Well-Being*, edited by Rae Lesser Blumberg et al. Boulder, CO: Westview Press.

———, ed. 1995b. *Gender and National Identity: Women and Politics in Muslim Societies.* London: Zed Books.

———. 1998a. "Gender and the Global Economy." Pp. 128–60 in *Revisioning Gender*, edited by Myra Marx Ferree, Judith Lorber, and Beth Hess. Thousand Oaks, CA: Sage.

———. 1998b. "The Feminization of Poverty in International Perspective." *Brown Journal of World Affairs* 5, no. 2: 225–48.

———. 2001. "Organizing Women: The New Women's Movement in Algeria." *Cultural Dynamics* 13, no. 2: 131–54.

———. 2003. *Modernizing Women: Gender and Social Change in the Middle East.* 2nd ed. Boulder, CO: Lynne Rienner.

———. 2005. *Globalizing Women: Gender, Globalization, and Transnational Feminist Networks*. Baltimore: Johns Hopkins University Press.

———. 2007. "Peace-Building and Reconstruction with Women: Reflections on Afghanistan, Iraq, and Palestine." Pp. 327–51 in *From Patriarchy to Empowerment: Women's Participation, Movements, and Rights in the Middle East, North Africa, and South Asia*, edited by V. M. Moghadam. Syracuse, NY: Syracuse University Press.

———. 2008. "Population Growth, Urbanization, and the Challenges of Unemployment." Pp. 281–308 in *Understanding the Contemporary Middle East*, edited by Jillian Schwedler and Deborah Gerner. 3rd ed. Boulder, CO: Lynne Rienner Publishers.

———. 2011a. "Algerian Women in Movement: Three Waves of Feminist Activism." Pp. 180–99 in *Confronting Global Gender Justice: Women's Lives, Human Rights*, edited by Debra Bergoffen, Paula Ruth Gilbert, Tamara Harvey, and Connie L. McNeely. Oxford: Routledge.

———. 2011b. "Women, Gender, and Economic Crisis Revisited: Perspectives on Global Development and Technology" [PGDT], vol. 10: 30–40. DOI: 10.1163/156914911X55508.

———. 2012. "Toward Human Security and Gender Justice: Reflections on Afghanistan and Iraq." In *Globalization, Social Movements and Peacebuilding*, edited by Jackie Smith and Ernesto Verdejo. Syracuse, NY: Syracuse University Press.

Moghadam, Valentine M., and Dilek Elveren. 2008. "The Making of an International Convention: Culture and Free Trade in a Global Era." *Review of International Studies* 34, no. 4 (October): 735–53.

Moghadam, Valentine M., Suzanne Franzway, and Mary Margaret Fonow, eds. 2011. *Making Globalization Work for Women: The Role of Social Rights and Trade Union Leadership*. Albany: State University of New York Press.

Moghadam, Valentine M., with Elham Gheytanchi. 2010. "Political Opportunities and Strategic Choices: Comparing Feminist Campaigns in Morocco and Iran." *Mobilization: An International Quarterly of Social Movement Research* 15, no. 3 (September): 267–88.

Moghadam, Valentine M., and Fatima Sadiqi. 2006. "Women and the Public Sphere in the Middle East and North Africa" (introduction to special issue). *Journal of Middle East Women's Studies* 2, no. 2 (spring).

Molyneux, Maxine. 2001. *Women's Movements in International Perspective: Latin America and Beyond*. London: Palgrave.

Monbiot, George. 2011. "The 1% Are the Best Destroyers of All Time." *Guardian Weekly*, November 18, 19.

Moore, Barrington. 1966. *Social Origins of Dictatorship and Democracy*. Boston, MA: Beacon Press.

Morozov, Evgeny. 2011. *The Net Delusion: The Dark Side of Internet Freedom*. New York: Public Affairs.

Naples, Nancy, and Manisha Desai, eds. 2002. *Women's Activism and Globalization*. London: Routledge.

Newman, Katherine S. 1999. *Falling from Grace: Downward Mobility in the Age of Affluence*. Berkeley: University of California Press.

Njehu, Njoki. 2004. "Cancel the Debt: Africa and the IMF." Pp. 94–110 in *A Movement of Movements: Is Another World Really Possible?*, edited by Tom Mertes. London: Verso.

O'Brien, Robert, Anne Marie Goetz, Jan Aart Scholte, and Marc Williams. 2000. *Contesting Global Governance: Multilateral Economic Institutions and Global Social Movements*. Cambridge: Cambridge University Press.

O'Donnell, Guillermo, and Philippe Schmitter. 1986. *Transitions from Authoritarian Rule: Tentative Conclusions about Uncertain Democracies*. Baltimore: Johns Hopkins University Press.

Okin, Susan Moller. 1989. *Justice, Gender, and the Family*. New York: Basic Books.

Olesen, Thomas. 2007. "Contentious Cartoons: Elite and Media-Driven Mobilization." *Mobilization* 12, no. 1: 37–52.

Oxfam. 2002. *Rigged Rules and Double Standards: Trade, Globalization, and the Fight against Poverty*. Oxford: Oxfam.

Pargeter, Alison. 2010. *The Muslim Brotherhood: The Burden of Tradition*. London: Saqi Books.

Pasha, Mustafa Kamal, and Ahmed I. Samatar. 1997. "The Resurgence of Islam." Pp. 187–201 in *Globalization: Critical Perspectives*, edited by James H. Mittelman. Boulder, CO: Lynne Rienner Publishers.

Payer, Cheryl. 1975. *The Debt Trap: The International Monetary Fund and the Third World*. New York: Monthly Review Press.

Peterson, V. Spike. 2003. *A Critical Rewriting of Global Political Economy: Integrating Productive, Reproductive, and Virtual Economies*. New York: Routledge.

Phillips, Kevin. 2003. *Wealth and Democracy: A Political History of the American Rich*. New York: Random House.

Pianta, Mario, and Raffaele Marchetti. 2007. "The Global Justice Movements: The Transnational Dimension." Pp. 29–51 in *The Global Justice Movement: Cross-National and Transnational Perspectives*, edited by Donatella della Porta. Boulder, CO: Paradigm Publishers.

Pieterse, Jan Nederveen. 1998. "Hybrid Modernities: Mélange Modernities in Asia." *Sociological Analysis* 1, no. 3: 75–86.

———. 2004. *Globalization or Empire?* London and New York: Routledge.

Pietila, Hilkka, and Jeanne Vickers. 1994. *Making Women Matter: The Role of the UN*. London: Zed.

Plastas, Melinda. 2011. *A Band of Noble Women: Racial Politics in the Women's Peace Movement*. Syracuse, NY: Syracuse University Press.

Podobnik, Bruce. 2005. "Resistance to Globalization." Pp. 51–68 in *Transforming Globalization*, edited by Bruce Podobnik and Thomas Reifer. Leiden, Netherlands: Brill Academic Publishers.

Podobnik, Bruce, and Thomas Ehrlich Reifer, eds. 2004. Special Issue: *Global Social Movements before and after 9–11. Journal of World Systems Research* 10, no. 1 (winter). http://jwsr.ucr.edu/archive/vol10/number1.

Polanyi, Karl. [1944] 2001. *The Great Transformation: The Political and Economic Origins of Our Time*. Boston: Beacon Press.

Polletta, Francesca. 2002. *Freedom Is an Endless Meeting: Democracy in American Social Movements*. Chicago: University of Chicago Press.

Przeworski, Adam, et al. 1995. *Sustainable Democracy*. Cambridge and New York: Cambridge University Press.

Rahman, Fazlur. 1982. *Islam and Modernity: Transformation of an Intellectual Tradition*. Chicago: Publications of the Center for Middle Eastern Studies, University of Chicago.

Rashid, Ahmed. 2000. *Taliban: Militant Islam, Oil and Fundamentalism in Central Asia.* New Haven, CT, and London: Yale University Press.

Reardon, Betty. 1993. *Women and Peace: Feminist Visions of Global Security.* Albany: State University of New York Press.

Reese, Ellen, Erika Gutierrez, and Christopher Chase-Dunn. 2007. "Labor and Other Anti-Systemic Movements in the World Social Forum Process." Institute for Research on World-Systems Working Paper 17. http://irows.ucr.edu.

Reid, Edna, and Hsinchen Chen. 2007. "Internet-Savvy U.S. and Middle Eastern Extremist Groups." *Mobilization* 12, no. 2 (June): 177–92.

Roberts, Hugh. 2003. *The Battlefield: Algeria 1988–2002, Studies in a Broken Polity.* London: Verso.

Roberts, J. Timmons, and Amy Bellone Hite, eds. 2007. *The Globalization and Development Reader.* London: Blackwell Publishers.

Robinson, William I. 2004. *A Theory of Global Capitalism.* Baltimore: Johns Hopkins University Press.

Robinson, William I., and Jerry Harris. 2000. "Towards a Global Class? Globalization and the Transnational Capitalist Class." *Science & Society* 64, no. 1 (spring): 11–54.

Roces, Mina. 2010. "Rethinking the 'Filipino Woman': A Century of Women's Activism in the Philippines, 1905–2006." In *Women's Movements in Asia: Feminisms and Transnational Activism,* edited by Mina Roces and Louise Edwards. London and New York: Routledge.

Round, Robin. 2002. "Controlling Casino Capital." Pp. 282–86 in *Global Backlash: Citizen Initiatives for a Just World Economy,* edited by Robin Broad. Lanham, MD: Rowman & Littlefield.

Roy, Olivier. 2004. *Globalized Islam: The Search for a New Ummah.* New York: Columbia University Press.

Roy, Sara. 2011. *Hamas and Civil Society in Gaza: Engaging the Islamist Social Sector.* Princeton, NJ: Princeton University Press.

Rubin, Barnett. 1997. "Arab Islamists in Afghanistan." Pp. 179–206 in *Political Islam: Revolution, Radicalism, or Reform?* edited by John Esposito. Boulder, CO: Lynne Rienner Publishers.

Rucht, Dieter, ed. 1991. *Research on Social Movements: The State of the Art in Western Europe and the United States of America.* Boulder, CO: Westview Press.

Rueschemeyer, Marilyn, ed. 1998. *Women in the Politics of Postcommunist Eastern Europe.* Armonk, NY: M. E. Sharpe.

Runyan, Anne Sisson. 2002. "Still Not 'at Home' in IR: Feminist World Politics Ten Years Later." *International Politics* 39 (September): 361–68.

Rupert, Mark, and M. Scott Solomon. 2006. *Globalization and International Political Economy.* Lanham, MD: Rowman & Littlefield.

Rupp, Leila. 1998. *Worlds of Women: The Making of an International Women's Movement.* Princeton, NJ: Princeton University Press.

Sabbah, Fatna A. [Fatima Mernissi]. 1984. *Woman in the Muslim Unconscious.* Translated by Mary Jo Lakeland. New York: Pergamon Press.

Sadiqi, Fatima, and Moha Ennaji. 2006. "The Feminization of Public Space: Women's Activism, the Family Law, and Social Change in Morocco." *Journal of Middle East Women's Studies* 2, no. 2 (spring): 86–114.

Salhi, Zahia Smail. 2011. "Algerian Women as Agents of Change and Social Cohesion." Pp. 194–272 in *Women in the Middle East and North Africa: Agents of Change*, edited by Fatima Sadiqi and Moha Ennaji. London and New York: Routledge.

Santos, Boaventura de Sousa. 2006. *The Rise of the Global Left: The World Social Forum and Beyond*. London: Zed Books.

Sater, James N. 2007. *Civil Society and Political Change in Morocco*. London: Routledge.

Scholte, Jan Aart. 2000. *Globalization: A Critical Introduction*. London: Palgrave.

Schwedler, Jillian. 2006. *Faith in Moderation: Islamist Parties in Jordan and Yemen*. New York: Cambridge University Press.

Schmitter, Philippe C., and Terry Lynne Karl. 1991. "What Democracy Is . . . and Is Not." *Journal of Democracy* 2, no. 3 (summer): 75–88.

Scott-Clark, Cathy, and Adrian Levy. 2010. "Lost Boys of Pakistan." *Guardian Weekly*, November 5, 25–27.

Shaheed, Farida. 1994. "Controlled or Autonomous: Identity and the Experience of the Network Women Living under Muslim Laws." Women Living under Muslim Laws Occasional Paper No. 5, July.

Shiva, Vandana. 2000. "War against Nature and the People of the South." Pp. 91–124 in *Views from the South: The Effects of Globalization and the WTO on Third World Countries*, edited by Sarah Anderson. Chicago: Food First and the International Forum on Globalization.

Sidahmed, A. Salam, and Anoushirvan Ehteshami, eds. 1996. *Islamic Fundamentalism*. Boulder, CO: Westview.

Sikkink, Kathryn. 2011. *The Justice Cascade*. New York: W. W. Norton.

Silva, Eduardo. 2010. *Challenging Neoliberalism in Latin America*. New York: Cambridge University Press.

Skalli, Loubna Hanna. 2007. "Women, Communications and Democratization in Morocco." In *Empowering Women: Participation, Rights, and Women's Movements in the Middle East, North Africa, and South Asia*, edited by Valentine M. Moghadam. Syracuse, NY: Syracuse University Press.

Sklair, Leslie. 1991. *A Sociology of the Global System*. Baltimore: Johns Hopkins University Press.

———. 2001. *The Transnational Capitalist Class*. Oxford: Blackwell Publishers.

———. 2002. *Globalization: Capitalism and Its Alternatives*. 3rd ed. Oxford: Oxford University Press.

Slyomovics, Susan. 2005. *The Performance of Human Rights in Morocco*. Philadelphia: University of Pennsylvania Press.

Smith, Jackie. 2008. *Social Movements for Global Democracy*. Baltimore: Johns Hopkins University Press.

Smith, Jackie, Charles Chatfield, and Ron Pagnucco, eds. 1997. *Transnational Social Movements and Global Politics*. Syracuse, NY: Syracuse University Press.

Smith, Jackie, and Hank Johnston, eds. 2002. *Globalization and Resistance: Transnational Dimensions of Social Movements*. Lanham, MD: Rowman & Littlefield.

Smith, Jackie, Marina Karides, Marc Becker, Dorval Brunelle, Christopher Chase-Dunn, Rosalba Icaza, Jeffrey Juris, Lorenzo Mosca, Donatella della Porta, Ellen Reese, Peter Jay Smith, and Rolando Vásquez. 2008. *The World Social Forums and the Challenge of Global Democracy*. Boulder, CO: Paradigm Publishers.

Smith, Jackie, and Dawn Wiest. 2005. "The Uneven Geography of Global Civil Society: National and Global Influences on Transnational Association." *Social Forces* 84: 621–51.

———. 2012. *Social Movements in the World-System: The Politics of Crisis*. Washington, DC: Russell Sage Foundation for the American Sociological Association, Rose Series.

Smith, Peter J., and Elizabeth Smythe. 2010. "(In)Fertile Ground? Social Forum Activism in Its Regional and Local Dimension." *Journal of World-Systems Research* 16, no. 1: 6–28.

Snow, David A. 2004. "Framing Processes, Ideology, and Discursive Fields." Pp. 380–412 in *The Blackwell Companion to Social Movements*, edited by David A. Snow, Sarah Soule, and Hanspieter Kriesi. Malden, MA: Blackwell.

Sparr, Pam, ed. 1994. *Mortgaging Women's Lives: Feminist Critiques of Structural Adjustment*. London: Zed Books.

Sperling, Valerie, Myra Marx Ferree, and Barbara Risman. 2001. "Constructing Global Feminism: Transnational Advocacy Networks and Russian Women's Activism." *Signs* 26, no. 4: 1155–86.

Standing, Guy. 1989. "Global Feminization through Flexible Labor." *World Development* 17, no. 7: 1077–95.

———. 1999a. "Global Feminization through Flexible Labor: A Theme Revisited." *World Development* 27, no. 3: 583–602.

———. 1999b. *Global Labour Market Flexibility: Seeking Distributive Justice*. Basingstoke, UK: Macmillan.

Starhawk. 2003. "Why We Need Women's Actions and Feminist Voices for Peace." *Off Our Backs* (March–April): 16–17.

Steger, Manfred. 2002. *Globalism*. Lanham, MD: Rowman & Littlefield.

———. 2003. *Globalization: A Very Short Introduction*. Oxford: Oxford University Press.

———. 2009. *Globalization: A Very Short Introduction*. 2nd ed. New York: Oxford University Press.

Steger, Manfred, and Ravi K. Roy. 2010. *Neoliberalism: A Very Short Introduction*. New York: Oxford University Press.

Stienstra, Deborah. 1994. *Women's Movements and International Organizations*. New York: St. Martin's Press.

———. 2000. "Dancing Resistance from Rio to Beijing: Transnational Women's Organizing and United Nations Conferences, 1992–1996." Pp. 209–24 in *Gender and Global Restructuring: Sightings, Sites and Resistances*, edited by Anne Sisson Runyan and Marianne Marchand. London: Routledge.

Strange, Susan. 1996. *The Retreat of the State: The Diffusion of Power in the World Economy*. Cambridge: Cambridge University Press.

Streeten, Paul. 1997. "Globalization and Competitiveness: Implications for Development Thinking and Practice?" Pp. 107–47 in *Economic and Social Development into the XXI Century*, edited by Louis Emmerij. Washington, DC: Inter-American Development Bank.

Subcomandante Marcos. 2004. "The Hourglass of the Zapatistas." Interview with Gabriel García Márquez and Roberto Pombo. Pp. 3–15 in *A Movement of Movements: Is Another World Really Possible?*, edited by Tom Mertes. London: Verso.

Tarrow, Sidney. 2001. "Transnational Politics: Contention and Institutions in International Politics." *Annual Review of Political Science* 4: 1–20.

———. 2005. *The New Transnational Activism.* Cambridge: Cambridge University Press.

Taylor, Lance. 1993. *The Rocky Road to Reform: Adjustment, Income Distribution and Growth in the Developing World.* Cambridge, MA: MIT Press.

———. 2000. "External Liberalization, Economic Performance, and Distribution in Latin America and Elsewhere." WIDER Working Papers No. 215, Helsinki, Finland, December.

Taylor, Rupert. 2004. "Interpreting Global Civil Society." Pp. 2–10 in *Creating a Better World: Interpreting Global Civil Society,* edited by Rupert Taylor. Bloomfield, CT: Kumarian Press.

Tessler, Mark. 2007. "Do Islamic Orientations Influence Attitudes toward Democracy in the Arab World? Evidence from the World Values Survey in Egypt, Jordan, Morocco, and Algeria." Pp. 105–25 in *Values and Perceptions of the Islamic and Middle Eastern Publics,* edited by Mansoor Moaddel. New York: Palgrave Macmillan.

Tickner, Ann. 1992. *Gender in International Relations: Feminist Perspectives on Achieving Global Security.* New York: Columbia University Press.

Tobin, James. 1978. "A Proposal for International Monetary Reform." *Eastern Economic Journal* 4, nos. 3–4 (July/October): 153–59.

Tugal, Cihan. 2009. "Transforming Everyday Life: Islamism and Social Movement Theory." *Theory and Society* 38, no. 5 (September): 423–58.

UNDP. 1999. *Human Development Report 1999: Globalization with a Human Face.* New York: Oxford University Press.

———. 2002. *Human Development Report 2002: Deepening Democracy in a Fragmented World.* New York: Oxford University Press.

———. 2005. *Human Development Report 2005: International Cooperation at a Crossroads: Aid, Trade and Security in an Unequal World.* New York: Oxford University Press.

———. 2011. *Human Development Report 2011: Sustainability and Equity: A Better Future for All.* New York: Oxford University Press.

Vargas, Virginia. 2005. "Feminisms and the World Social Forum: Space for Dialogue and Confrontation." *Development* 48, no. 2: 107–10.

———. 2009. "International Feminisms: The World Social Forum." Pp. 145–64 in *Feminist Agendas and Democracy in Latin America,* edited by Jane Jaquette. Durham, NC: Duke University Press.

Vieceli, Jacqueline M. 1997. "Assessing the Impact of Structural Adjustment on Prospects for Democracy in the 'Third World'." *Comparative Studies of South Asia, Africa, and the Middle East* 17, no. 2: 82–99.

Waddington, David, and Mike King. 2007. "The Impact of the Local: Police Public-Order Strategies during the G8 Justice and Home Affairs Ministerial Meetings." *Mobilization* 12, no. 4 (December): 417–30.

Walgrave, Stefaan, W. Lance Bennett, Jeroen Van Laer, and Christian Breunig. 2011. "Multiple Engagements and Network Bridging in Contentious Politics: Digital Media Use of Protest Participants." *Mobilization: An International Journal* 16, no. 3: 325–49.

Wallerstein, Immanuel. 1991. *Geopolitics and Geoculture: Essays on the Changing World-System.* Cambridge: Cambridge University Press.

———. 2000. "Globalization or the Age of Transition? A Long-Term View of the Trajectory of the World-System." *International Sociology* 15, no. 2: 249–65.

———. 2003. *The Decline of American Power: The U.S. in a Chaotic World*. New York: New Press.

Walton, John, and David Seddon. 1994. *Free Markets and Food Riots: The Politics of Global Adjustment*. Oxford: Blackwell.

Waylen, Georgina. 1994. "Women and Democratization: Conceptualizing Gender Relations in Transition Politics." *World Politics* 46, no. 3: 327–54.

———. 2007. *Engendering Transitions: Women's Mobilizations, Institutions, and Gender Outcomes*. London and New York: Oxford University Press.

Wejnert, Barbara. 2005. "Diffusion, Development, and Democracy, 1800–1999." *American Sociological Review* 70 (February): 53–81.

Weldon, S. Laurel. 2011. *When Protest Makes Policy: How Social Movements Represent Disadvantaged Groups*. Ann Arbor: University of Michigan Press.

Welzel, Christian, and Ronald Inglehart. 2009. "Development and Democracy: What We Know about Modernization Today." *Foreign Affairs* (March–April): 33–41. http://www.worldvaluessurvey.org/wvs/articles/folder_published/publication_593/files/inglehart-welzel-modernization-and-democracy.pdf.

White, Jenny B. 2003. *Islamist Mobilization in Turkey: A Study in Vernacular Politics*. Seattle: University of Washington Press.

Wichterich, Christa. 1999. *The Globalized Woman: Notes from a Future of Inequality*. London: Zed Books.

Wickham, Carrie Rosefsky. 2002. *Mobilizing Islam: Religion, Activism, and Political Change in Egypt*. New York: Columbia University Press.

Wiest, Dawn. 2007. "A Story of Two Transnationalisms: Global Salafi Jihad and Transnational Human Rights Mobilization in the Middle East and North Africa." *Mobilization* 12, no. 2 (June): 137–60.

Wiktorowicz, Quintan, ed. 2000. "The Salafi Movement in Jordan." *International Journal of Middle East Studies* 32: 219–40.

———. 2001. *The Management of Islamic Activism: Salafis, the Muslim Brotherhood, and State Power in Jordan*. Albany: State University of New York Press.

———. 2004a. "Introduction: Islamic Activism and Social Movement Theory." Pp. 1–36 in *Islamic Activism: A Social Movement Theory Approach*, edited by Quintan Wiktorowicz. Bloomington: Indiana University Press.

———. 2004b. *Islamic Activism: A Social Movement Theory Approach*. Bloomington: Indiana University Press.

———. 2005. *Radical Islam Rising: Muslim Extremism in the West*. Lanham, MD: Rowman & Littlefield.

Wilkinson, Richard, and Kate Pickett. 2009. *The Spirit Level: Why Greater Equality Makes Societies Stronger*. New York and London: Bloomsbury Press.

Women in Development Europe (WIDE). 1998. *Trade Traps and Gender Gaps: Women Unveiling the Market. Report on WIDE's Annual Conference held at Jarvenpaa, Finland, May 16–18, 1997*. Brussels: WIDE.

Women Living under Muslim Laws (WLUML). 2005. "WLUML Appeal against Fundamentalisms: There Is No Such Thing as the 'Clash of Civilizations': The Clash in the

World Today Is between Fascists and Antifascists." http://www.wluml.org/english/ newsfulltxt.shtml?cmd%5B157%5D=x-157-103376 (accessed January 16, 2008).

Wuthnow, Robert. 1986. "Religious Movements and Counter-Movements in North America." Pp. 1–28 in *New Religious Movements and Rapid Social Change*, edited by James Beckford. Beverly Hills, CA, and Paris: Sage Publications and UNESCO.

Yaghmaian, Behzad. 2001. "The Political Economy of Global Accumulation and Its Emerging Mode of Regulation." In *Labor and Capital in the Age of Globalization: The Labor Process and the Changing Nature of Work in the Global Economy*, edited by Berch Berberoglu. Lanham, MD: Rowman & Littlefield.

Young, Kate, ed. 1992. *Gender and Development Reader*. Ottawa: Canadian Council for International Cooperation.

Zeghal, Malika. 2008. *Islamism in Morocco: Religion, Authoritarianism, and Electoral Politics*. Princeton, NJ: Markus Wiener.

Zey, Mary. 1993. *Banking on Fraud: Drexel, Junk Bonds, and Buy-outs*. Piscataway, NJ: Transaction Books.

Zivkovic, Andrea, and John Hogan. 2007. "Virtual Revolution? ICTs and Networks." Pp. 182–98 in *Revolution in the Making of the Modern World*, edited by John Foran, David Lane, and Andreja Zivkovic. London: Routledge.

Zubaida, Sami. 1993. *Islam, the People and the State: Political Ideas and Movements in the Middle East*. London: I. B. Taurus.

INDEX

abortion, women's movement and, 148, 169

action directes Islamists, 128–30

Adbusters, 92

Afghanistan, 50–51, 107, 111, 139, 142, 152

Afkhami, Mahnaz, 150, 154

Africa, 68. *See also* Middle East and North Africa

Agha-Soltani, Neda, 89

Ahmadiyya Muslim Community, USA, 102

Akef, Mohamed Mahdi, 122

Al Arabiyya, 127, 160

al-Awlaki, Anwar, 165

Al-Azhar University, 121

al-Azm, Sadik, 102, 104, 128–30

al-Banna, Hassan, 17, 105, 120

Alexander, Amanda, 163

Alger, Chadwick, 56

Algeria, 16, 48, 78–79, 115–17, 152

Alive in Egypt, 90

Al Jazeera, 89–90, 127, 160

Allende, Salvadore, 33

al-Muhajiroun, 126, 227n37

al-Qaeda, 49, 100, 107, 111–12, 118, 127

al-Sahib, 127

al-Zawahiri, Ayman, 112, 127

American Civil Liberties Union, 165

American Society for Muslim Advancement (ASMA), 102

Amin, Samir, 104, 218n11

Amnesty International, 165

an-Nahda, 17, 100, 118–19, 131

Anonymous collective, 11

Anonymous Iran, 89

antislavery movement, 16

antisystemic resistance, 14, 15t

Anwar, Zainah, 230n48

April 6 Youth Movement, 70, 87, 89

Arab Human Development Report, 80, 82

Arab Spring, 9, 17, 61; and democratization, 80–91; diffusion and, 70; emotions and, 24; future of, 215–16; women's movements and, 167

Arab Women's Solidarity Association (AWSA), 140t

Argentina, 33, 68, 73t, 199

Arjomand, Said Amir, 1–5

Assange, Julian, 10–11, 218n15

Association Démocratique des Femmes du Maroc (ADFM), 85

Association des Femmes Tunisiennes pour la Recherche et le Développement (AFTURD), 86

Association for the Taxation of Financial Transactions and for Citizens' Action (ATTAC), 186–87, 196–98, 221n12

Association for Women's Rights in Development (AWID), 140*t*, 153, 167
Association of Women of the Mediterranean Region (AWMR), 141*t*
Association Tunisienne des Femmes Démocrates (ATFD), 86
Ataturk, Kemal, 118
Atkinson, Anthony, 40
austerity measures, 35, 173
Avaaz.org, 9

Babones, Salvatore, 25
Bach, Amandine, 162
Bahrain, 115
bankocracy, Marx on, 53
Bank of the South, 199–200
Baobab, 151
Barber, Benjamin, 5, 49, 64, 78, 206
Barkawi, Tarak, 45
Battle of Seattle, 6, 76–77, 173, 179, 184
Bayat, Asef, 80
Beck, Ulrich, 44
Begg, Moazzam, 165
Beijing Platform for Action, 134, 143, 168, 228n4
Beijing World Conference on Women, 55, 135, 144, 181*t*
Beinin, Joel, 80
Belarbi, Aicha, 84
Bello, Walden, 40, 96, 175, 182, 198
Benali, Driss, 91
Ben Ali, Zine El Abidine, 31, 86–87
Bendjedid, Chadli, 116
Benjamin, Medea, 159, 192, 218n11
Ben Mhenni, Lina, 89
Bennani, Farida, 85
Bennoune, Karima, 165
Berger, Suzanne, 44
Bhagwati, Jagdish, 37
Bhavnani, Kum-Kum, 24
bin Laden, Osama, 24, 49, 111–12
biographical availability, 81–82, 219n16
Blair, Tony, 178, 184
Blee, Kathleen, 4
blogs, 89, 93, 127
Blunt, Gary, 127

Boko Haram, 227n39
Bolivian Alternative for the Americas (ALBA), 199
Bollen, Kenneth, 69
boomerang effect, 46
Borland, Elizabeth, 191
Born, Brooksley, 53–54
Boswell, Terry, 14
Bouazizi, Mohammed, 24
Boumedienne, Houari, 79
bourgeoisie, modernizing, and democratization, 69
Brazil, 73*t*, 199; Porto Alegre, 48, 96; Workers' Party, 59, 179, 182, 188
Brigadas Lilas, 192
Brim, Sand, 159
Brown, Nathan, 120–22
Bunch, Charlotte, 228n19
Bush, George H. W., 50
Bush, George W., 47, 50–51, 127, 184

Cameron, David, 114
capitalism: contradictions of, 42–43; disaster, 33; and globalization, 32–43; history of resistance to, 14, 15*t*; and women's movement, 137. *See also* neoliberal capitalism
casino capitalism, 43
Cassen, Bernard, 187
Castells, Manuel, 44, 208
categorical terrorism, 116–17
Cavtat Roundtable, 34
Center for Constitutional Rights, 165
Center for the Study of Islam and Democracy, 102
Center for Women's Global Leadership, 151, 167
Center on Transnational Corporations, 33
Chabaka, 84
charitable foundations, and recruitment, 125–26
Chase-Dunn, Christopher, 14, 26, 39, 189, 194
Chávez, Hugo, 199
Chen, Hsinchen, 26
Cherifati-Merabtine, Doria, 213

Chile, 33, 36, 40, 73*t*, 74
China, 19, 46–48
Chua, Amy, 78
Citizens Coalition for Economic Justice, 64
Citizens' Coalition for Participatory Democratic Society, 64
citizenship: and democracy, 64; rights of, 65
civil society: definitions of, 57; Hamas and, 125–26; and social movements, 63, 206
Clark, Janine, 125
class: and Islamist movements, 108–10; neoliberalism and, 38–39
Clinton, Bill, 50, 178
Code Pink, 141*t*, 145*t*, 159–60, 218n11
Cold War, 33, 136; end of, 36, 50, 107, 117–18
Collectif Maghreb Egalité 95, 8, 85–86
collective action, transnational, 54–60, 209
collective action repertoires, 16, 21, 205; diffusion of, 70; of first-wave feminism, 18; of women's movement, 145*t*, 166–69
commercialization, creep of, 178, 197
communalism, 49
communication: and social movement activism, 207. *See also* information and commmunication technologies
communism, and Islamism, 106
complex multilateralism, 94
conditionalities, 35; and democratization, 67–69
conflict. *See* violence; war
Connell, R. W., 51–52
consent, and democratization, 67
contagion, and democratization, 67, 69
control, and democratization, 67
Convention on the Elimination of All Forms of Discrimination Against Women (CEDAW), 87, 134, 168
Conway, Jane, 26, 163
Cooley, John, 107
cooperation, women's movements and, 167–68

corporate domain: capture of government by, 75, 78; global justice movement and, 175; women and, 53–54
Creasap, Kimberly, 4
cultural globalization, characteristics of, 41*t*
Curtis, Mark, 107
Czech Republic, 184

Danaher, Kevin, 159, 195
Danish cartoons of Muhammad, 105, 114
da Silva, Luiz Ignacio "Lula," 182
debt forgiveness, 147, 177–78
debt trap, 34
deglobalization, 198
della Porta, Donatella, 26, 96, 186, 189
Delphy, Christine, 165
democracy(ies): global justice movement and, 189; social movements and, 205; state and, 215; types of, 64–65; WSF and, 193–95
democratic globalization network, 94–95
democratic Islam, 101–2, 103*t*
democratization: characteristics of, 62–64; deficits of, 75–79; factors affecting, 69–71; MENA protests and, 80–91; processes in, 67–69; social movements and, 61–98; wave theory of, 12, 64–71, 72*t*–73*t*
demographic transition, and Islamist movements, 109
dependency theory, 2
development: cuts in, and women's movement, 137–38; and democratization, 69; and globalization, 32–38; SAPs and, 174–75
Development Alternatives with Women for a New Era (DAWN), 139, 140*t*, 145*t*, 151, 177
Development Group for Alternative Policies (D-Gap), 177
Diamond, Larry, 80
diffusion, and democratization, 67, 69
Di Marco, Graciela, 63

disaster capitalism, 33
Dore, Ronald, 44
double-movement, 14
Dufour, Pascale, 148
Dunn, John, 77–78

Eckstein, Susan, 54
economic conditions: 2008 crisis, 42–45, 53; and democratization, 69; and development of neoliberalism, 32–38; and Islamist movements, 107–8; and MENA protests, 81; and women's movement, 136, 146–49, 155–56, 168
economic globalization, characteristics of, 41t
Egypt, 17, 61, 69, 80–91, 118; emotions in, 25; and Internet, 47, 90t; Kefaya movement, 73t; moderate Islamism and, 120–22
Egyptian Center for Women's Rights (ECWR), 122
Eisenstein, Zillah, 162
El-Ghobashy, Mona, 122
elites: neoliberalism and, 38–39; and social movements, 47–48; in United States, factions within, 51
Elveren, Dilek, 77
emotions: global justice movement and, 189; and social movements, 22–25, 207
emphasized femininity, 52
empire: term, 50; women's movements and, 155–62
Engels, Friedrich, 2
Enloe, Cynthia, 53, 162
Ennahda. See an-Nahda
Entelis, John, 108, 115
Environment et Développement du Tiers Monde (ENDA), 182
Equality Now, 140t
Eschle, Catherine, 26
Estrada, Joseph, 9
European Union, 3, 197
Eurozone, 45, 68
Evans, Jodie, 159
extremist Islamist movements, 23t, 100, 103t

Facebook, 9, 89–90
failed states, and recruitment, 126
family law, 46, 112–13, 116, 149–50
Faroohar, Rana, 42
Fédération des Femmes du Québec, 147
feminist action, term, 134
Feminist Alliance for International Action, 167
feminist humanitarianism, 160–62
Feminist Majority, 142, 157
feminist movement, global, 7–8, 133–70, 204–5; emotions and, 22–24; features of, 23t; globalization and, 59; and Islam, 102; rationale for study of, 14; and state, 46
feminist movement, term, 133
Ferree, Myra Marx, 134
50 Years Is Enough, 177
financial instruments, complexity of, 35, 43
first wave of democratization, 18, 65, 72t
Focus on the Global South, 182
Foran, John, 24
formal democracy, 65
Fourest, Caroline, 230n48
fourth wave of democratization, 66, 72t–73t
Fox, Vicente, 177
frame alignment, 21
frames/framing processes, 21, 23t, 70, 93, 205; global justice movement and, 195–200; Islamist movements and, 17–18, 118, 124–28; women's movements and, 139, 143–44, 166–69
France, 54
Fraser, Nancy, 71
free market. See neoliberal capitalism
Free Muslims, 102
Friedman, Milton, 36
Front Islamique du Salut (FIS), 16, 48, 79, 115, 152
Fukuyama, Francis, 65
Fuller, Graham, 123
fundamentalism, 49; definition of, 102–4; Islamic, 4–5, 102; women's movement and, 134, 138–42, 149–55, 164–65, 168

GABRIELA, 71
Gadahn, Adam, 127
Gama'a Islamiyya, 48, 115
Gambia, 68
gender issues: and development, 139; global justice movement and, 192; reaction and, 49, 51–53; and social movements, 212
Genoa G8 protests, 183
George, Susan, 187, 192, 196–98, 230n6, 232n41
Gerges, Fawaz, 101, 111–12
Gerlach, Luther, 21–22
Ghaddafi, Muammar, 8, 48
Ghana, 175
Ghannouchi, Rachid, 90, 118–19
Ghonim, Wael, 89
Giraud, Isabelle, 148
global, term, 111
global civil society, 7, 56–57; definitional issues, 57–58; and transnational social movements, 206
Global Day of Action, 185
Global Exchange, 159
global feminist activism, definition of, 134
globalization: from above versus from below, 25–29, 171, 180; advantages and disadvantages of, 37–38, 37t, 75–79; alternatives to, 195–200; characteristics of, 6–7, 41t; and collective action, 31–60; definition of, ix; development and, 32–38; and diffusion, 69–70; future of, 203–16; and Islamist movements, 111–18; MENA protests and, 80–91; reactions to, 49–54; and social movements, 1–29; and state, 43–49; study of, 25–29, 31–32; WSF on, 193–94
global justice movement (GJM), 2, 7, 23t, 59, 171–201, 172t, 204–5; cycle of protests, 179, 182–85, 185t; emotions and, 22–24; future of, 214; and inequality, 40; origins of, 174–79; rationale for study of, 14; state allies and, 48; women's movement and, 162–65; world-system theory and, 20

global networks, neoliberal versus democratic, 94–95
global social movements: definition of, 56; as interconnected, 59–60. See also transnational social movements
Goodwin, Jeff, 116
governance structures: global, democracy deficit and, 77; new, 3
government, capture by business sector, 75, 78
Gramsci, Antonio, 99
Grandmothers for Peace International, 141t
gray zones: definition of, 120; moderate Islam and, 118–24
Greece, 45, 68, 73t, 77
Greenpeace, 177
Group Islamique Armée, 79, 115–18, 152
Guidry, John, 56, 62, 206
Gulalp, Haldun, 119–20
Gulen movement, 102
Gulf War, 161

Habermas, Jurgen, 78
Hafez, Mohammed, 5, 101, 104, 115
Hamas, 48, 100, 115, 125–26, 227n35
Hamzawy, Amr, 120–22
Hanafi, Hassan, 102
Hardt, Michael, 50
Harik, Judith, 125
Harvey, David, 33, 38
Hawkesworth, Mary, 134
Heckscher, Zahara, 13
hegemonic masculinities, 51–53, 192
Hegghammer, Thomas, 107
Hélie-Lucas, Marieme, 150
Hezbollah, 48, 100, 125
Hirst, Paul, 44
Hizb ul-Tahrir, 100
homosexuality, women's movement and, 148, 169
honor killings, 161
Htun, Mala, 70
humanitarianism, feminist, 160–62
Huntington, Samuel, 12, 65–66, 78, 131
Hussein, Saddam, 111
hybridization, 7

Ibn Abd-al-Wahhab, 17
Ibn Taymiyyah, 17
Ibrahim, Saad Eddin, 87, 101, 108
identities: transnational, 208; women's movements and, 166–69
identity politics, 49
Imam, Ayesha, 150
India, 42, 169
Indonesia, 73t, 78, 106, 118
Indymedia, 180
inequality: globalization and, 75–76; MENA protests and, 91; neoliberal capitalism and, 40, 42; Occupy Wall Street and, 92–93
information and commmunication technologies (ICTs): and social movements, 8–13; and women's movements, 142–44. See also Internet
Institute for Research on World-Systems (IROWS), 26
International Alliance of Women (IAW), 19
International Conference on Population and Development (ICPD), 54–55, 143, 151, 181t
International Council, WSF, 186, 189–91
International Council of Women (ICW), 19
International Criminal Court (ICC), 47, 160
International Forum on Globalization, 198
International Gender and Trade Network (IGTN), 191–92
International Labour Organization (ILO), 34, 38, 137, 175
International Monetary Fund (IMF), 3, 34–36, 146, 174–75, 197, 200
international nongovernmental organizations, women's movement and, 144
international nongovernmental organizations (INGOs), 3–4
International Woman Suffrage Alliance (IWSA), 18
International Women's Tribune Center (IWTC), 140t, 144

Internet: disadvantages of, 11, 47; and global justice movement, 180; and Islamist movements, 126–28; mobilizing role of, 207–10; and social movements, ix–x, 8–13, 56, 90, 204; use in Egypt, Morocco, and Tunisia, 90, 90t; and women's movements, 153–55, 167–68. See also social media
Iran, 17, 47, 82, 88–91, 122–23; Green Protests, 9, 46, 73t, 80–91
Iraq War, 47, 51, 157–60, 179, 183–84
Ireland, 45
ISIS International Women's Information and Communication Service, 144
Islah, 100
Islamic Action Front, 131
Islamic activism, definition of, 104
Islamic fundamentalism, 4–5, 102. See also fundamentalism
Islamism: definition of, 102–5; goal of, 99
Islamist movements, 5, 23t, 99–132, 204–5; action directes, 128–30; and democratization, 80–91; emotions and, 22; future of, 212–13, 215–16; globalization and, 58–59, 111–18; grievances of, 117–18; origins of, 16–18, 105–11; reaction and, 49–51; state allies and, 48; study of, 14, 101–5; types of, 103t; women's movements and, 8, 79, 108, 110, 122, 138, 149–55. See also extremist Islamist movements; moderate Islamist movements
Israel, 46–47, 110

jahiliyya, 17, 112
Jang Roko Abhiyan, 157
Jaquette, Jane, 74
Jayawardena, Kumari, 18
Jbabdi, Latifa, 84, 223n34
jihad, 5, 49–50, 206. See also extremist Islamist movements
Johnston, Hank, 45, 63
Jordan, 131
Jubilee 2000, 147, 177–78
justice. See global justice movement

Justice and Development Party (AKP), 17, 100, 119–20
justice cascade, 47, 70

Kaldor, Mary, 57
Karides, Marina, 22, 189
Karl, Terry Lynn, 65
Keane, John, 74
Keck, Margaret, 6, 16, 22, 46
Kennedy, Michael, 56, 62, 206
Kepel, Gilles, 101
Keynesian economic models, shift away from, 3, 34–36, 107–8, 137, 179
Khamenei, ayatollah, 83
Khan, Daisy, 102
Khatami, Mohammad, 83
Khomeini, ayatollah, 48, 105, 114
Khosrokhavar, Farhad, 128
Klatch, Rebecca, 4
Klein, Naomi, 33, 192, 199
KOFAVIV, 161

labor issues, 35, 87–88, 136–37, 147, 178
Landless Workers' Movement (MST), 199
Langman, Lauren, 10, 52, 208
Langohr, Vickie, 123
language, and social movement activism, 207
Latin America: pink tide in, 66, 70, 199; women's movements in, 71, 169
La Via Campesina, 163, 192
left-wing terrorism, versus Islamist, 128–30
liberal democracy, 64–65
liberal Islam, 101–2, 103t
liberation theology, 119–20
Libya, 8, 48, 51, 80, 218n11
Lizardo, Omar, 26
lobbying, women's movement and, 167
Lukacs, John, 78
Lula da Silva, 182

Maddison, Angus, 40
MADRE, 140t–141t, 145t, 158, 160–62
Mahdi Army, 100

Mahdism, 16
Mahfouz, Asma, 89
Mair, Lucille Mathurin, 155–56, 229n26
Manifesto of Porto Alegre, 198
Marche Mondiale des Femmes, 140t–141t, 145t
Marchetti, Raffaele, 56, 182, 184, 195
Marcos, Ferdinand, 71
Marcos, Subcomandante, 177
marginalization, democratization and, 78–79
Markoff, John, 61, 75
Marshall, T. H., 65
martyrdom, Islamic versus Christian, 128
Marx, Karl, 1–2, 14, 53, 203
Marxist analysis, 13, 22, 34, 39, 42
masculinities: hegemonic, 51–53, 192; and social movements, 212
Matthews, Jessica, 43–44
Mawdudi, Abul Ala, 17
Mbali, Mandisa, 163
McAdam, Doug, 81
McBride, William, 96
media: and democratization, 76; and emotion, 22; and Islamism, 114, 117, 127–28; and MENA protests, 89–90; and Occupy Wall Street, 92–93; and WikiLeaks, 10–11; and women's movement, 160. See also social media
Medica Mondiale, 141t, 157–58
Mercosur Feminist Articulation, 162
Mernissi, Fatima, 108
Mertes, Tom, 188
Messaoudi, Khalida, 151
Mexico, 73t
Meyer, David, 63
Middle East and North Africa (MENA), 12, 61, 82; future of, 215–16; protests in, 80–91; women's movement in, 8, 147
migration, and globalization of Islamism, 113–14
Milanovic, Branko, 40
militarism, 50–51
Millennium Development Goals (MDGs), 38, 168
Moaddel, Mansoor, 16

mobile phones, and activism, 9
mobilizing structures, 20–21, 23*t*; global justice movement and, 186–87; Internet and, 207–10; Islamist movements and, 124–28; women's movements and, 139
moderate Islamist movements, 100, 103*t*, 118–24, 131, 230n48; features of, 23*t*; future of, 204; obstacles to, 123
modernization: and democratization, 69; and Islamist movements, 111
Mohammad, Omar Bakri, 227n37
Mohammed VI, king of Morocco, 83, 85
Moi, Daniel arap, 11
Monbiot, George, 42
Moore, Barrington, 62, 69
Morgan, Robin, 150, 158
Morgenson, Gretchen, 54
Morocco, 61, 80–91, 90*t*
Morozov, Evgeny, 47
Morris, Douglas, 10, 52
Mossadegh, Mohammad, 17, 106–7
Mothers and Grandmothers of the Plaza de Mayo, 191
MoveOn.org, 8–9
Mubarak, Hosni, 47, 87–88, 121
Muhammad, prophet, 16, 105, 114
multiculturalism, and Islamism, 113–14
Multilateral Agreement on Investment (MAI), 6, 178–79
multilateralism: complex, 94; women's movements and, 143, 166
Mumtaz, Khawar, 150
Murphy, Gael, 159
Muslim Brotherhood, 17, 88, 100, 104, 106, 112–13, 118, 120–22
Muslim Wake-Up, 102

Nader, Ralph, 178
Najibullah, Mohammed, 107
Nasr, Seyyid Hossein, 101
Nasser, Gamal Abdel, 17, 107, 121
National Organization for Women, 160
nation-state. *See* state/nation-state
Negri, Antonio, 50
neoconservativism, 50–51

neoliberal capitalism: alternatives to, 199–200; and democratization, 66; development of, 33–38; and Egypt, 87; features of, x; and globalization, 39; and global justice movement, 173; and Islamist movements, 109; state and, 45; Washington Consensus and, 19, 36–37; and women's movement, 137, 139, 146–49. *See also* global justice movement
neoliberal globalization network, 94–95
Network Women in Development Europe (WIDE), 139, 140*t*, 145*t*, 149, 151, 163, 166–67, 177; and Internet, 207, 209
New International Economic Order (NIEO), 34
new media. *See* social media
No Bases Initiative, 184
Nobel Women's Initiative, 160
Nobre, Miriam, 163
nongovernmental organizations (NGOs), 3–4, 144, 181*t*
nonviolence, global justice movement and, 197–98
norm diffusion, 70
North American Free Trade Agreement (NAFTA), 3, 175, 177
Norway, 54
Nour, Ayman, 87
Nouri, Fazlollah, 17

Obama, Barack, 47, 51
O'Brien, Robert, 94
Occupy Wall Street (OWS), 31, 62, 77, 91–96, 173, 214; emotions and, 24–25; and Global Day of Action, 185; social media and, 10
O'Donnell, Guillermo, 64
Olesen, Thomas, 114
One Million Signatures Campaign, 83, 210
opportunities, 23*t*; analysis of, 20; global justice movement and, 179–82
Organization for Economic Cooperation and Development (OECD), 42, 178

Organization of Women's Freedom in Iraq (OWFI), 161
Osanloo, Mansour, 82
other world, global justice movement on, 195–200, 212–16
Otpor, 70
Ottaway, Marina, 120–22
Oxfam-U.K., 38

Pahlavi, Mohammad Reza, 106
Pakistan, 51, 115, 152, 157
Palestine, 110, 184
Paley, Grace, 159
Papandreou, Andreas, 68
Pargeter, Alison, 122
Parliamentarian Islamist movements. See moderate Islamist movements
Parti de la Justice et du Développement (PJD), 100
patriarchy, 49, 51–53, 147–48, 163, 168
Paul, Alice, 18
Payer, Cheryl, 34
Peterson, Spike, 38, 219n32
Philippines, 9, 71, 73t
Pianta, Mario, 56, 182, 184, 195
Pickett, Kate, 42
Pieterse, Jan Nederveen, 7
pink tide, 66, 70, 199
Podobnik, Bruce, 183
Polanyi, Karl, 14
political globalization, characteristics of, 41t
political Islam, 104, 212
polycentric, social movements as, 21–22
Porto Alegre, Brazil, 48, 96, 182, 188, 198. See also World Social Forum
Portugal, 45, 73t
poverty, feminization of, 138
privatization, 38, 137–38
protests: cycles of, 175, 176t; global justice movement and, 173, 182–85, 185t; in Middle East and North Africa, 9, 46, 73t, 80–91
Przeworski, Adam, 78
Public Citizen, 178
public sphere, transnational, 208–9

punishments, Muslim public opinion and, 124

Qutb, Sayyid, 17, 105, 111–12, 121

radical democracy, 63
radical Islamists, 100, 103t
Rahman, Fazlur, 101, 225n2
Ramadan, Tariq, 102, 124, 165, 230n48
Rattah, Israa Abdel, 89
Rauf, Feisal Abdul, 102
Reagan, Ronald, 36
recruitment: Internet and, 207–10; Islamic movements and, 124–26
Reese, Ellen, 194
Refah Party, 79, 119
Reid, Edna, 26
religion: in Algeria, 79; and antislavery movement, 16; in Egypt, 17–18; global revivals and, 4–5, 138–39; reaction and, 49–50. See also under Islam
representative democracy, 63
resistance: antisystemic, 14, 15t; to globalization, 40; to war, 51. See also protests
resources, 23t; analysis of, 20
reticulate, social movements as, 21–22
Rice, Condoleezza, 159
Rida, Rashid, 17, 105
Risman, Barbara, 134
Roberts, Hugh, 16
Robinson, William I., 39
Rodrik, Dani, 37
Roy, Arundhati, 192
Roy, Olivier, 101
Roy, Sarah, 125, 227n35
Rubin, Barnett, 107
Runyan, Anne Sisson, 52
Rushdie, Salman, 105, 114
Russia, 48

Saadawi, Nawal, 87
Saadi, Mohammad Said, 84–86
Sachs, Jeffrey, 37
Sadat, Anwar, 106

Sadiki, Larbi, 86
Sahgal, Gita, 165
Said, Khaled, 89
Salafiyists, 16, 100–101, 219n21
Santos, Boaventura de Sousa, 48, 189, 192–93
Saud, Muhammad Ibn, 17
Saudi Arabia, 17, 106–7, 111–12
Savage, Catherine, 218n15
Schmitter, Philippe, 64–65
Scholte, Jan Aart, 7
Schwedler, Jillian, 80, 101, 123
Seattle, Battle of, 6, 76–77, 173, 179, 184
second wave of democratization, 65, 72t, 135–36
secularization, 4–5
Seddon, David, 175
segmentary, polycentric, and reticulate (SPR) thesis, 21–22
Sem Terre, 188
Seneca Falls Convention, 18
September 11, 2001, 112, 117, 157, 183
sexual identity, women's movement and, 148, 169
Shaheed, Farida, 150
sharia law, 17, 79, 85, 99, 112–13, 121, 153
Shirkat Gah, 151–52
Shiva, Vandana, 192, 198–99
Siddiqui, Mona, 124
Sikkink, Kathryn, 6, 16, 22, 46, 70
Sisterhood Is Global Institute (SIGI), 139, 150
Sisters in Islam (SIS), 102, 151
Skaba, Shallo, 163
Sklair, Leslie, 39, 44
Smeal, Ellie, 158
Smith, Jackie, 22, 26, 77, 94–95, 189
Smith, Peter, 190
Smythe, Elizabeth, 190
Sobhan, Salma, 150
socialism, 15t; and democracy, 65; and women's movement, 18, 71
Socialist International, 18
social media: and MENA protests, 88–91; and Occupy Wall Street, 92–93; and

social movements, 8–13; and world culture, 4
social movement organizations (SMOs), 18
social movements: in 2011, x–xi, 61–62; definition of, ix, 45; and democratization, 61–98; future of, 203–16; globalization and, 1–29; Internet and, ix–x, 8–13; SPR thesis on, 21–22; and state, 45; world-system theory and, 19–25
social movement theory, 2, 20–22, 25–26, 180, 206–7
Society for International Development, 33
solidarity economy, 96, 200
Solidary Economy Network (SEN), 200
Soroush, Abdolkarim, 101–2
South, Global: neoliberalism and, 34–35; SAPs and, 174–75, 179; and women's movement, 136, 138
South Africa, 63, 73t
South Center, 33
South Korea, 9, 63–64, 73t
Soviet Union, 50, 107, 117, 220n3
Spain, 9, 45, 68, 73t, 183
Sperling, Valerie, 134
Standing, Guy, 38, 137
Starhawk, 158
state/nation-state: continuing importance of, 45–48; future of, 214–15; and globalization, 43–49; and Islamism, 114–17; and social movements, 210–11; women's movement and, 165; in world-system theory, 19–20
Steger, Manfred, 39, 127
Steinem, Gloria, 158
Stiglitz, Joseph, 38
Strange, Susan, 44
strategies. See collective action repertoires
Streeten, Paul, 37
structural adjustment policies (SAPs), 33, 35, 67–68, 138, 173–75
substantive democracy, 65
Sudan, 17

Suharto, 106
Syria, 48, 80

Tablighi Jamaat, 100, 126
tactics. *See* collective action repertoires
Taiwan, 73*t*
Talcott, Molly, 24
Taliban, 51, 142, 152
Tarrow, Sidney, 13, 45, 63
Taseer, Salmaan, 114–15
Tax, Meredith, 165
Taylor, Lance, 40, 174
Taylor, Rupert, 57–58, 206
technology. *See* Internet; social media
terrorism, 5, 116–17; Islamist movements
    and, 128–30; women's movement and,
    165
Tessler, Mark, 79
Thatcher, Margaret, 36, 107
third wave of democratization, 12, 65–
    66, 72*t*–73*t*
Third World: debt forgiveness, 147,
    177–78; development and, 33–35;
    SAPs and, 174–75; and women's
    movement, 136
Third World Network, 182
Thompson, Grahame, 44
Tiananmen Square movement, 16
Tobin, James, 187, 221n12
Tobin tax, 40, 148, 187, 221n12
transnational advocacy network (TAN),
    6–7
transnational capitalist class (TCC), 39,
    221n18
transnational collective action, 54–60, 209
transnational feminist networks
    (TNFs), 133–70; definition of, 134;
    development of, 135–44; and global
    justice movement, 177; and Internet,
    209–10; types of, 140*t*–141*t*. *See also*
    women's movement, global
transnational networks, definition of, 186
transnational public sphere, 208–9
transnational social movements, 6–13;
    definition of, ix, 7, 55–56; functions
    of, 56; history of, 13–19, 15*t*; making

of, 55*f*; study of, 5–6, 25–29. *See also*
    social movements
transnational state apparatus (TSA), 39
Troubled Assets Relief Program (TARP),
    54
Tugal, Cihan, 120
Tunisia, 24, 61, 69, 73*t*, 74, 80–91, 90*t*;
    an-Nahda, 17, 118–19, 131
Turkey, 17, 79, 106, 118–20
Twitter, 9, 47, 89–90

Underground Railroad for Iraqi Women,
    161
Union Socialiste des Forces Populaires
    (USFP), 84
United for Peace and Justice (UFPJ),
    159–60
United Kingdom, 33, 36, 68–69, 107
United Nations, 34, 54–55, 77, 143;
    Charter, 94; Children's Fund
    (UNICEF), 161, 175; Conference on
    Trade and Development (UNCTAD),
    33; Development Programme
    (UNDP), 42, 75; Educational,
    Scientific and Cultural Organization
    (UNESCO), 33–34, 36, 220n7; global
    justice movement and, 180–82,
    181*t*; Population Fund (UNFPA),
    143; reform proposals for, 95, 148;
    Security Council Resolution 1325,
    156–57, 168; women's movement
    and, 136, 142–44, 155, 166–67
United States: and democratization, 76;
    and globalization, 33; as hegemon,
    19; and Internet, 47; limits to power
    of, 50–51; and reactive movements,
    50, 107
United States Social Forum (USSF), 76,
    200
Universal Declaration of Human Rights,
    91

Vallejo, Camila, 171, 185, 230
Vargas, Virginia, 169, 186, 192
veiling, 79, 108, 113–14, 164, 226n16,
    230n48

Venezuela, 199
violence, 128, 211–12; global justice
    movement and, 189, 192, 197–98;
    Islamist movements and, 13, 85,
    105, 113, 115–18, 128–30; women's
    movements and, 22–24, 143, 155–62
virtual public spheres, 208
Voll, John, 16

Wahhabism, 16–17, 100
Walgrave, Stefaan, 10
Wallach, Lori, 178
Wallerstein, Immanuel, 19, 39
Walton, John, 175
war: global justice movement and,
    184; Islamism and, 115; women's
    movements and, 143, 155–62, 168.
    See also violence
Warren, Elizabeth, 54
Washington Consensus, 19, 36–37
Watkins, Sherron, 53
wealth gap. *See* inequality
Weber, Max, 4
Wejnert, Barbara, 69
Weldon, Laurel, 62–63, 70
welfare, cuts in, and women's movement,
    137–38
White, Jenny B., 101
Wickham, Carrie Rosefsky, 101, 125
Wickham-Crowley, Timothy, 54
Wiest, Dawn, 26
WikiLeaks, 10–11, 47, 86, 89, 218n15
Wiktorowicz, Quintan, 5, 101, 104, 112,
    115
Wilkinson, Richard, 42
women: and corporate domain, 53–54;
    democratization and, 78–79
Women for Women International
    (WWI), 140t–141t, 145t, 160
Women in Black, 141t, 160
Women in Conflict Zones Network, 160
women-in-development (WID)/women-
    and-development (WAD), 2, 35, 139,
    228n6
Women Living under Muslim Laws
    (WLUML), 57, 102, 139, 140t, 145t,
    150–53, 164; and Internet, 207, 209
Women's Caucus for Gender Justice, 140t

Women's Environment and Development
    Organization (WEDO), 139, 140t
Women's Human Rights Network
    (WHRNet), 140t, 153
Women's Initiatives for Gender Justice,
    141t, 160
Women's International Democratic
    Federation (WIDF), 19
Women's International League for Peace
    and Freedom (WILPF), 19, 141t, 155
Women's Learning Partnership (WLP),
    140t, 145t, 154–55, 209
women's movement, global, 7–8, 83–87,
    133–70, 204–5; and democratization,
    71–75; development of, 135–44;
    future of, 213; and global justice
    movement, 162–65, 177; and Islamist
    movements, 8, 79, 108, 110, 122,
    138, 149–55; origins of, 18–19;
    terminology in, 133–34; and WSF,
    148, 160, 162–65, 169, 190–93
women's movement, term, 133
Women's Social and Political Union, 18
Women Waging Peace, 160
Workers' Party, Brazil, 59, 179, 182,
    188
World Bank, 3, 34–36, 138, 174–75;
    global justice movement and, 197,
    200; women's movement and, 146,
    148
World Conference on Human Rights, 54
World Council for Economic and
    Financial Security, 148
World Economic Forum (WEF), 59,
    183
World March of Women, 133, 147–48,
    162–63
world polity theory, 3–4
World Social Forum (WSF), 7,
    31, 73t, 95–96, 179, 188–95;
    Charter of Principles of, 193; and
    democratization, 66; global justice
    movement and, 184, 186; participants
    in, 189–91; state allies and, 48;
    studies of, 26; women's movement
    and, 148, 160, 162–65, 169, 190–93
World Summit on Social Development,
    55, 143, 181t

world-system theory, 2, 14; on democratization, 66–67; on globalization, 39; and Islamist movements, 108; and social movements, 19–25

World Trade Organization (WTO), 3, 77, 178; global justice movement and, 179, 200; women's movement and, 146–47

Wuthnow, Robert, 4

Yaghmaian, Behzad, 39

Yemen, 80, 107

Young Women's Christian Association (YWCA), 19

Youssefi, Abdelrahman, 84

youth, in MENA protests, 81–82, 219n16

Zald, Mayer, 56, 62, 206

Zapatista movement, 24, 73t, 177

Zeghal, Malika, 101

Zenab for Women in Development, 161

Zeyd, Nasr Hamed Abou, 102, 225n2

Zuckerberg, Mark, 218n15

About the Author

Valentine M. Moghadam is director of the International Affairs Program and professor of sociology at Northeastern University, Boston. Born in Tehran, Iran, she received her higher education in Canada and the United States. In addition to her academic career, Dr. Moghadam has been a senior researcher with the WIDER Institute of the United Nations University, Helsinki, Finland, and a section chief at UNESCO in Paris. The author of many books and journal articles, she has lectured widely and consulted many international organizations.